For Bart Friedman,

With all best wishes

to a wise counselor

with unusually broad-based

interests,

Marty [illegible]

June 8, 2004

Praise for

Inside the Yield Book

The Classic That Created the Science of Bond Analysis

by Sidney Homer and Martin L. Leibowitz, Ph.D.

"**For active fixed-income investors, this book has always been the holy writ, where it all began.** Leibowitz's revisions make certain that the book will continue in that role. But for all investors, of any stripe, *Inside the Yield Book* is the essential work for understanding what the entire investment process is all about."

—Peter L. Bernstein
Author of *Against the Gods* and *Capital Ideas*
President, Peter L. Bernstein, Inc.

"**It's pure pleasure to revisit this innovative and authoritative bedrock of modern bond analysis.** The new edition demonstrates how the authors' pioneering approach can be applied broadly. You can ignore the analysis if you'd like; however, the description of Wall Street's original 'rocket scientist' encountering Salomon Brothers' trading floor is worth the price of admission."

—John Lipsky
Chief Economist, JPMorgan Securities Inc.

"This book transformed the markets' understanding of bonds. **The new material in this expanded edition extends those insights to equities and other investments—and the investment world is indebted anew to Sidney Homer and Martin Leibowitz.**"

—Frank J. Fabozzi, Ph.D., CFA
Editor of the *Journal of Portfolio Management*
Frederick Frank Adjunct Professor of Finance at Yale University's School of Management

"*Inside the Yield Book* may not be where it all began, but it certainly is where it all began to be understood. **The clarity and elegance of language and thought is startling.** The new material will not disappoint. This book will live forever!"

—Jack R. Meyer
President and CEO, Harvard Management Company

"As someone who's been in the business for forty-eight years and still makes good use of the original edition, **I'm very pleased to see *Inside the Yield Book* back in print with the very helpful addition on present value**."

—Gedale Horowitz
Senior Managing Director, Citigroup Global Markets Inc.

"In the 1970s and 1980s, we built strong fixed-income franchises both at the Harris Bank and Lincoln Capital based on Marty's work contained in *Inside the Yield Book*. Few, if any, mathematical studies have had the impact on an industry that this book has. **More than thirty years later, it still should be must reading for every investment professional.**"

—Kenneth R. Meyer
Chairman, Lincoln Capital Management Company
A Lehman Company

"***Inside the Yield Book* brought bond trading out of the Dark Ages and the investment world's brightest stars into bond trading.** Its enduring popularity reflects the authors' rare ability to provide sound solutions to practical concerns in clear, economical prose."

—Martin Fridson
Publisher of *Leverage World*
Member of the Fixed Income Analysts Society Hall of Fame

"**The new edition gives us the best of both worlds**: the complete classic that helped launch a golden age for fixed-income investing, and completely new sections that show how **relevant and essential** its wisdom remains today."

—Lewis S. Ranieri
Chairman, Hyperion Partners

"When I was a young mortgage security trader in the mid 1970s, I found *Inside the Yield Book* to be an absolutely essential reference tool. Today, as fixed-income markets grow even more complex and global risk management becomes mandatory, **every participant in the fixed-income market needs to read and then reread this authoritative work.**"

—Laurence Fink
Chairman and CEO, BlackRock

"**There have been many developments in fixed-income analysis, and they all benefit from the seminal publication *Inside the Yield Book.*** The foundation that was established supports and inspires the work which has followed. Marty's additional material adds to the legacy of his path-breaking efforts."

—H. Gifford Fong
President, Gifford Fong Associates

"Just as thousands of years ago, the Greeks measured the diameter of the earth quite accurately; and just as the Chinese circumnavigated the globe long before Columbus and Magellan; so Sidney Homer charted the constellation of bond mathematics long before modern computers. Since bonds finance human activity, this book is full of fascinating history, and it is not only Sidney's. Marty Leibowitz's fingerprints are all over it, too. **Sidney was the historian, and Marty is the poet, of the most important financial market on earth: bonds.**"

—Andrew M. (Andy) Carter
Vice Chairman, Hyperion Capital Management, Inc.

"**This expanded version of the classic study continues to make a significant contribution to our understanding of interest rates and debt pricing. It should be required reading for both practitioners and academics.** Marty has the ability to explain complex relationships in the debt markets in a logical and often intuitive way, and to then back the intuition with rigorous mathematics."

—Martin J. Gruber
Nomura Professor of Finance, Stern School of Business
New York University

"*Inside the Yield Book* is *the* fixed income classic, and it has been updated with a fascinating chapter of bond market history. **Some books get better with age, and this is one of them.**"

—Brian S. O'Neil
Chief Investment Officer, Robert Wood Johnson Foundation

"When my son earned his MBA, I gave him an engraved wristwatch and a dog-eared copy of *Inside the Yield Book.* The watch will help him get to work on time, but the book was the real gift. **You cannot succeed as an investor without understanding the concepts *Inside the Yield Book* teaches. Marty Leibowitz has done a great service to all investors by bringing back this classic.**"

—Brian F. Wruble, CFA
General Partner, Odyssey Partners, L.P.
Past Chairman, Institute of Chartered Financial Analysts

"With the global nature of today's investment management process and the increasing complexity of financial instruments, we seem far removed from the bond markets that Sidney Homer and Marty Leibowitz first wrote about in 1972. However, Sidney's intuition and Marty's mathematical rigor gave all of us the foundation from which all of today's analytical approaches emanate. **Their work was innovative at the time but, if anything, may be even more relevant today.**"

—Thomas E. Klaffky
Managing Director and Head of the Yield Book Group, Citigroup

INSIDE THE YIELD BOOK

INSIDE THE YIELD BOOK

The Classic That Created
the Science of Bond Analysis

SIDNEY HOMER
and MARTIN L. LEIBOWITZ, Ph.D.

With a Foreword by Henry Kaufman
and two new sections by Martin L. Leibowitz

Bloomberg PRESS
PRINCETON

Printed in the United States of America

1 3 5 7 9 10 8 6 4 2

Library of Congress Cataloging-in-Publication Data

Homer, Sidney, 1902–1983
Inside the yield book : the classic that created the science of bond analysis / Sidney Homer and Martin L. Leibowitz ; with a foreword by Henry Kaufman and two new sections by Martin L. Leibowitz.
p. cm.
Includes bibliographical references and index.
ISBN 1-57660-159-5 (alk. paper)
1. Bonds--United States. 2. Bond market. I. Leibowitz, Martin L., 1936– II. Title.

HG4936.H65 2004
332. 63 ' 23--dc22

2004006036

To the memory of my coauthor, Sidney Homer,
who first introduced me to the financial marketplace
with its intriguing challenges, its colorful personalities,
and its many fascinating problems that I am still
struggling to more fully understand.

Martin L. Leibowitz

Contents

Foreword
by Henry Kaufman

I STILL RECALL when in 1969 Sidney Homer asked me to meet with Martin Leibowitz in order to ascertain how he might fit into our research effort at Salomon Brothers. Sidney Homer had joined Salomon in 1960 to set up a bond market research department. He had hired me a year later. My role eventually expanded to assuming overall research responsibilities. By the time Marty arrived, Sidney had already published his monumental book, *A History of Interest Rates,* followed by a number of papers on the behavior of interest rates from a portfolio management perspective. However, Sidney and I concluded that the time was now ripe for a more quantitative approach to evaluating the opportunities and pitfalls in the bond market. With a doctorate in mathematics, Marty was well prepared to join with us in this new pursuit.

I should explain the title *Inside the Yield Book.* Market veterans will understand the title, but newcomers generally will not. Back in those days, the "yield book" was a compilation of numerical tables of prices and yields for a wide range of bond maturities. Traders and investors would agree on the yield basis for a trade and then laboriously plow into these tables to determine the corresponding price.

There were two problems that became increasingly troublesome as the bond market began to experience enormous growth in the size and breadth of new issues. The first problem was that, with the increasing range of interest rates during the 1960s and 1970s, these volumes became thicker and thicker, resulting in an ever longer time required to find the interpolated price and then negotiate a given trade. Today, the computer has basically solved this problem. The second problem was that bond market participants—portfolio managers as well as broker/

dealers—had come to rely upon these yield books as gospel, with all too little understanding of the underlying mathematical and financial concepts. Sidney Homer had long been urging market participants to move toward a more total-return orientation that would be consistent with modern financial theory.

When Sidney's insight and experience were combined with Marty's ability to probe beyond the rigid tabulations of the yield book, they were able to coauthor a series of studies that opened a wider and more compelling vista into this new world of bond analysis. These studies soon came to have a profound impact on the bond community, and it was that reception that led to the publication of this book's first edition in 1972.

The insights and observations in *Inside the Yield Book* are as true today as they were then. Virtually every one of the fifteen chapters, starting with the first part that deals with "Bond Yields, Bond Prices, and Bond Investment" and concluding with the chapters on "The Mathematics of Bond Yields," have stood the test of time. In particular, the chapters on present value, interest on interest, and the different rates of return have often been cited as among the clearest exposition of these key concepts, which are fundamental to understanding the analysis of cash flows not only in the bond world but in any area of finance.

Following the publication of *Inside the Yield Book*, Marty's career blossomed. He became the head of an important division (in research) known as the Bond Portfolio Analysis Group. After I left Salomon Brothers in 1988, Marty became director of global research, responsible for all of the firm's research activities in equities as well as fixed income. Marty attracted a number of highly competent quantitative analysts, many with Ph.D. degrees, not just in economics, but in mathematics, engineering, and even astronomy. Their work became vital to the firm's trading desk and was responsible for many client transactions. Many of these analysts went on to achieve wide recognition on their own.

Marty led the research effort by example. Over the course of the years, there was an outpouring of writings. Many were published in book form in *Investing: The Collected Works of Martin L. Leibowitz* (1991), *Franchise Value and the Price/Earnings Ratio* (1994), and *Return Targets and Shortfall Risks* (1996). The range of subjects covered in these pages is truly breathtaking. Throughout their combined 2,000 pages, Marty's great intellect and broad range of knowledge is ever present.

In 1995, Marty joined one of the largest retirement funds in the world, TIAA-CREF, as chief investment officer. In this capacity, he was able to put many of his investment ideas and theories into practice.

Marty's career has been characterized by the persistent search for a deeper understanding of the most basic investment concepts, an approach that first came to light in his work on *Inside the Yield Book*.

Preface to the 2004 Edition: A Historical Perspective

by Martin L. Leibowitz

When first published in 1972, *Inside the Yield Book* made a big splash in a very shallow pond. From today's vantage point, fixed-income activities back in those days can seem somewhat naïve, and perhaps even rather dull. But when I first found myself on the bond trading floor at Salomon Brothers and Hutzler (SB & H), it was anything but. In fact, it had some asylum characteristics, with traders and partners shouting and screaming, banging phones down in frustration, arguing bitterly with traders across the aisle, sometimes holding their heads in despair or, when a dynamite trade was consummated, giving everyone "high fives" and even occasionally jumping on the desk for a victory dance.

Perhaps the most striking feature was the trays of half-eaten lunches, several days old, that could be stacked three and four high on the trading desks. The traders always ate at their desks and rarely had time to clear away their uneaten sandwiches. As a freshly minted Ph.D. in mathematics, this was not exactly my expectation of high finance. Especially not after riding up in the oak-paneled elevator, entering the elegantly oak-paneled foyer, and stealing a yearning glimpse into the elegantly oak-paneled Partner's Dining Room, with its—yes, elegant oak-paneled table. Nor was this what I was expecting after learning about Salomon Brothers and Hutzler from Sidney Homer.

Sidney Homer was remarkable on many counts. First of all, he was my wife's uncle, which is how I first met him. In fact, when my wife, Sarah, and I were married in 1966, it was Sidney who accompanied her down the aisle in lieu of her father who had passed away years earlier. Sidney was a man with a patrician presence. He was very intelligent, finishing an education in classics at Harvard in three years, and was an embarrassingly gifted writer (at least, he embarrassed me on repeated occasions with his uncanny knack for turning an initially awkward phrase into an eloquent statement). His parents were both musicians of the first rank. His father, also named Sidney Homer, was a composer of superb classical art songs, and his mother, Madame Louise Homer, was a renowned mezzo-soprano with a long career at the Metropolitan Opera, singing with the greats such as Enrico Caruso. Sidney's parents were so exalted in their artistic sphere and so broadly revered that they mingled with the upper crust of New York society. Alas, as is almost always the case with the arts, talent and funding follow separate paths: Sidney may have had an aristocratic upbringing, but his family was far from wealthy. So when Sidney fell in love and married at a very young age, he had to go to work. And the only work that he could find at the time was to join a Wall Street bond firm—a crass descent into commercialism by his family's standards.

But quality shines through. Sidney became a highly skilled bond manager, spending the larger part of his career at Scudder, Stevens and Clark. Along the way, his inquiring mind led him not just to participate in the bond market, but to study it deeply and write about his findings. Sidney's literary skills were exceptional by financial market standards, and his bond market studies gained a wide following. He soon became known as the "bard of the bond market"—an honorary title that no one else has ever held since (or perhaps ever aspired to). He wrote several books that became classics in their day. One of his books, *The Bond Buyer's Primer,*[1] was a tongue-in-cheek story describing how a bond salesman should go about selling bonds, and how a bond buyer should go about resisting him. It is now out of print but highly prized by those who have a copy.

One of Sidney's enduring works is his monumental study, *The History of Interest Rates*.[2] Most financial writers would have been content with covering the last two centuries, but Sidney's classical training and avocational interest led him to extend his history back to pre-Biblical times. He managed to take a potentially tedious subject and make it into a fascinating story relating cyclical sweeps in interest rates to grand societal changes. The book has been through several editions, with the latest updated by Henry Kaufman and Richard Sylla, an eminent financial historian from New York University. The publication of *The History* added a touch of class to the bond market, and every serious participant had a copy. Its most thorough reader was undoubtedly the young Dr. Henry Kaufman who, after being hired by Sidney at SB & H, actually "volunteered" to proofread all 472 pages.

In the early 1960s, SB & H was the premier bond trading firm, but it was basically just that—a bond trading firm. One of the senior partners, Charles Simon, realized that for the firm to flourish, it needed to provide services beyond the best price to its customers. He hit upon the idea of creating a bond market research department—the first on Wall Street—and he enticed Sidney to head it up.

Back in those days, bond trading was an arcane backwater. I had literally never heard of SB & H, nor had a lot of other generally well-informed people. My wife and I had visited Sidney's Gramercy Park home on numerous occasions, but we never discussed Wall Street until one evening when Sidney learned that I would soon complete my doctorate in mathematics. He pulled me aside and dug out a file that contained about fifty handwritten pages of a never-finished book entitled *The Mathematics of Bonds*. He explained that this project was begun many years before, but it had foundered into filedom. He had started the book by setting forth a number of principles that he (and virtually every other bond market participant) was sure were true. One of these principles was that longer-maturity bonds have greater price volatility than shorter bonds. However, as he developed numerical examples, he found that they contradicted his "rock certain" principles. After years of letting his manuscript collect dust, he now wondered if I would take a look at it to see if my mathematical background could help untangle the paradox.

I must confess that, at that point, my knowledge of bonds was nonexistent. But I gamely took the pages home and worked up the (relatively straightforward) algebra that defined yield-to-maturity and related it to a bond price. When I presented my findings, he was duly appreciative and gracious, as he always was. However, at this point neither Sidney nor I was particularly excited by my explanations. They might be illuminating, but neither of us saw how they could prove really useful. Out of curiosity, I asked Sidney why he hadn't taken the problem to the "house mathematician" at SB & H. He found great humor in my question, because no one at SB & H came close to fitting that description. That surprised me. I would have thought that the premier bond firm, trading instruments that had so many mathematical facets, would surely have some in-house expertise of that sort. As I pondered his response, it dawned upon me that maybe I could become that "house mathematician."

My route into SB & H was more circuitous than one might imagine. At first, Sidney was not encouraging. His research department was very compact at that point, and he certainly did not have room for someone not steeped in the financial markets. But persistence pays off (sometimes), and one day Sidney heard that two of his associates, Morris Offit and Harry Peterson, were looking for someone to develop computer-based analyses that could facilitate various trading activities. One thing led to another and I eventually found myself manning the single, time-shared computer terminal on the trading floor at 60 Wall Street (the one with the stacks of old lunch trays).

My first two weeks at SB & H were spent going through their rudimentary training program. This consisted of sitting next to various traders, plugging into their phone lines, and listening to their dialogues. Because trade talk is almost always highly compressed, clipped, super-fast, and replete with market jargon (and other specialty words), this was an arduous learning experience. Coincidentally, on my very first day, I was assigned to sit next to a young but clearly up-and-coming equity trader by the name of Mike Bloomberg.

Work on the trading floor was hectic, but it gave me a great education about the financial markets and the transaction process. The traders and salesmen were generally kind to me. They became even kinder when I was able to develop a package of computer programs that facilitated a number of trades. Also, with my little time-sharing terminal, I could determine the yield for any given price with great speed and accuracy. However, the traders were themselves very adept at using the look-up tables—their so-called "yield books"—to find the yield values required to complete their trades. So, at first, my "high-tech" yield calculator was just a curiosity. But in 1970, when interest rates moved higher than the levels available in any of the traders' yield book tables, I became the only game in town. Senior partners lined up in front of my terminal, desperate for the number that could confirm their latest trade. Needless to say, this boosted my standing on the floor, although it put me in a harrowing position in which any mistake could prove fatal. In a curious sense, one might say that I benefited from interest rates moving "outside" the yield book.

It is said that need is the mother of invention. In the financial world, the gestation period can be very compressed. It was not many weeks before computer terminals and clunky special-purpose hand-held yield calculators sprouted up all over the trading floor. My reign as the sole "yield keeper" came to an abrupt end, allowing me to return to developing models for analyzing portfolio improvements involving corporate bonds and convertibles.

The broad-based use of computers to replace the yield book tables did nothing to further the general understanding of what a bond yield was all about. In fact, the great facility of the computer may have been a step backward. Traders could punch in a few numbers and the desired yield value would pop up. There was no need to ponder what it all meant, or what would happen if you changed the coupon or the maturity. At least the old yield book procedure required a table look-up and an interpolation that forced the trader to move a finger up and down the yield rows and across the maturity columns. So, in a sense, the advent of the computer capability actually reduced the need for an appreciation of what a yield really meant. This may be a general problem of our computer age. The computer *can* be an effective facilitator in all sorts of areas, but its use on a rote basis also dulls the desire to seek a deeper understanding.

At that time, most bond portfolios were long-term oriented, and our analytical models typically focused on the long-term benefits of holding one type of bond versus another. The alternative bonds were usually of the same credit quality but differed in coupon, maturity, sinking fund, and/or call features, thereby creating different patterns of cash flow over time. In order to make fair comparisons, we had to assume that cash receipts were reinvested at a common set of hypothetical interest rates. We soon began to notice that the return from a given bond investment depended critically on the assumption of a common reinvestment opportunity *and* on the choice of that reinvestment rate. This finding greatly surprised many of the bond veterans.

Basically, their confusion stemmed from the widespread belief that a bond's yield described the accumulation of wealth that would be generated over its life. From my earlier discussions with Sidney, I knew that this was not the case. Now the computer models validated the idea that reinvested rates played a critical role in the wealth buildup. Moreover, the computer output made this finding visible through numerical examples that would be hard to argue with, although that didn't stop many of my trading floor neighbors from trying. A number of paths converged when I realized that (1) the reinvestment effect was *theoretically* important, (2) this effect was also *practically* important (i.e., it could affect investment decisions), (3) virtually every bond trader, salesperson, and portfolio manager was woefully unaware of this fact, and (4) perhaps most important, my computer could provide a compelling demonstration of this result. This realization signaled opportunity, and I went to visit Sidney in his off-the-floor office (oak-paneled, naturally).

Sidney was very interested. When I expressed my surprise at how little known this reinvestment effect seemed to be within the bond market (after all, this was not "rocket science"), Sidney observed that there are many myths and half-truths (some of them useful) embedded in daily practice. Sidney's vast experience gave him a unique vantage point: He knew what was "known" and what was "not known." It was this meeting that really gave birth to *Inside the Yield Book,* although I didn't know that at the time.

A week later, while I was on vacation in Florida, Sidney tracked me down to tell me that he had been ruminating on my reinvestment results. He had already put together a draft "Memorandum to Portfolio Managers," as he termed his research reports. He said that we would be coauthors of the finished product.

The first memorandum in the series, entitled "Interest on Interest," was published on October 5, 1970. It was viewed by many readers as an attack on the sanctity of the standard yield measure. There was considerable outrage among many of the crustier members of the bond community (and there were a lot of crusty members!). Sidney received many indignant calls and letters from valued friends and even more valued customers. All of these communications were turned over to me, and Sidney charged me with the job of responding to—and convincing—each and every complainant. The bad news was that undercutting the long-held views of our best customers did not exactly endear me to the firm's senior partners. This hardly seemed like the ideal way to launch a fledging financial career. The good news was that as I methodically chewed through the correspondence that Sidney piled on my desk, I found myself coming into contact with the pillars of the bond community.

Some were soothed by my written explanations, but many were not, which resulted in some pretty nervous grumbling within SB & H about potential damage to the firm's standing. Sidney was steadfast in his support. Moreover, he put his prestige on the line by personally making appointments for us to visit the offices of the remaining recalcitrant customers. With my mathematical arguments, thankfully reinforced by Sidney's credibility, we were finally able to attain a level of acceptance sufficient to keep SB & H's reputation intact.

The next two memoranda, on price volatility, received a more gracious reception, even though they surprised many readers by pointing out that low-coupon bonds could be more volatile than par bonds with much longer maturities.

There is one paragraph in Chapter 2 that was based on two questions Sidney posed to me. First, if a Roman centurion at the time of Christ had invested one drachma and allowed it to compound at just 4 percent through the centuries, what would be the accumulated amount? I was able to perform this calculation and it turned out to be a huge number of drachmas, which, at virtually any exchange rate, would exceed all the capital wealth now visible in the world's financial markets. His second question I found not so easy to answer: What happened to all that potential wealth? Sidney had a way with the Big Ideas and answered this succinctly, if not wholly satisfactorily, on page 32 of *Inside the Yield Book:* "Aside from the destructive effects of wars, revolutions and inflations, and the incidence of taxes, there is a very human propensity to consume." This question is still well worth the pondering, notwithstanding its rather depressing implications.

Subsequent memoranda dealt with a variety of subjects—zero-coupon bonds (long before zero-coupon bonds actually existed), callable bonds, and the total-return concept for bonds of different maturities and coupons. These new efforts were readily digested by a growing readership.

It was the last memorandum that had the greatest impact on the actual practice of bond portfolio management. At the time, virtually every trade that involved selling one bond and buying another was called a swap. The failure to differentiate among different types of swaps often led to serious confusion among market participants. The final memorandum proposed a classification system that segregated these trades into four distinct categories: (1) yield pick-up swaps, (2) substitution swaps, (3) sector swaps, and (4) rate-anticipation swaps. This terminology proved useful as a way of distinguishing one activity from another and rapidly worked its way into the standard vocabulary of the bond market.

As they gained broader acceptance, the five memoranda were widely redistributed both in the United States and internationally (they were quickly translated into Japanese and German). They also found their way into investment training programs, not only at SB & H but at many other Wall Street firms, sometimes in photocopied form with the SB & H banner removed. It was not long before the New York Institute of Finance and Prentice-Hall urged us to expand the memoranda into a book.

We added a few more chapters and a technical appendix that described the basic mathematics involved in calculating present values, yields, and rates of return. Such appendices are usually backwaters rarely dipped into, so we were surprised to hear many readers comment that our simple, step-by-step mathematical development in the appendix helped them to understand the present value concept for the first time.

THE RESULTING VOLUME was published in 1972 under the title *Inside the Yield Book*. It subsequently went through more than twenty-five reprintings.

The occasion of this new edition is an opportunity for some additional acknowledgments. As we proceeded from one memorandum to the next, we came into contact with market participants as well as scholars who had given deep thought to the fundamental nature of the bond market. We learned from all these individuals things that enlightened us and enriched our endeavors. Among many who helped to move us forward, there were several who, for one reason or another, played a particularly special role.

First of all, it turned out that the London gilt firms were far ahead of the U.S. market in terms of their sophistication and even in their use of computer tools. Unlike U.S. firms, those in the United Kingdom had many senior staff members who were broadly trained actuaries with powerful mathematical backgrounds. Through his network in the United Kingdom, Sidney Homer was able to send me to London with introductions to key bond people at firms such as Greenwell and Co., Phillips and Drew, and Grieveson Grant. Our British friends were not used to such visits, but they received me with great warmth. (The three-hour luncheon meetings were unlike any I ever experienced—before or since. I think they may now be ancient history in London.) Everyone in these firms was extraordinarily forthcoming about their analytic approaches to the market. Although most of their techniques would not have worked in the United States without considerable reworking, we went to great lengths to incorporate what we could of their thinking into our analytical tools, and some of their ideas surely improved our later memoranda.

I mentioned earlier that Sidney Homer had spent the bulk of his long career as a bond manager at the firm of Scudder, Stevens, and Clark. One of his intellectual soul mates there was Herman Liss, a brilliant and creative student of the bond and convertible markets. At an early point, Sidney Homer sent me to meet with Herman for a series of lunches. Herman spoke so quickly and sparkled with so many intriguing ideas that he was hard to follow. I soon learned that I had to excuse myself from the lunch table for a few minutes and sneak off to some corner to quickly scribble down notes on his many outpourings. I hesitate to conjecture as to how Herman interpreted those interruptions; needless to say, many of his thoughts found their way into our work.

In the academic sphere, there was at that time relatively little interest in bonds, although there were some notable studies by Peter Williamson at Dartmouth[3] and by Larry Fisher and Roman Weil at the University of Chicago.[4] The classic work of Frederick Macaulay[5] was, of course, invaluable. And many of us came amicably to terms with the Treasury yield curve through a wonderful book by Princeton's Burton Malkiel, *The Term Structure of Interest Rates*.[6]

Finally, it would be unfair not to recognize that many SB & H customers were well ahead of the pack. We were fortunate to be able to benefit from our dialogue with these thought leaders who helped to shape our work.

To sum it up in the language of the bond world, we all owe many more debts of intellectual gratitude than we can ever redeem.

Acknowledgments

I WOULD LIKE TO EXPRESS my deep gratitude to my associates Dr. Brett Hammond and Dr. Stanley Kogelman for their many valuable comments and suggestions that have found their way into the new material presented in this volume.

At Bloomberg L.P., I am grateful to Thomas Keene, Bloomberg News editor at large, for championing this new edition, and to my editor at Bloomberg Press, Jared Kieling, and associate editor Tracy Tait for guiding us smoothly around the inevitable problems that arise in any editorial and publication process.

I must also express my deepest appreciation to my assistant, Celia Blancaflor, without whose tireless and meticulous effort in the preparation of this manuscript this new work would never have seen the light of day.

Finally, I would like to salute my former partner at Salomon Brothers, Michael R. Bloomberg, for having the vision to create an organization that can produce and disseminate such worthy publications for the financial community.

MARTIN L. LEIBOWITZ

Some Topics That Didn't Make It into the 1972 Edition

by Martin L. Leibowitz

The concept of present value (*PV*) is basically a simple one that plays a key role in virtually every area of finance. Yet some surprising points of confusion and gaps in understanding remain, even among experienced financial analysts. In *Inside the Yield Book,* we addressed some of these issues within the bond domain. The original appendix represented a deliberate attempt to move beyond the simple mathematics of present value and provide a more comprehensive feeling for the underlying motivations and assumptions. In particular, we tried to relate *PV* to the more intuitive concept of a basic compounding process that generates future value (*FV*) over time. The following discussion explores a number of topics regarding the *PV* concept and how it interacts with a cash flow's future value over a prescribed time horizon. For completeness, the equations are developed in the Technical Appendix.

In the final section of this chapter, we go beyond the fixed-income realm and suggest some generalizations of the *PV* concept that can be useful in thinking about the value of equities or virtually any other types of investment. (Some readers may wish to first move to these generalizations and then later back into the more mathematical treatment of the fixed-income topics.)

The Basic Concept of Present Value

Every investment is an exchange of current resources for some future flow of payments. In the broadest sense, the concept of *PV* is a gauge of the value of those future payments in current terms. One could argue that the *PV* concept is at work (at least implicitly) in every investment decision, both in the primary and the secondary market. The *PV* idea is a very old concept, and every investor has some intuitive sense of how it works. In fact, it is such a basic tool, and so widely used and taught, that its application has become all too second nature. The problem with this is that use of common yardsticks (as we saw in *Inside the Yield Book*) can easily become rote, that is, used routinely without any thoughtful application of their roots—or limitations.

The fundamental element in the *PV* calculation is the discount rate—the rate of interest that relates what an investor is willing to pay currently to receive a future payment at some specified point in time. This subject of discount rates can quickly become very complicated. Discount rates can vary due to a variety of factors: the time to each cash payment, the risk associated with the payments, the volatility of the discount rate itself, and so forth. For clarity of exposition, we shall keep it simple and assume throughout that the market applies the single, flat discount rate of 8% to all investments.

With this heroic assumption, any flow of payments can be discounted at this 8% rate to determine a *PV* that should exactly correspond to its fair market price. In a very real sense, a market discount rate is a measure of society's time value of money, and more generally, the time value of scarce resources in general. (And one *could* obviously go on at great length about the relationship of inflation, growth prospects, resource scarcity, consumption patterns, etc.)

Seen another way, the discount rate is equivalent to the basic market return on a fair value investment. This returns view of the discount rate (just the other face of the same coin) leads to a slightly different interpretation of the *PV:* The *PV* is the dollar amount that, if invested and compounded at the discount rate, could produce the exact same pattern of future flows as the original investment. It should be noted that both of the above interpretations of the *PV*—as a time exchange of current for future dollars, and as an invested amount that would mimic the original investment's flow—make no reference to what happens to those future flows once they are received. The future payment may be spent, reinvested, or just given away. Whatever the fate of the future payments, the *PV* would be the same.

As an example, throughout this discussion, we will consider the simplest possible cash flow: a 10-year annuity consisting of 10 annual pay-

TABLE 1

Cumulative Present Value

10 Annual Payments of $10
8% Discount Rate

Horizon, *H*	Payments	Present Value of Each Payment, *PV*(*H*,*H*)	Cumulative Present Value, *PV*(1,*H*)
0	$0	$0.00	$0.00
1	10	9.26	9.26
2	10	8.57	17.83
3	10	7.94	25.77
4	10	7.35	33.12
5	10	6.81	39.93
6	10	6.30	46.23
7	10	5.83	52.06
8	10	5.40	57.47
9	10	5.00	62.47
10	10	4.63	67.10
11	0	0.00	67.10
12	0	0.00	67.10
13	0	0.00	67.10
14	0	0.00	67.10
15	0	0.00	67.10

ments of $10 each, subject to our discount rate of 8%. We will use this same cash flow example to illustrate a number of analytic points, most of which apply quite generally to any cash flow. In *Table 1,* the third column labeled *PV*(*H*,*H*) shows the *PV* of the payment received in year *H*. (More precise definitions and more complete development of the mathematical concepts are presented in the Technical Appendix.) Thus, the first $10 payment at the end of year 1 has a *PV*(1,1) of $9.26 in current dollar terms. We could also turn this around and note that a $9.26 deposit would have grown to $10 when invested for one year at an 8% rate of interest:

$$\$9.26 \times 1.08 = \$10.$$

The second $10 payment has a *PV*(2,2) of $8.57, and so on up until the last payment in the 10th year which has a *PV*(10,10) of only $4.63. The next column, labeled *PV*(1,*H*), is the accumulation of all payments from the first year up to and including the one in year *H*. Thus, the *PV*(1,2) for the first two $10 payments is $9.26 + $8.57 = $17.83. The *PV*(1,5) of the flow's first 5 years is $39.93, and the *PV*(1,10) for the entire cash flow is $67.10.

The Reinvested Future Value

However, it is very useful to move beyond this strictly "discounting" framework to think in terms of a generalized future value (*FV*) of an investment. As with most things, it's easy to fall into an overly complicated discussion. So, keeping it simple, we can define a reinvested future value *RFV*(1,*H*) at some horizon *H* as the total funds that would have accumulated if *all* of an investment's payments from year 1 to *H* were reinvested (and compounded) at a given reinvestment rate. For the moment, assume that time horizon *H* coincides with the last payment from the original investment. Returning to our basic annuity example, *Table 2* illustrates the reinvestment process for the 10-year $10 annuity. The first $10 payment is received at the end of year 1 and is immediately reinvested at the assumed 8% rate. This reinvestment generates an additional $0.80 interest, so that together with the second $10 payment, the accumulated reinvested value *RFV*(1,2) = $20.80. The reinvestment process then continues year by year until the end of the 10th year, at which point the *RFV*(1,10) = $144.87. Note that this sum implies the investor will receive $44.87 in interest in addition to the underlying $100 from the original 10 payments.

The *RFV* concept paves the way to a particularly simple (and useful) interpretation of an investment's *PV*. Consider the total *RFV*(1,*H*) that would be built up as of the *H*th year. When this *RFV*(1,*H*) amount is discounted back to the present, it will always just equal the *PV*(1,*H*) of the original investment. Turning this idea around, any investment's *PV*(1,*H*) reflects the magnitude of the required investment that would grow on a fully compounded basis to the given *RFV*(1,*H*), again assuming that a single market interest rate is used for both discounting and reinvestments. (See the Technical Appendix following this section.)

For the simplest possible example, consider the *RFV*(1,1) = $10 for the first payment. When discounted back to the present 8%, the *PV*(1,1)

TABLE 2

Reinvested Future Value

10 Annual Payments of $10
8% Discount Rate

Horizon, H	Payments	Carryforward Amount	New Interest	Reinvested Future Value, $RFV(1,H)$
0	$0	$0.00	$0.00	$0.00
1	10	0.00	0.00	10.00
2	10	10.00	0.80	20.80
3	10	20.80	1.66	32.46
4	10	32.46	2.60	45.06
5	10	45.06	3.60	58.67
6	10	58.67	4.69	73.36
7	10	73.36	5.87	89.23
8	10	89.23	7.14	106.37
9	10	106.37	8.51	124.88
10	10	124.88	9.99	144.87
11	0	144.87	11.59	156.45
12	0	156.45	12.52	168.97
13	0	168.97	13.52	182.49
14	0	182.49	14.60	197.09
15	0	197.09	15.77	212.86

= $9.26 is obtained. And as in the preceding section, this $PV(1,1) = \$9.26$ grows to exactly the $RFV(1,1) = \$10$ when invested at 8%. Similarly, for $H = 7$, Table 2 shows that the $RFV(1,7) = \$89.23$. From Table 1, this 7-year flow has a cumulative $PV(1,7) = \$52.06$. A simple computation shows that

$$\$52.06 \times (1.08)^7 = \$89.23.$$

More generally, as demonstrated in the Technical Appendix,

$$PV(1,H) \times (1.08)^H = RFV(1,H).$$

Like the *PV*, the *FV* has the appeal of great simplicity. Rather than think through a complex pattern of payments, we can just observe that all investments with the same last payment date will have the same *RFV*(1,*H*) for each dollar of *PV*(1,*H*):

$$\frac{RFV(1,H)}{PV(1,H)} = (1.08)^H$$

In other words, any investment's *RFV*(1,*H*) can be reproduced by simply deploying its *PV* amount into a savings account that is then compounded forward at the given rate.

In the preceding, the *RFV*'s horizon was defined to coincide with the last payment date. Suppose that is not the case, that is, suppose we want to consider a 15-year horizon but the investment's payments only cover 10 years? There is an easy fix. After the last payment in the 10th year, the accumulated value *RFV*(1,*H*) would simply be reinvested and compounded forward at the market rate until the 15th-year horizon, thereby growing to the *RFV*(1,15) = \$212.86 as shown in Table 2.

The Horizon Present Value (*HPV*)

In the preceding discussion, when the horizon *H* matches or exceeds the investment's life, there is no further cash flow beyond the horizon. However, a somewhat more complex situation arises when the horizon date falls *before* the cash flow's last payment. For example, consider a 7-year horizon that falls in the midst of our 10-year cash flow. In the 7th year, there will remain a 3-year "tail" consisting of the three \$10 payments in years 8, 9, and 10. Now, the most natural way to put a number on this tail is to again use the *PV* approach. Thus, at the time of the 7th-year horizon, the tail is treated as a new 3-year investment and the remaining flows are discounted back to a *PV*, which we may call the horizon *PV*, with the symbol *HPV*(8,10).

In general terms, for an investment having its last (maturity) payment in year *M*, we can express the horizon *PV* of the next (*M*-*H*) payments as *HPV*(*H*+1, *M*), representing the *PV* as of time *H* (i.e., just *after* the *H*th payment).

For the basic case of a level-pay annuity, the *HPV* is a pretty simple

TABLE 3

Horizon Present Value

10 Annual Payments of $10
8% Discount Rate

Horizon, H	Payments	Present Value of Each Payment, (H,H)	Cumulative Present Value $PV(1,H)$	Horizon Present Value, $HPV(H+1,10)$
0	$0	$0.00	$0.00	$67.10
1	10	9.26	9.26	62.47
2	10	8.57	17.83	57.47
3	10	7.94	25.77	52.06
4	10	7.35	33.12	46.23
5	10	6.81	39.93	39.93
6	10	6.30	46.23	33.12
7	10	5.83	52.06	25.77
8	10	5.40	57.47	17.83
9	10	5.00	62.47	9.26
10	10	4.63	67.10	0.00
11	0	0.00	67.10	0.00
12	0	0.00	67.10	0.00
13	0	0.00	67.10	0.00
14	0	0.00	67.10	0.00
15	0	0.00	67.10	0.00

calculation. At the outset, $H = 0$ and the entire 10-year annuity remains ahead of us, so that the $HPV(1,10)$ is just the same as the $PV(1,10)$ for the entire annuity. In Table 1, $PV(1,10)$ = $67.10, and in *Table 3*, $HPV(1,10)$ is also $67.10. However, at the end of the first year, for $H = 1$, there are only 9 remaining payments. In other words, Table 3's $HPV(2,10)$ = $62.47 is the same as Table 1's $PV(1,9)$, that is, the *PV* for a level flow with 9 annual payments. We can continue in this fashion until we reach a horizon $H = 9$, at which point there is only the one remaining $10 payment to be received. Thus, Table 3's $HPV(10,10)$ = $9.26 is just the discounted value of a $10 payment one year forward, $PV(1,1)$, which we could have read from the third column of Table 1.

The exceptionally simple relationship between Tables 1 and 3 holds only for level cash flows. For more complex cash flows, the $HPV(H{+}1, M)$ must be adjusted to reflect the PV of the cash flow's remaining payments from year $(H + 1)$ to the maturity year M.

The Total Future Value *TFV*(*H*)

To find the total future value at a given horizon $TFV(H)$, we must add the going-forward $HPV(H{+}1, M)$ of the tail flows to the accumulated $RFV(1,H)$ from the reinvestment process. Note that two concepts are combined here: (1) reinvesting (and compounding) the payments from the first H years, that is, $RFV(1,H)$, and (2) discounting the tail payments for the next $(M\text{-}H)$ years, that is, the $HPV(H{+}1, M)$. However, with both reinvesting and discounting taking place at the same market rate, we will obtain a consistent $TFV(H)$ for any investment stretching over any span of years:

$$TFV(H) = RFV\,(1,H) + HPV(H{+}1, M)$$

The numerical illustration of the TFV concept *(Table 4)* requires combining the reinvested value $RFV(\mathrm{H}{+}1, M)$ from Table 2 with the going-forward $HPV(\mathrm{H}{+}1, M)$ values from Table 3. At the outset, when $H = 0$, there will have been no payments as yet and hence, no $RFV\,(0,0) = 0$, and the $TFV(0)$ is simply the $PV(1, M)$. Similarly, at the 10th-year horizon, there are no further payments, so that $HPV(11,10) = 0$, and the $TFV(10)$ consists solely of the accumulated reinvestment $RFV(1,10) = \$144.87$. At the intermediate horizon $H = 3$, there is a reinvested accumulated $RFV(1,3) = \$32.46$ and an $HPV(4,10) = \$52.06$, so that $TFV(3) = \$32.46 + \$52.06 = \$84.53$.

The Technical Appendix following this section demonstrates that, when both discounting and reinvestment take place at the same rate, the $TFV(H)$ can be directly determined from the $PV(1, M)$ for the *entire* cash flow:

$$TFV(H) = (1.08)^{H}\,\mathrm{PV}(1, M)$$

or

TABLE 4

Total Future Value

10 Annual Payments of $10
8% Discount Rate

Horizon, H	Payments	Reinvested Future Value $RFV(1,H)$	Horizon Present Value $HPV(H+1,10)$	Total Future Value $TFV(H)$
0	$0	$0.00	$67.10	$67.10
1	10	10.00	62.47	72.47
2	10	20.80	57.47	78.27
3	10	32.46	52.06	84.53
4	10	45.06	46.23	91.29
5	10	58.67	39.93	98.59
6	10	73.36	33.12	106.48
7	10	89.23	25.77	115.00
8	10	106.37	17.83	124.20
9	10	124.88	9.26	134.13
10	10	144.87	0.00	144.87
11	0	156.45	0.00	156.45
12	0	168.97	0.00	168.97
13	0	182.49	0.00	182.49
14	0	197.09	0.00	197.09
15	0	212.86	0.00	212.86

$$\frac{TFV(H)}{PV(1,M)} = (1.08)^H$$

With the preceding assumptions and the definition of $TFV(H)$, we have achieved the ultimate in oversimplification: Per dollar invested, *every* investment will produce the exact same $TFV(H)$ at any specified horizon date H! And just as any investment will have the same FV per dollar invested today, so at a given horizon, any investment will have the same PV per dollar of FV. This hypothetical world—with a common fixed discount rate that suits every market participant and fits all investments—is a very dull one indeed. At any future point in time (including today), a dollar invested in *any* vehicle will always generate the same *TFV*. Thus, every investment outcome could be replicated by the most trivial action of simply deploying the comparable *PV* into a savings account that then compounds at the specified discount rate.

In such a market, there would be basically no point in choosing one investment over another, and hence no real incentive to trade. It would be the financial equivalent of an ultimate state of entropy, where informed judgment counted for naught—like a bleak, flat desert without any distinguishing features. (Some might argue that it would be the ultimate in efficient markets, but most of us would want to be spared any such deadening form of efficiency!)

Given this finding, one might wonder about the utility of the *RFV* and *HPV* measures. However, the *RFV* and *HPV* are very general concepts that can apply to general cash flows subject to different (and possibly more complex) discounting and reinvestment rates. In these more general cases, the appropriately defined $RFV(1,H)$ and the $HPV(H+1,M)$ will still sum to the $TFV(H)$, even when the compounding relationship,

$$TFV(H) = (1.08)^H \, PV(1,M),$$

may fail to hold.

The *FV* versus the *PV*

In some ways, the *FV* is more intuitively appealing than the *PV*. However, the *FV* does have the disadvantage that it must be pinned to a specific point in time, whereas the *PV* is always uniquely defined in current dollar terms. At the same time, it could be argued that the *FV* is the more general concept, with the *PV* just being a special case of the *FV* with the current time specified as the reference date.

One question that arises is what happens to the *FV* concept when future payments are consumed rather than reinvested? The theoretician's answer would be to look back to the fundamental idea of a discount rate as the exchange between a current dollar (which could be invested or consumed today) and a future payment (where consumption would have been deferred). To the extent that a payment is consumed, the investor is making a trade-off implying that the consumption is worth the "sacrifice" of that many *FV* dollars at a future date. With this generalized notion of value combining literal dollars with psychic reward, the *PV* (or *FV*) of any investment will always be the same, whether the payments are reinvested or just consumed.

Bond Prices and Yields

The reader will notice that we've gotten to this point without specifically addressing the subject of a bond's yield—that which *Inside the Yield Book* is presumably all about. A bond's yield-to-maturity (*YTM*) is that discount rate which generates a *PV* equal to the bond's price. In our flat world of a single market discount rate, the bond's price would always be set by that discount rate, so the *YTM* would always just be this discount rate itself.

One of a bond's basic attributes is its par value, which (roughly) corresponds to the initial funds received by the issuer. In the most idealized bond with neither call features nor sinking funds, the final "principal payment" at maturity will also be generally equal to this par value. The par value is typically set at $1,000, with the bond's price and coupon payment then expressed as a percentage of this $1,000 standard. Thus, for a coupon rate that coincides with our fixed market discount rate of 8%, the *PV* of $1,000 would just match the par value, the price ratio would just be 100% and the bond would be called—not surprisingly—a "par bond." For coupon rates higher than the discount rate (generally, for bonds that had been issued earlier during a higher rate environment), the *PV* would exceed the par value, so the price ratio would be greater than 100%, and such a bond would be called a "premium bond." Similarly, lower coupon rates and lower *PV*s would give rise to price ratios below 100%—hence, "discount bonds."

Now, all this is pretty old hat. Why go through this entire discussion of a flat discount world only to come to these standard descriptions of the three bond types? The point is that these characterizations are really somewhat misleading. *All* these bonds are *fairly* priced in the sense that their *PV* corresponds to their market price. A "discount bond" is not a bargain, nor is a "premium bond" really worth more than a par bond. Only when some differentiating features are incorporated into the analysis does any investment look cheap or dear to a specific investor.

To really understand the *YTM,* our flat-world assumption must be replaced by the more realistic situation where bond prices are based on a host of differentiating factors such as credit quality, maturity, coupon level, sinking funds, call features, market liquidity, and so forth. In this environment, one can argue about whether the bond's price or the *YTM* is the primary determinant of value. The basic fact is that a bond's price, and its *YTM,* are defined in a circular fashion.[7] Thus, for any given bond, the *YTM* is the specific discount rate that generates a *PV* equal to the bond's market price. Different pricing effects can then also be expressed as different *YTM*s. Over the years, this *YTM* approach has proven to be a very convenient comparative yardstick. For example, it has now become commonplace to characterize the incremental return of corporate bonds in terms of their *YTM* "spread" over the U.S. Treasury bond curve.

PV Volatility

A central issue in virtually all *PV* analysis is the level of the *PV*'s sensitivity to changes in the basic discount rate. In the bond world, such *PV* changes in response to changing interest rates are the primary source of price volatility in high-grade bonds. Naturally, this question has major significance for bond market investors and traders.

Let us first examine *PV* volatility in the simple case of the 10-year level-pay annuity. *Table 5* departs from the standard assumption of a fixed discount rate to show, in the third and fourth column, the *PV* of each payment first under our standard 8%, and then a 9% discount rate. The next column contains the percentage change in the *PV* derived from moving from the 8% to the 9% rate.

Table 5 illustrates two key points about the *PV* volatility of single lump-sum payments. First of all, at the higher 9% discount rate, it takes fewer *PV* dollars to grow to a magnitude that matches any given future payments. Thus, the *PV* always declines with higher rates. Moreover, moving out towards later payments, these percentage declines become even greater.

The next two columns show the accumulated *PV*(1,*H*) for the payments from the first to the *H*th year, first calculated at the standard 8% and then at the new rate of 9%. As might be expected, with the move to 9%, the *PV*(1,*H*) value declines for every horizon *H,* with greater percentage declines associated with the longer horizons. Thus, *PV* volatility increases with the length of the time to the annuity's last payment. This result is true for level annuities, but it does not hold when comparing any two cash flows. As an illustration that longer flows are not always more volatile, the single payment in the 7th year shows a far greater percentage *PV* change of –6.25% (shown in the fifth column of Table 5) than the full 10-year annuity's percentage *PV* change of –4.36%.

Table 6 has exactly the same format as Table 5, except that the lower rate levels of 4% and 5% have been substituted for the beginning and ending discount rates. By comparing the entries for the percentage price decline in the two tables, one can immediately see that a lower-rate environment engenders somewhat greater *PV* volatility.

These annuity examples provide a clear basis for understanding the basic principles that determine *PV* volatility in more complex cash flows such as bonds. There are a number of surprises in this area. For example, as an extension of the point made previously, bonds with longer maturities are not always more volatile than bonds with shorter maturities. A typical bond has a stream of coupon payments stretching out to its ultimate maturity payment. If these interim coupon payments loom large relative to the longer maturity payment (as in a premium bond), then the net effect will be some reduction in the bond's volatility. On the other hand, if the coupon flows are small (as in discount bonds), then the larger maturity payment with its greater *PV* volatility will be dominant. At the limit where all coupon payments vanish, one has a highly volatile, pure zero-coupon discount bond that consists solely of a lump-sum payment at maturity. The *PV* price volatility of these zero-coupon bonds *will* increase with each extension in the maturity date. Moreover, the *PV* volatility of zero-coupon bonds will always exceed that of comparable-maturity "normal" bonds with positive coupon flows. It was shown in *Inside the Yield Book* that long enough zero-coupon or discount bonds can have rate sensitivities that exceed that of the longest par bonds. Because the very longest bonds are the so-called "perpetuals" that provide the same coupon flow forever (in theory), this finding came as quite a shock in some parts of the bond world (although not in the United Kingdom, where perpetual government bonds have been a market staple for many years).

TABLE 5

Percentage *PV* Change under +1% Rate Move

10 Annual Payments of $10
8% Starting Discount Rate

Horizon, *H*	Payments	Present Value of Each Payment @ 8%	Present Value of Each Payment @ 9%	Percentage *PV* Change
0	$0	$0.00	$0.00	0.00%
1	10	9.26	9.17	–0.92
2	10	8.57	8.42	–1.83
3	10	7.94	7.72	–2.73
4	10	7.35	7.08	–3.62
5	10	6.81	6.50	–4.50
6	10	6.30	5.96	–5.38
7	10	5.83	5.47	–6.25
8	10	5.40	5.02	–7.11
9	10	5.00	4.60	–7.96
10	10	4.63	4.22	–8.80
11	0	0.00	0.00	0
12	0	0.00	0.00	0
13	0	0.00	0.00	0
14	0	0.00	0.00	0
15	0	0.00	0.00	0

The Macaulay Duration

One of the concepts just discussed is that a bond's maturity date—or more generally, the date of any cash flow's last payment—is a poor gauge of the flow's "life." As one might suspect, the problem of finding a good measure of a flow's life is closely related to the problem of determining its *PV* volatility. One natural way is to simply compute an "average life" by just determining the time to each payment, weighted by the size of the payment. However, a little experimentation quickly reveals a number of problems with this approach. For example, a perpetual bond has an infi-

Cumulative Present Value, *PV*(1,*H*) @ 8%	Cumulative Present Value, *PV*(1,*H*) @ 9%	Percentage Change in Cumulative Present Value
$0.00	$0.00	0.00%
9.26	9.17	–0.92
17.83	17.59	–1.35
25.77	25.13	–1.78
33.12	32.40	–2.19
39.93	38.90	–2.58
46.23	44.86	–2.96
52.06	50.33	–3.33
57.47	55.35	–3.69
62.47	59.95	–4.03
67.10	64.18	–4.36
67.10	64.18	–4.36
67.10	64.18	–4.36
67.10	64.18	–4.36
67.10	64.18	–4.36
67.10	64.18	–4.36

nite maturity and an infinite average life as well on this payment-weighted basis. But, as noted above, the perpetual's *PV* volatility is generally lower than that of a 15-year zero-coupon bond.

A somewhat more sophisticated approach entails again finding the average time to the flow's payments, but now weighted by the *PV* of each payment. This approach was first suggested by Frederick Macaulay in 1938.[8] In his treatise (which covered a broad range of topics), Macaulay addressed the problem of finding a useful "half-life" measure for railroad bonds, where the cash flows were complicated by the presence of strong mandatory sinking funds. He finally decided on *PV*-weighted aver-

TABLE 6

Percentage *PV* Change under +1% Rate Move

10 Annual Payments of $10
4% Starting Discount Rate

Horizon, *H*	Payments	Present Value of Each Payment @ 4%	Present Value of Each Payment @ 5%	Percentage *PV* Change
0	$0	$0.00	$0.00	0.00%
1	10	9.62	9.52	–0.95
2	10	9.25	9.07	–1.90
3	10	8.89	8.64	–2.83
4	10	8.55	8.23	–3.76
5	10	8.22	7.84	–4.67
6	10	7.90	7.46	–5.58
7	10	7.60	7.11	–6.48
8	10	7.31	6.77	–7.37
9	10	7.03	6.45	–8.25
10	10	6.76	6.14	–9.13
11	0	0.00	0.00	0.00
12	0	0.00	0.00	0.00
13	0	0.00	0.00	0.00
14	0	0.00	0.00	0.00
15	0	0.00	0.00	0.00

age life as the best yardstick. It has since become known as the "Macaulay Duration," and it has proven to be an extremely useful concept.

The Macaulay Duration $D(1,H)$ is determined by weighting the time to each payment by that payment's percentage of the flow's overall *PV*. In *Table 7,* this calculation is carried out by first multiplying the time to each payment (the first column) by the payment's *PV* (the third column), to obtain a product (the fifth column), which is then accumulated over the horizon period (the sixth column). The Duration $D(1,H)$ (the seventh column) is then found by dividing this accumulated value by the flow's $PV(1,H)$ to that horizon (the fourth column).

Cumulative Present Value, $PV(1,H)$ @ 4%	Cumulative Present Value, $PV(1,H)$ @ 5%	Percentage Change in Cumulative Present Value
$0.00	$0.00	0.00%
9.62	9.52	–0.95
18.86	18.59	–1.41
27.75	27.23	–1.87
36.30	35.46	–2.31
44.52	43.29	–2.75
52.42	50.76	–3.18
60.02	57.86	–3.59
67.33	64.63	–4.00
74.35	71.08	–4.40
81.11	77.22	–4.80
81.11	77.22	–4.80
81.11	77.22	–4.80
81.11	77.22	–4.80
81.11	77.22	–4.80
81.11	77.22	–4.80

Thus, the Duration $D(1,1)$ of the first year's payment is just $D(1,1) = (1 \times 9.26) \div 9.26 = 1$. The Duration $D(1,2)$ of the 2-year flow is found by adding 1×9.26 to the product of 2 times the \$8.57 *PV* of the second year payment, to obtain $(1 \times 9.26) + (2 \times 8.57) = 26.41$, and then dividing by $PV(1,2) = \$17.83$. In this case, the result $D(1,2) = 26.41 \div 17.83 = 1.48$ is close to the 2-year flow's simple unweighted average life of

$$\frac{1 \times 10 + 2 \times 10}{(10 + 10)} = 1.50.$$

TABLE 7

The Macaulay Duration

10 Annual Payments of $10
8% Discount Rate

Horizon, *H*	Payments	Present Value of Each Payment, *PV*(*H*,*H*)	Cumulative Present Value, *PV*(1,*H*)	Time to Payment Multiplied by *PV* of Each Payment *H* × *PV*(*H*,*H*)
0	$0	$0.00	$0.00	$0.00
1	10	9.26	9.26	9.26
2	10	8.57	17.83	17.15
3	10	7.94	25.77	23.81
4	10	7.35	33.12	29.40
5	10	6.81	39.93	34.03
6	10	6.30	46.23	37.81
7	10	5.83	52.06	40.84
8	10	5.40	57.47	43.22
9	10	5.00	62.47	45.02
10	10	4.63	67.10	46.32
11	0	0.00	67.10	0.00
12	0	0.00	67.10	0.00
13	0	0.00	67.10	0.00
14	0	0.00	67.10	0.00
15	0	0.00	67.10	0.00

However, as the time is extended, the gap between the weighted Macaulay Duration and the simple average life becomes more pronounced. For the full 10-year flow, the Duration $D(1,10) = 4.87$ is considerably less than the flow's 5.5-year payment-weighted average life. Generally, the longer the annuity, the larger this gap will grow as the more distant payments are discounted ever more severely. In the extreme limit, the infinite annuity has an infinite average life, but it can be shown to have a duration of 13.5 years.

The annuity is a stream of fixed annual payments over some span of time. Without a large, bond-like principal payment at maturity, the annu-

Cumulative *PV*-Weighted Life	Macaulay Duration $D(1,H)$ Cum. *PV*-Weighted Life as % of Cum. $PV(1,H)$	*PV* Volatility $PV\text{-}VOL(1,H) = -D(1,H)/(1+y)$
$0.00	0.00%	0.00%
9.26	1.00	–0.93
26.41	1.48	–1.37
50.22	1.95	–1.80
79.62	2.40	–2.23
113.65	2.85	–2.64
151.46	3.28	–3.03
192.31	3.69	–3.42
235.53	4.10	–3.79
280.55	4.49	–4.16
326.87	4.87	–4.51
326.87	4.87	–4.51
326.87	4.87	–4.51
326.87	4.87	–4.51
326.87	4.87	–4.51
326.87	4.87	–4.51

ity would always have a Macaulay Duration that is shorter than its payment-based half-life. This annuity example provides a clear illustration of the original Macaulay insight. All the payments of an annuity have the same dollar value (by definition). However, when the *PV*-weighted average of each payment is considered, the earlier payments naturally loom larger. Consequently, the annuity's Macaulay Duration will always be shorter than the midpoint of its equal-dollar cash flow. (For general cash flows, all that can be said is that the duration will never be longer than the time to the last payment.)

The annuity example also provides a good intuitive illustration of how duration itself depends on the level of discount rates. At very low interest rates approaching zero, the *PV* of a single payment converges on its raw dollar value. Thus, at ever-lower discount rates, the Macaulay Duration ultimately does coincide with the literal half-life. In contrast, at higher interest rates, the later payments are discounted more severely and the stream of *PV*s is more "front-loaded," resulting in generally shorter durations.

As noted earlier, this result holds quite generally: The Macaulay Duration of any cash flow becomes larger as interest rates fall. One might be tempted to conclude from this observation that very low interest rate environments can be very treacherous. When rates can only go up, and when the price sensitivity of any given cash flow is near its maximum, it's a pretty toxic combination.

PV Volatility and the Modified Duration

Macaulay was quite happy with his half-life interpretation of the duration measure. (Indeed, he only devoted a few pages to its derivation before moving to other matters in a 591-page book.) However, it was subsequently discovered that with a slight adjustment factor, the Macaulay Duration could act as a gauge of the *PV* volatility for a general cash flow.

Table 7 illustrates how the duration $D(1,H)$ can be used to approximate the percentage price sensitivity. Dividing $D(1,H)$ by $(1+y)$ where y is the discount rate results in a value that is often referred to as the "modified Duration." Thus for our 8% discount rate, the 10-year Macaulay Duration $D(1,10) = 4.87$ is reduced to a modified Duration,

$$\frac{4.87}{1.08} = 4.51.$$

It is worth noting that this adjustment results in a 4.51 value that is another step smaller than the annuity's simple average life of 5.5 years. It can be shown (see the Technical Appendix following this section) that this value of 4.51 corresponds to the derivative of the percentage change in the *PV*. In Table 5, the $PV(1,10)$ drops from \$67.10 at the original 8% discount rate to \$64.18 at 9%. This percentage loss of –4.36% is closely approximated by the negative of the modified Duration value of 4.51. Thus, the modified Duration can be seen to be a reasonable approximation for the magnitude of the percentage price loss resulting from a +1% move in the discount rate.

With smaller and smaller moves in the discount rate, the percentage *PV* change per unit rate move converges (in absolute value) to the negative of the modified Duration value (see the Technical Appendix). For this reason, we can refer to the negative value of the modified Duration as the *PV* volatility, *PV-VOL* (1,*H*).

In many ways, it was remarkable that Macaulay failed to see the broader use of his discovery as a volatility measure. It is even more remarkable that more than forty years elapsed before this measure came into common usage in the U.S. bond market. In fact, this double level of discovery forms a fascinating case study in how theoretical findings can take a circuitous path before ultimately finding their way into practice.[9,10]

Reinvestment Volatility

When we move from the *PV,* which declines with higher discount rates, to the *RFV,* which increases with higher reinvestment rates, another "volatility" measure becomes important. The reinvestment volatility (*RFV-VOL*) is rarely characterized in the same quantitative way as the Duration concept, but doing so leads to some interesting results that should be more widely appreciated and that may be particularly useful for long-term holders of fixed-income exposures such as insurance companies and pension funds.

The first step in such a discussion is to focus on some prescribed future date as the *RFV* horizon. For bonds, as discussed in *Inside the Yield Book,* the reference *RFV* horizon *H* is almost always the bond's maturity date. We noted earlier how premium bonds with their higher coupon flows are more reinvestment-sensitive than discount bonds. In contrast, the zero-coupon bond is the ultimate in terms of reinvestment insensitivity: When its maturity is taken as the reference point, it will always have its maturity payment as the *RFV* regardless of the level of intervening interest rates. In other words, it has absolutely no sensitivity to changing reinvestment rates. (Incidentally, for all bonds having the same maturity date, the zero-coupon has the *highest PV* sensitivity to discount rate changes, but the *lowest RFV* sensitivity to reinvestment rates changes.)

It turns out that the percentage volatility $RFV\text{-}VOL(1,H)$ bears a very simple relation to the Duration value. For a cash flow stretching out to a given horizon *H,* the *RFV* volatility can be shown to be just the gap between the horizon and the flow's Macaulay Duration, adjusted by one plus the interest rate:

$$\begin{aligned} RFV\text{-}VOL(1,H) &= \frac{[H - D(1,H)]}{(1+y)} \\ &= \left(\frac{H}{1+y}\right) + PV\text{-}VOL(1,H) \end{aligned}$$

This result is developed in the Technical Appendix. As one might expect from the earlier discussion of the duration measure, this *RFV-VOL* finding is essentially derivative-based, that is, it acts as a better approximation for ever-smaller rate moves.

At the outset, it can be seen that for $H = 0$, before any payment whatsoever, there is no cash flow, and so the Duration $D(1,0)$ has the trivial value of zero. Similarly, there is no reinvestment volatility:

$$\begin{aligned} RFV\text{-}VOL(1,10) &= \frac{[H - D(1,H)]}{(1+y)} \\ &= \frac{(0\text{–}0)}{(1.08)} \\ &= 0. \end{aligned}$$

Moreover, for the single lump-sum payment at the horizon, the Duration $D(1,H)$ just equals the horizon *H:*

$$\begin{aligned} D(1,H) &= D(H,H) \\ &= H, \end{aligned}$$

and again there is no reinvestment sensitivity because

$$\begin{aligned} RFV\text{-}VOL(H,H) &= \frac{[H - D(1,H)]}{(1+y)} \\ &= \frac{[H - H]}{(1+y)} \\ &= 0. \end{aligned}$$

However, moving from single lump-sum payments toward more general cash flows stretching out over time, the reinvestment volatility grows with longer horizons. Thus in *Table 8,* the annuity develops a significant exposure to changing reinvestment rates as the horizon lengthens. Taking the 7-year horizon as an example, Table 8 provides a value of $D(1,7) = 3.69$, so that

$$\begin{aligned} RFV\text{-}VOL(1,7) &= \frac{[H - D(1,H)]}{(1+y)} \\ &= \frac{7 - 3.69}{1.08} \\ &= \frac{3.31}{1.08} \\ &= 3.06. \end{aligned}$$

To see how well this measure approximates an actual shift in reinvestment rates, refer to Table 2, which shows that $RFV(1,7) = \$89.23$ at the 8% rate. If the reinvestment rate is raised to 9%, the $RFV(1,7)$ becomes \$92.10, a 3.22 percentage increase, which is reasonably approximated by the derivative-based value of 3.06.

Turning the above finding around, note that in general, when a flow's maturity M is taken as the FV horizon, the Duration and the $RFV\text{-}VOL(1,M)$ volatility add up to the flow's life,

$$M = D(1,M) + (1+y) \times [RFV\text{-}VOL(1,M)].$$

Thus, for the annuity with $M = 10$, Table 8 provides values of $D(1,10) = 4.87$ and $RFV\text{-}VOL(1,10) = 4.75$, so that

$$\begin{aligned} M &= D(1,10) + (1+y) \times [RFV\text{-}VOL(1,10)] \\ &= 4.87 + 1.08 \times 4.75 \\ &= 10. \end{aligned}$$

It turns out that this relationship holds for any cash flow. For the 10-year annuity, the Duration and reinvestment volatility turn out to be nearly equal. However, this will not be true for more general cash flows, even though their sum will always equal the time to the last payment.

TABLE 8

Reinvestment Volatility

10 Annual Payments of $10
8% Discount Rate

Horizon, H	Reinvested Future Value $RFV(1,H)$	Macaulay Duration $D(1,H)$	Horizon-to-Duration Gap $H - D(1,H)$	Reinvestment Volatility $RFV\text{-}VOL(1,H) = [H - D(1,H) / (1+y)]$
0	$0	0.00	0.00	0.00%
1	10.00	1.00	0.00	0.00
2	20.80	1.48	0.52	0.48
3	32.46	1.95	1.05	0.97
4	45.06	2.40	1.60	1.48
5	58.67	2.85	2.15	1.99
6	73.36	3.28	2.72	2.52
7	89.23	3.69	3.31	3.06
8	106.37	4.10	3.90	3.61
9	124.88	4.49	4.51	4.17
10	144.87	4.87	5.13	4.75
11	156.45	4.87	6.13	5.67
12	168.97	4.87	7.13	6.60
13	182.49	4.87	8.13	7.53
14	197.09	4.87	9.13	8.45
15	212.86	4.87	10.13	9.38

The Total Future Value Volatility at Longer Horizons

The preceding development of an $RFV\text{-}VOL(1,H)$ volatility also provides an answer to the question of the volatility $TFV\text{-}VOL(H)$ of a cash flow's $TFV(H)$ with a horizon H that coincides with the flow's last payment M, that is, where $H = M$. With horizons that match the flow's last payment, there are by definition no tail flows and so the total future value, *TFV,* consists of just the reinvestment-driven $RFV(1,H)$. Because the reinvestment effect is always positive,

$$TFV\text{-}VOL(M) = RFV\text{-}VOL(1,M)$$
$$= \frac{[M - D(1,M)]}{(1 + y)},$$

higher rates will always lead to higher *TFV*s (except for the case of a single lump-sum payments in the *M*th year).

Even when the *FV* horizon is extended beyond the last payment date, this relationship continues to hold. The Duration value remains stable, but the horizon gap increases by the exact length of the extension. For example, if we look at a 12-year horizon with the 10-year annuity, the Duration $D(1,12) = D(1,10)$ remains unchanged at 4.87, but the $RFV\text{-}VOL(1,12)$ volatility now increases to 6.60:

$$RFV(1,12) = \frac{[H - D(1,M)]}{(1 + y)}$$

$$= \frac{12 - 4.87}{1.08}$$
$$= 6.60$$

as shown in Table 8 for $H = 12$.

Moreover, this *TFV* volatility result will hold for any horizon longer than the last payment date:

$$TFV\text{-}VOL(H) = \left(\frac{1}{1+y}\right)[H - D(1,M)]$$

for any $H \geq M$.

Horizon Duration and the Generalized *TFV* Volatility

As noted earlier, one can also have horizon *H* dates that precede the last payment date, that is, $H<M$. Recall that in such cases, the total $TFV(H)$ will be the sum of the reinvested flows to that date $RFV(1,H)$, together with the going-forward $HPV(H+1,M)$ of the remaining flows. These two terms react in opposite ways to rate changes, so that the *TFV*

sensitivity will depend on the balance between the two volatility terms. As might be expected, for relatively short horizons, the *TFV* is dominated by the Duration effect (i.e., a negative response to positive interest rate changes), whereas relatively long horizon *TFV*s are more subject to positive rate sensitivity from the reinvestment effect.

In the preceding sections, we developed volatility concepts for the reinvestment effect *RFV*. However, to provide for a complete understanding of the total volatility of the *TFV* at intermediate horizons $H < M$, we must also develop a measure for the rate sensitivity of the $HPV(H{+}1, M)$ for the cash flows beyond the horizon. This measure of *HPV* volatility can be readily formed as a straightforward extension of the basic *PV* volatility and Duration concepts.[11]

The $HPV(H{+}1, M)$ is basically the *PV* at *H* of the remaining cash flow beyond a given horizon point *H*, and its volatility $HPV\text{-}VOL(H{+}1, M)$ reflects the investment's continuing volatility at the end of a specified investment period. As one can imagine, this measure is an important tool in many fixed-income analyses. In our particularly simple case of a level 10-year annuity, this Horizon Duration $HD(H{+}1,10)$ just corresponds to the duration of the remaining $(10–H)$ payments. Thus, as shown in *Table 9*, for a horizon $H = 6$, there remain 4 annual payments, and the Horizon Duration $HD(7,10) = 2.40$ can basically be read from the earlier Duration value for $D(1,4)$.

This easy "reversal" of the Duration holds only for level annuities, where the tail years have the same level cash flow pattern as the early years. In the case of a general cash flow, the Horizon Duration can be calculated as the *PV*-weighted average life, as of the horizon *H* of the tail flows remaining after the horizon (see the Technical Appendix).

In these cases where the horizon falls within the span of the flow, both the reinvestment rate and the future estimated discount rate are part of the analytic process. In analyzing scenarios that entail changing both of these rates, one sometimes assumes that both rates are equal, and that they remain in lockstep under the changing rate scenario. Moreover, the greatest simplicity is achieved under the further assumption that the rate change occurs at the outset.

In the previous sections, it is shown that, for horizons equal to or longer than the last payment, the *TFV* volatility could be approximated by a simple "horizon-to-Duration gap" formula. Now, with this assumption of

TABLE 9

Horizon Duration and Horizon Volatility

10 Annual Payments
8% Discount Rate

Horizon, *H*	Horizon Present Value *HPV*(*H*+1,10)	Macaulay Duration *D*(1,*H*)	Horizon Duration *HD*(*H*+1,*M*)	Horizon Volatility *HPV-VOL*(*H*+1,*M*) = −*HD*(*H*+1,*M*) / (1+*y*)
0	$67.10	0.00	4.87	−4.51%
1	62.42	1.00	4.49	−4.16
2	57.47	1.48	4.10	−3.79
3	52.06	1.95	3.69	−3.42
4	46.23	2.40	3.28	−3.03
5	39.93	2.85	2.85	−2.64
6	33.12	3.28	2.40	−2.23
7	25.77	3.69	1.95	−1.80
8	17.83	4.10	1.48	−1.37
9	9.26	4.49	1.00	−0.93
10	0.00	4.87	0.00	0.00
11	0.00	4.87	0.00	0.00
12	0.00	4.87	0.00	0.00
13	0.00	4.87	0.00	0.00
14	0.00	4.87	0.00	0.00
15	0.00	4.87	0.00	0.00

lockstep rate changes, it can be shown that the "horizon-to-Duration gap" relationship holds not only for longer horizons, but indeed for *any FV* horizon regardless of its placement relative to the investment's span of flows (see the Technical Appendix). More precisely, for *any FV* horizon *H,* the percentage volatility in the *TFV*(*H*) can be approximated by the extent that the horizon *H* exceeds the Macaulay Duration $D(1, M)$ of the entire flow; that is, for any *H,*

$$TFV\text{-}VOL(H) = \left[\frac{1}{1+y}\right][H - D(1, M)].$$

This formulation (sometimes known as the "Babcock rule"[12]) can be used to ascertain the *TFV* sensitivity for *any* horizon point, regardless of whether it falls within or after the span of the cash flow. This finding is quite general, holding for any cash flow (i.e., not just level annuities). However, staying with our basic example of the 10-year annuity, *Table 10* shows how the *TFV-VOL* changes from an initially negative value for short horizons to positive values for longer horizons. For example, consider the 10-year annuity with a Duration of 4.87. With a horizon of zero, that is, where the *TFV*(10) equals the *HPV*(1,10), the adjusted horizon gap is,

$$\begin{aligned} TFV\text{-}VOL(0) &= \frac{1}{1+y}[H - D(1,M)] \\ &= \frac{1}{(1.08)}[0 - D(1,10)] \\ &= \frac{1}{(1.08)}(0 - 4.87) \\ &= -4.51 \end{aligned}$$

When the horizon is extended to 3 years, the gap becomes 3 – 4.87 = –1.87, and

$$\begin{aligned} TFV\text{-}VOL(3) &= \frac{1}{1.08}(-1.87) \\ &= -1.73, \end{aligned}$$

so that *TFV*(3) is still more sensitive to price moves from the remaining 7-year flows than to the reinvestment effects from the first three years. In other words, a +1% rate move would create about – 1.73% change in *TFV*. In contrast, when the *FV* horizon is extended to 7 years, the gap becomes 7 – 4.87 = +2.13, and

$$\begin{aligned} TFV\text{-}VOL(7) &= \frac{2.13}{1.08} \\ &= +1.97, \end{aligned}$$

TABLE 10

The Total Future Value Volatility

10 Annual Payments of $10
8% Discount Rate

Horizon, H	Reinvested Future Value, $RFV(1,H)$	Horizon Present Value, $HPV(H+1,10)$	Total Future Value, $TFV(H)$	Horizon-to-Duration Gap $H - D(1,10) = H\text{-}4.87$	Total Future Value Volatility $TFV\text{-}VOL(H) = [H\text{-}D(1,10)]\,/\,(1.08)$
0	$0.00	$67.10	$67.10	−4.87	−4.51%
1	10.00	62.47	72.47	−3.87	−3.58
2	20.80	57.47	78.27	−2.87	−2.66
3	32.46	52.06	84.53	−1.87	−1.73
4	45.06	46.23	91.29	−0.87	−0.81
5	58.67	39.93	98.59	0.13	0.12
6	73.36	33.12	106.48	1.13	1.05
7	89.23	25.77	115.00	2.13	1.97
8	106.37	17.83	124.20	3.13	2.90
9	124.88	9.26	134.13	4.13	3.82
10	144.87	0.00	144.87	5.13	4.75
11	156.45	0.00	156.45	6.13	5.67
12	168.97	0.00	168.97	7.13	6.60
13	182.49	0.00	182.49	8.13	7.53
14	197.09	0.00	197.09	9.13	8.45
15	212.86	0.00	212.86	10.13	9.36

and the reinvestment effect now dominates. And, of course, at the flow's 10-year maturity, the $TFV\text{-}VOL(10)$ sensitivity just corresponds to reinvestment volatility $RFV\text{-}VOL(1,10)$, and has the +4.75 value noted earlier.

Now consider a horizon $H = 4.87$ years, which exactly corresponds to the Duration. The horizon-to-Duration gap vanishes, and the *TFV* sensitivity becomes negligible. At this point, the positive reinvestment from the first 4.87 years' flow is just offset by the negative rate response in the *PV* for the flow from the next 5.13 years. In other words, with a horizon matching the flow's Duration, a stable *TFV* can essentially be achieved in the face of interest rate movements—up or down! (Of course, there are many caveats that should surround this overly strong statement, especially the ones that restrict rate movement to our assumption of a small lockstep move that occurs at the outset.)

The above result suggests that the *TFV*(*H*) at a given horizon can be stabilized by investing in a fixed-income portfolio having a Duration that matches the horizon date. This observation leads to a discussion of the subject of "immunization."

Immunization

A common investment problem is to provide a given dollar payment at a specified future point in time. Obviously, with zero-coupon bonds, this problem has a simple solution: Just use a zero-coupon bond that matures at the specified horizon. However, back when *Inside the Yield Book* was written, the zero-coupon bond was only a hypothetical construct (although Sidney Homer and I made considerable use of the zero-coupon concept as an analytic tool in several of the *Inside the Yield Book* chapters).

At that time, without the availability of zero-coupon bonds, the lump-sum payment problem could be solved only by finding a portfolio of coupon-bearing bonds that would provide the desired *TFV*, even in the face of upward or downward moves in the interest rate. Because this problem involved creating a portfolio whose outcome was protected against the "disease" of changing rates, it came to be called the immunization problem.

Although now there are many zero-coupon bonds of all maturities, they are primarily U.S. government bonds (or their components). Accordingly, they may have the highest credit quality, but they also have the disadvantage of providing the most conservative yields available. Thus, even today, when the problem arises of achieving a stable lump-sum payment with higher yielding bonds, the immunization process remains relevant.

In 1952, the basic immunization problem was solved by a U.K. actuary named F. M. Redington.[13] Essentially, his finding was a generalization of the above result that the *TFV* sensitivity vanishes at the cash flow's Duration. Turning this around, the immunization problem can be solved by constructing a bond portfolio with a Duration that *continuously* matches the specified time at which the lump-sum payment is needed. In essence, with such a portfolio, the reinvestment boost from a higher rate shock is offset by the lower price of the tail flows, and vice versa for lower rates.

As time passes and with each interest rate movement, the Duration of an immunized portfolio will generally shift away from its initially "matched" position. Thus a continual rebalancing back to a matched Duration posture is an intrinsic feature of the immunization process.

Because of this requirement for continuous rebalancing, the immunization concept can be recast in strictly *PV* terms. Recall that with a uniform interest rate assumption, the *PV* and *TFV* are connected via the relationship,

$$TFV(H) = (1 + y)^H \times PV(1, M).$$

Thus, as long as the *PV*s of the assets and the liabilities are matched at the outset, and can stay matched under various interest rate movements, they will both compound forward to approximately the same *TFV(H)*. The key to maintaining this match is (1) to have the *PV*s be equal at the outset, and (2) to have the *PV* volatility of the assets match that of the liabilities. With these two basic conditions (and some other secondary conditions that need not be delved into here), the *PV*s will move in lockstep, and hence both *TFV*s will always evolve along a common path.

A more generalized form goes beyond the problems of a single payment at a point in time to the immunization of a stream of liabilities that stretch out *over* time. Many pension liabilities have this form.[14,15] An analogous approach to the zero-coupon bond solution is to find a "cash-match" portfolio that provides a cash flow that coincides with the specified liability schedule.[16] However, this cash-matching technique is a rather restrictive approach. A more general and more optimal solution is to achieve an immunization where changing interest rates affect *both* the fixed-income portfolio and the liability flows in approximately the same way (see Technical Appendix). Redington addressed this more general immunization problem and found that the same basic technique worked once again: Construct a fixed-income portfolio so that its Duration matches the Duration of the liability stream.[17,18,19] (As always, although this is the basic idea, there are second-order conditions and complications that arise, especially when more complex forms of rate movements are allowed.[20])

Horizon Analysis

The preceding discussion assumed that the reinvestment rate and the discount rate are always equal and always move in a lockstep fashion. However, there is an important form of total return analysis for fixed-income portfolios where these assumptions break down. As demonstrated earlier, the total value $TFV(H)$ of a cash flow at any given horizon H consists of the $RFV(1,H)$ plus the $HPV(H+1,M)$. Viewing the $TFV(H)$ in terms of these two basic components has the advantage of allowing for reinvestment rates over an initial period that may differ from the discount rate that applies at the end of that period.

Of course, in this more general case where the reinvestment and discount rates may take different paths, the Babcock formula cited earlier fails to hold, and the $TFV(H)$ (and its volatility) have to be estimated using more appropriately tailored measures for the *RFV* and the *HPV*. More specifically, in this "horizon analysis" approach, the current rate structure is often assumed to persist throughout the initial horizon period, thereby largely determining the reinvestment effect.[21] The impact of future rate changes is then focused on the going-forward discount rate that applies as of the horizon point. In such scenarios, the *RFV* remains stable, whereas the *HPV* volatility bears the brunt of the overall volatility in *TFV* (see the Technical Appendix).

One alternative approach is to assume that the reinvestment rate moves uniformly up or down to reach the rate level assumed at the horizon. For horizons that are short relative to the length of the investment's overall cash flow, both these horizon analysis approaches enable the analyst to focus on the future rate levels at the horizon as the primary source of return variability.

A similar technique can be used when a yield curve is assumed to maintain its shape, resulting in a bond having a "rolling yield" as it captures the capital gain (or loss) from moving to the yield curve position at the horizon.[22]

In a sense, this horizon analysis approach attempts to separate the nearer-term probable results from the more hypothetical future outcomes. This two-phase structure can be seen in many areas of investment analysis (e.g., two-stage *DDM* models, horizon-matching immunizations, etc.).

For example, consider an investor who plans to hold an investment for 3 years. The *RFV* over that short period will be relatively insensitive to reinvestment rate changes. For our basic 10-year annuity example, the *RFV-VOL*(1,3) volatility will only be about +0.97%, as can be seen in Table 8. The primary source of risk will then be the *HPV* volatility, which in Table 9 is quite significant at *HPV-VOL*(4,10) = –3.42%. At the same time, it is worth noting that this *HPV* volatility of –3.42% is more moderate than the cash flow's original *PV* volatility of *PV-VOL*(1,10) = –4.51% (Table 7). In essence, by settling in advance on a 3-year holding period, the investor has reduced the price volatility risk to this lower level that applies at the 3-year horizon. These two observations illustrate how the horizon analysis enables the investor to incorporate his planned holding period into his assessment of the probable return and relevant risks associated with a given investment.

Generalizing the *PV* Model to Equities

The *YTM* is a well-defined measure because the coupon flows over the maturity of high-grade noncallable bonds are well defined. Therefore, for a given market price, there is only one uniform rate that can discount these fixed flows back to the given price. However, turning to investments with less well-defined flows, such as equities or callable bonds, the problem becomes more complex on a number of counts. At the outset, there needs to be some process for estimating the flows themselves. Such estimates, even when they presume a single scenario without risk considerations, are essentially subjective estimates.

One basic model for estimating the fair value of an equity investment is the so-called dividend discount model (*DDM*). Basically, the *DDM* assigns a uniform growth rate to the stock's dividend, thereby producing a growing stream of payouts. In a fairly standard version, this growth is assumed to continue indefinitely, with an appropriate market discount rate then translating the growth flows into a fair price—or "intrinsic value" as it is sometimes called.[23,24] In its basic form, the *DDM* treats dividend growth as organic (or magical, depending on one's viewpoint). However, the *DDM* can also be formulated as an "earnings model," in which the firm earns a given return on its asset base, distributes some portion as dividends, but then retains the remainder as reinvested capital. It is the compounding of these additional reinvested funds that then generates the further growth in earnings, and hence the growth in dividends as well.

In a sense, the earnings model treats the stock with its cash flows as if it were a bond, albeit a rather complex one. Many variants of these cash flow models are applied in equity valuation. However, there is one particular approach—the "franchise value"—that gives rise to some rather different applications of the *PV* concept.[25] These applications are worth mentioning because they can be useful in addressing a wide variety of financial problems.

In the franchise value approach to modeling equity cash flows, the earnings are notionally segregated into two different streams. The first is the current sustainable earnings stream that would continue without any further investment by the firm. (Hypothetically, if the firm were to forgo all investment-driven growth, these earnings could be fully distributed as dividends.) The second earnings stream arises from the firm's ability to find investments that provide "franchise" level returns, that is, returns in excess of the cost of capital.

Spread Flows and Opportunity *PVs*

The opportunity for such franchise investments exists because of the firm's presumed special presence in the marketplace, its various cost efficiencies, patents and knowledge base, distribution network, and so forth. The earnings from these new investments produce a stream of "net-net" profits above and beyond the cost of capital, and it is the present value of this net-net profit flow that leads to the firm's franchise value. The firm's total present value—or intrinsic value—is the sum of the tangible value from the base level of sustainable earnings together with the net-net franchise value derived from these new investments.

By further deconstructing the franchise value, one finds two additional *PV* concepts that can prove both interesting and useful. The first is the idea of a flow of net-net profits above and beyond cost of funding. In essence, this flow is based on a *spread* between the return on new investments and the cost of financing those investments. In some form, this notion of the availability of a positive "spread flow" can be found in many financial analyses. But the spread flow itself can be further decomposed into two *PV* components: (1) the normalized *PV* per dollar invested in the spread flow, and (2) the "opportunity *PV*" reflecting the total stream of dollars that can be invested at this advantageous spread. The product of these two *PV*s corresponds to the franchise value.

Because advantageous spread flows are, well, advantageous, an investor would be well-advised to invest in them as fully as possible. Hence, by their very nature, these opportunities are intrinsically limited in magnitude. For example, in the standard *DDM* models, the new advantageous investments are implicitly limited to some fraction of the earnings at each point in time.

One can find many forms of spread flow opportunities in today's capital markets. Basically, a spread flow potential is present in any opportunity where a special edge—large or small—can lead to a stream of profits that exceed the cost of capital. In essence, this world of potential franchise spreads might be viewed as comprising an invisible meta-market that exists side-by-side with the more visible capital markets. When brought to fruition, these franchise spread opportunities presumably provide some social and/or economic value. From this vantage point, one could argue that the ultimate mission of a modern financial market is to steer capital to truly worthwhile franchise opportunities so that their potential value can be realized.

The *PV* as a Hypothetical Ratio

The *PV* concept can be generalized to a very simple ratio form that is helpful in thinking about the valuation of financial securities. The numerator in this ratio basically reflects the cash flows from a given investment. Obviously, these flows can be quite complex. However, a "perpetualization" technique can be used to represent any given cash flow as a *PV*–equivalent annuity with infinite life. (Note that the other characteristics—such as the Duration—of the original cash flow will generally be lost in this transformation.)

Now, the *PV* of a perpetual annuity is the simplest of all *PV* formulas—it is just the ratio of the annual payment to the discount rate. With this formulation, the *PV* of any financial instrument can be cast in terms of a ratio with a numerator reflecting the cash flow and a denominator consisting of the appropriate (risk-adjusted) discount rate.

Movements in the investment value can then be viewed as the net result of changes in the estimated flows in the numerator and changes in the discount rates. Any changes in the numerator would generally reflect altered estimates of the investment's cash flows, whereas discount rate changes would correspond to movements in the market structure of interest rates. However, although the discount rate has been designated as a single flat number for illustrative purposes, it should be recognized that the *appropriate* discount rate for a given investment will really be an amalgam of many factors—the placement of the investment's flow along the yield curve, its credit risk, its optionality, and so forth. As a result, when there is a shift in the estimated value or riskiness of an investment's flows, it shouldn't come as a surprise to see changes in the appropriate discounting process as well.

Nonetheless, it can be very useful to retain this mental framework of the *PV* as a basic ratio. It can then be helpful to try to identify whether the initial stimulus for *PV* movements arises primarily from the revised flows in the numerator or from a changing discount rate in the denominator (even when both ultimately adjust to a new equilibrium).

This ratio model applies to equities as well as to bond investments. Indeed, it could be argued that the ratio model provides useful insights into the structure of the franchise value approach. By combining the sustainable current earnings together with the opportunity-weighted franchise spread, one obtains a hypothetical perpetual annuity for the numerator. When discounted by the cost of capital in the denominator, the result is the estimated intrinsic value of the firm.

Market-Based versus Subjective Estimates

The hypothetical *PV* ratio can also serve as a framework for distinguishing between market-based versus personal estimates for the numerator or the denominator. First, consider a financial market that is totally, deadeningly efficient with all information shared and agreed upon by all participants. With total consensus both on flows in the numerator and in the discount rates in the numerator, all investments would presumably sell at their uniquely determined *PV*. There would be no bargains, no rip-offs, no disagreements about valuation, and probably very little trading. However, investors are not homogenous in either their needs or their preferences. In addition, they may have different estimates of the probable flows from any given investment. From all these sources of heterogeneity, one can see how different investors may generate some very distinct *PV* values for identical investments:

1. a market/market *PV* based on market-estimated flows in the numerator and market-based discount rates in the denominator,
2. a personal/market *PV* based on subjective estimates of the investment flows, but still using market-based discount rates,
3. a market/personal *PV* that makes use of the market's flow estimates but uses a personal discount rate that reflects the special predilections and circumstances of the investor, and
4. a personal/personal *PV* that uses both subjective flow estimates and personal discount rates.

These four combinations are displayed in *Table 11*.

The first—the market/market *PV*—should generally coincide with the market-determined cost of the investment. In contrast, the personal/market *PV* is based on a presumed special insight into the investment flows and could be the source of relatively short-term gains—*if* the market comes to agree with the subjectively estimated flows. The market/personal *PV* situation is one where there is no quarrel with the market-based estimates of the flows, but where the investment fits the investor's specific needs more effectively than those of the market in general. The benefit to the investor here tends to be longer term in nature. Finally, the personal/personal *PV* case incorporates both the subjective cash flow estimates and the investor's individual discounting preferences. Thus, to the extent that this personal/personal *PV* exceeds the market price, the investor believes that a gain in present value can be captured. (In a sense, this personal/personal *PV* could also serve as the most general case, with each of the preceding decision factors viewed as special cases.)

Of course, the increments from a market-based *PV* to one of the three personalized *PV*s could be negative as well as positive, and one could argue that many transactions consist of holders with low personal *PV*s selling to buyers with high personal *PV*s. However, it is probably more convenient to think of the great market/market *PV* marketplace as acting as an intermediary in all transactions. Then, all transactions could be thought of as taking place at a price set by the "market" with buyers and sellers both deriving some personal *PV* benefit.

If one accepts this framework, then it's surely advisable for any market participant to try to understand how "Mr. Market" sets the price on any given investment, that is, to appreciate the market estimate of the

TABLE 11

A Classification of Present Value Concepts

DISCOUNT RATE	FLOW ESTIMATE: Market	FLOW ESTIMATE: Personal
Market	***Market/Market*** Generally same as cost (when broadly market-priced)	***Personal/Market*** Value-based on special insights into investment flows
Personal	***Market/Personal*** Fair investment providing special value to investor	***Personal/Personal*** Value-based on special insights *and* special needs

flows and to have a sense of the discount rate that the market applies to these flows. With this knowledge, thoughtful investors can then begin to see where their personal estimates and discount rates differ from the market's, and then assess whether their view incorporates all the considerations embedded in the market price. These investors will then have a much more comprehensive basis for feeling that their departures from the market view are truly justified.

A Final Note

Even though this new "chapter" has gone far beyond its original intent, there are many important topics left totally untouched (e.g., option-adjusted duration, statistical duration, yield curve analysis, and tax effects, to name but a few). The key take-away should be an appreciation of the many ways that present value concepts can be used in the analysis of financial cash flows. For it is my belief, just as it was Sidney Homer's belief as we wrote the original *Inside the Yield Book,* that a deep understanding of the many facets of present and future value represents an essential analytic foundation for any disciplined investment process.

Technical Appendix to "Some Topics"

Present Value (PV)

C_i = cash flow at end of year
y = discount rate
M = years to flow's maturity (i.e., time to last payment)
$PV(1, H)$ = present value of flows received from first through the Hth year (the "present" value is taken here as of the beginning of the first year, or equivalently, as of the end of the 0th year).

$$PV(1, H) = \sum_{i=1}^{H} C_i (1+y)^{-i}$$

For the special case of a level annuity,

$$C_i = C$$

and,

$$\begin{aligned} PV(1, H) &= C \sum_{i=1}^{H} (1+y)^{-i} \\ &= \left(\frac{C}{1+y}\right) \sum_{i=1}^{H} (1+y)^{-i+1} \\ &= \left(\frac{C}{1+y}\right) \left[\frac{(1+y)^{-H} - 1}{(1+y)^{-1} - 1}\right] \\ &= C \left[\frac{(1+y)^{-H} - 1}{1-(1+y)}\right] \\ &= \left(\frac{C}{y}\right) \left[1-(1+y)^{-H}\right] \end{aligned}$$

Reinvested Future Value (*RFV*) at Horizon *H*

$RFV(1,H) \equiv$ accumulated reinvested value from payments in years 1 through year H (after the Hth year payment has been received).

$$\begin{aligned} RFV(1,H) &= \sum_{i=1}^{H} C_i (1+y)^{H-i} \\ &= (1+y)^H \sum_{i=1}^{H} C_i (1+y)^{-i} \\ &= (1+y)^H \, PV(1,H) \end{aligned}$$

The last equality is intended to relate the *RFV* back to the earlier *PV* concepts. We shall try to show these "throwback" relationships whenever possible. Also, for the special case of a level annuity,

$$\begin{aligned} RFV(1,H) &= (1+y)^H \left\{ \frac{C}{y} \left[1-(1+y)^{-H} \right] \right\} \\ &= \left(\frac{C}{y} \right) \left[(1+y)^H - 1 \right] \end{aligned}$$

Horizon Present Value (*HPV*) of "Tail" Cash Flow at Horizon *H*

$HPV(H{+}1,M) \equiv PV$ of flows in years $H{+}1$ to M with discounting to end of Hth year (after Hth year payment).

$$\begin{aligned} HPV(H+1,M) &= \sum_{i=1}^{M-H} C_{i+H} (1+y)^{-i} \\ &= (1+y)^H \sum_{i=1}^{M-H} C_{i+H} (1+y)^{-i-H} \\ &= (1+y)^H \sum_{i=H+1}^{M} C_i (1+y)^{-i} \\ &= (1+y)^H \, PV(H+1,M) \end{aligned}$$

where $PV(H{+}1,M)$ = the *PV* of flows received in years $(H{+}1)$ through M evaluated as of the beginning of the *first* year.

For the special case of a level annuity,

$C_i = C$ for all i and

$$HPV(H+1, M) = \sum_{i=1}^{M-H} C_{i+H} (i+y)^{-i}$$

$$= C \sum_{i=1}^{M-H} (1+y)^{-i}$$

$$= PV(1, M-H)$$

Total Future Value (*TFV*) at Horizon *H*

In general, when the pre-H reinvestment rate y_1 and the post-H discount rate y_2 differ,

$$TFV(H) \equiv RFV_{y_1}(1, H) + HPV_{y_2}(H+1, M)$$

For the case when the reinvestment rate and going-forward discount rate both equal y,

$$TFV(H) = (1+y)^H \; PV(1, H) + (1+y)^H \; PV(H+1, M)$$

$$= (1+y)^H \left[PV(1, H) + PV(H+1, M) \right]$$

$$= (1+y)^H \; PV(1, M)$$

For the special case of a level annuity,

$$TFV(H) = (1+y)^H \; PV(1, M)$$

$$= (1+y)^H \left\{ \left(\frac{C}{y} \right) \left[1 - (1+y)^{-M} \right] \right\}$$

$$= \left(\frac{C}{y} \right) \left[(1+y)^H - (1+y)^{H-M} \right]$$

Macaulay Duration $D(1,H)$

$$D(1,H) \equiv \frac{1}{PV(1,H)} \sum_{i=1}^{H} iC_i (1+y)^{-i} \qquad H \geq 1$$

PV Volatility $PV\text{-}VOL(1,H)$

$$\begin{aligned} PV\text{-}VOL(1,H) &\equiv \frac{1}{PV(1,H)} \frac{d}{dy}\left[PV(1,H)\right] \qquad H \geq 1 \\ &= \frac{1}{PV(1,H)} \frac{d}{dy}\left[\sum_{i=1}^{H} C_i (1+y)^{-i}\right] \\ &= \frac{-1}{PV(1,H)}\left[\sum_{i=1}^{H} iC_i (1+y)^{-i-1}\right] \\ &= \left(\frac{-1}{1+y}\right)\frac{1}{PV(1,H)} \sum_{i=1}^{H} iC_i (1+y)^{-i} \\ &= \left(\frac{-1}{1+y}\right) D(1,H) \end{aligned}$$

Reinvestment Volatility $RFV\text{-}VOL(1,H)$

The assumption here is that a single immediate rate move impacts all reinvestment throughout the horizon period.

$$RFV\text{-}VOL(1,H) \equiv \frac{1}{RFV(1,H)} \frac{d}{dy}\left[RFV(1,H)\right] \qquad H \geq 1$$

$$= \frac{1}{RFV(1,H)} \frac{d}{dy} \left[\sum_{i=1}^{H} C_i (1+y)^{H-i} \right]$$

$$= \frac{1}{RFV(1,H)} \left[\sum_{i=1}^{H} (H-i) C_i (1+y)^{H-i-1} \right]$$

$$= \left(\frac{1}{1+y} \right) \frac{1}{RFV(1,H)} \left[\sum_{i=1}^{H} (H-i) C_i (1+y)^{H-i} \right]$$

$$= \left(\frac{1}{1+y} \right) \frac{(1+y)^H}{RFV(1,H)} \left[H \sum_{i=1}^{H} C_i (1+y)^{-i} - \sum_{i=1}^{H} iC_i (1+y)^{-i} \right]$$

$$= \left(\frac{1}{1+y} \right) \frac{(1+y)^H}{RFV(1,H)} \left[H \times PV(1,H) - D(1,H) PV(1,H) \right]$$

$$= \left(\frac{1}{1+y} \right) \left[\frac{(1+y)^H \, PV(1,H)}{RFV(1,H)} \right] \left[H - D(1,H) \right]$$

$$= \left(\frac{1}{1+y} \right) \left[\frac{RFV(1,H)}{RFV(1,H)} \right] \left[H - D(1,H) \right]$$

$$= \left(\frac{1}{1+y} \right) \left[H - D(1,H) \right]$$

Horizon Duration *HD*(*H*+1, *M*)

$$HD(H+1,M) \equiv \left[\frac{1}{HPV(H+1,M)} \right] \left[\sum_{i=1}^{M-H} iC_{i+H} (1+y)^{-i} \right] \qquad H \le M-1$$

For $H \geq M$, there are no future payments and so *HPV* and *HD* both have a value of zero.

When the same discount/reinvestment rate applies from year 1 through year *M*, the Horizon Duration can be expressed as a "throwback" to the earlier Duration expressions, but the resulting general formula is somewhat more complicated:

$$HD(H+1,M)=\left[\frac{1}{HPV(H+1,M)}\right]\left[\sum_{i=1}^{M-H} iC_{i+H}(1+y)^{-i}\right]$$

$$=\left[\frac{1}{HPV(H+1,M)}\right]\left[\sum_{i=H+1}^{M}(i-H)C_i(1+y)^{-i+H}\right]$$

$$=\left[\frac{1}{HPV(H+1,M)}\right]\left[\sum_{i=H+1}^{M} iC_i(1+y)^{-i+H}-H\sum_{i=H+1}^{M} C_i(1+y)^{-i+H}\right]$$

$$=\left[\frac{1}{HPV(H+1,M)}\right]\left\{(1+y)^H\left[\sum_{i=1}^{M} iC_i(1+y)^{-i}-\sum_{i=1}^{H} iC_i(1+y)^{-i}\right]-\right.$$

$$\left.-H \times HPV(H+1,M)\right\}$$

$$=\left[\frac{1}{HPV(H+1,M)}\right]\left\{(1+y)^H\left[PV(1,M)\times D(1,M)-\right.\right.$$

$$\left.\left.-PV(1,H)\times D(1,H)\right]-H\times HPV(H+1,M)\right\}$$

$$=\left[\frac{1}{HPV(H+1,M)}\right]\left\{(1+y)^H\left[\left[PV(1,M)-PV(1,H)\right]D(1,M)-\right.\right.$$

$$\left.\left.-PV(1,H)\left[D(1,H)-D(1,M)\right]\right]-H\times HPV(H+1,M)\right\}$$

and since $HPV(H+1,M)=(1+y)^H\left[PV(1,M)-PV(1,H)\right]$,

we obtain the following general expression in Duration terms,

$$HD(H+1,M)=\left[\frac{1}{HPV(H+1,M)}\right]\left\{HPV(H+1,M)\times D(1,M)-\right.$$

$$\left.-RFV(1,H)\left[D(1,H)-D(1,M)\right]-H\times HPV(H+1,M)\right\}$$

$$=\left[D(1,M)-H\right]+\left[\frac{RFV(1,H)}{HPV(H+1,M)}\right]\left[D(1,M)-D(1,H)\right]$$

The above formulation holds for all forms of cash flow. However, for the special case of a level annuity,

$$C_i = C,$$

and one obtains the following far simpler but narrower result,

$$\begin{aligned} HD(H+1,M) &= \frac{1}{HPV(H+1,M)} \sum_{i=1}^{M-H} Ci(1+y)^{-i} \qquad H \le M-1 \\ &= \left[\frac{1}{C \sum_{i=1}^{M-H} (1+y)^{-i}}\right]\left[C \sum_{i=1}^{M-H} i(1+y)^{-i}\right] \\ &= \left[\frac{1}{PV(1,M-H)}\right]\left[PV(1,M-H) \times D(1,M-H)\right] \\ &= D(1,M-H) \end{aligned}$$

Horizon Present Value Volatility *HPV-VOL(H+1,M)*

$$\begin{aligned} HPV\text{-}VOL(H+1,M) &\equiv \frac{1}{HPV(H+1,M)} \frac{d}{dy}\left[HPV(H+1,M)\right] \qquad H \le M-1 \\ &= \frac{1}{HPV(H+1,M)}\left[\sum_{i=1}^{M-H} -iC_{i+H}(1+y)^{-i-1}\right] \\ &= \frac{-(1+y)^{-1}}{HPV(H+1,M)}\left[\sum_{i=1}^{M-H} iC_{i+H}(1+y)^{-i}\right] \\ &= -(1+y)^{-1} HD(H+1,M) \end{aligned}$$

Total Future Value Volatility *TFV-VOL(H)*

The assumption here is a simple immediate rate move that impacts reinvestment throughout the horizon period and also affects the tail pricing at the horizon.

$$
\begin{aligned}
TFV\text{-}VOL(H) &\equiv \frac{1}{TFV(H)}\frac{d}{dy}\left[TFV(H)\right] \\
&= \frac{1}{TFV(H)}\frac{d}{dy}\left[(1+y)^{H} PV(1,M)\right] \\
&= \frac{1}{TFV(H)}\left\{\left[H(1+y)^{H-1} PV(1,M) + \right.\right. \\
&\quad \left.\left. + (1+y)^{H}\left[\frac{d}{dy}PV(1,M)\right]\right]\right\} \\
&= \frac{(1+y)^{H-1}}{TFV(H)}\left\{H \times PV(1,M) - (1+y)\left[\frac{PV(1,M)D(1,M)}{(1+y)}\right]\right\} \\
&= \frac{(1+y)^{H-1}PV(1,M)}{(1+y)^{H}PV(1,M)}\left[H - D(1,M)\right]
\end{aligned}
$$

or finally,

$$
TFV\text{-}VOL(H) = \left[\frac{H - D(1,M)}{(1+y)}\right]
$$

This result could also be obtained using the earlier expressions for $HD(H+1,M)$ and $RFV\text{-}VOL(1,H)$ under the same assumption of a single rate movement,

$$
\begin{aligned}
TFV(H) \times \left[TFV\text{-}VOL(H)\right] &= RFV(1,H) \times \left[RFV\text{-}VOL(1,H)\right] + \\
&\quad + HPV(H+1,M) \times \left[HPV\text{-}VOL(H+1,M)\right] \\
&= \frac{RFV(1,H)}{(1+y)}\left[H - D(1,H)\right] - \\
&\quad - \frac{HPV(H+1,M)}{(1+y)}HD(H+1,M)
\end{aligned}
$$

$$=\frac{RFV(1,H)}{(1+y)}\left[H-D(1,H)\right]-\frac{HPV(H+1,M)}{(1+y)}\left\{\left[D(1,M)-H\right]+\right.$$

$$\left.+\frac{RFV(1,H)}{HPV(H+1,M)}\left[D(1,M)-D(1,H)\right]\right\}$$

$$=\frac{RFV(1,H)}{(1+y)}\left[H-D(1,H)\right]-\frac{HPV(H+1,M)}{(1+y)}\left[D(1,M)-H\right]-$$

$$-\frac{RFV(1,H)}{(1+y)}\left[D(1,M)-D(1,H)\right]$$

$$=\frac{RFV(1,H)}{(1+y)}\left[H-D(1,M)\right]+\frac{HPV(H+1,M)}{(1+y)}\left[H-D(1,M)\right]$$

$$=\left[RFV(1,H)+HPV(H+1,M)\right]\left[\frac{H-D(1,M)}{(1+y)}\right]$$

$$=TFV(H)\left[\frac{H-D(1,M)}{(1+y)}\right]$$

or finally,

$$TFV\text{-}VOL(H)=\left[\frac{H-D(1,M)}{(1+y)}\right]$$

The Babcock Rule

Under the earlier assumption that interest rates move from y_1 to y_2 at the *very outset,* with rates remaining stable thereafter, the total *TFV* volatility is needed.

$$TFV(H)\cong TFV_{y_1}(H)\left[1+TFV\text{-}VOL_{y_1}(H)\times(y_2-y_1)\right]$$

$$=TFV_{y_1}(H)\times\left\{1+\left[\frac{H-D(1,M)}{(1+y)}\right]\times(y_2-y_1)\right\}$$

Immunization

Under the same assumption as the Babcock rule, immunization is said to occur when *TFV* remains stable under an immediate interest rate shift from y_1 to y_2, i.e.,

$$TFV_{y_2}(H) \cong TFV_{y_1}(H)$$

or from the Babcock rule,

$$TFV\text{-}VOL_{y_1}(H) = 0$$

$$= \left(\frac{1}{1+y}\right)\left[H - D(1,M)\right]$$

In other words, immunization occurs when

$$D(1,M) = H$$

If the liabilities consist of a stream of payouts, then the asset portfolio will immunize the liability flow when

$D(1,M)$ of Assets $= D(1,M)$ of Liabilities.

The above are first-order conditions. There are various second-order conditions that must be applied under a broader range of assumptions regarding the structure of rate movements.

Horizon Analysis

In one form of horizon analysis, the pre-horizon rate y_1 is typically assumed to be stable, and the movement to a second rate y_2 is assumed to be concentrated *at* the horizon. Thus, the only volatility term involved is *HPV*.

$$TFV(H) \cong RFV_{y_1}(1,H) + HPV_{y_1}(H+1,M)\left[1 + HPV\text{-}VOL_{y_1}(H+1,M) \times \times (y_2 - y_1)\right]$$

$$\approx TFV_{y_1}(H) + HPV_{y_1}(H+1,M) \times HPV\text{-}VOL_{y_1}(H+1,M) \times \times (y_2 - y_1)$$

References

Preface to the 2004 Edition

1. Sidney Homer, *The Bond Buyer's Primer* (New York: Salomon Brothers Hutzler, 1968).

2. Sidney Homer, Richard Sylla, and Henry Kaufman, *A History of Interest Rates* (New Brunswick, NJ: Rutgers University Press, 1996).

3. J. Peter Williamson, "Computerized Approaches to Bond Switching," *Financial Analysts Journal* (July/August 1970).

4. Lawrence Fisher and Roman L. Weil, "Coping with the Risk of Interest Rate Fluctuations: Returns to Bondholders from Naïve and Optimal Strategies," *Journal of Business* 44, no. 4 (October 1971), 408–431.

5. F. R. Macaulay, *Some Theoretical Problems Suggested by the Movements of Interest Rates, Bond Yields and Stock Prices in the U.S. Since 1856* (New York: National Bureau of Economic Research, 1938).

6. Burton Malkiel, *The Term Structure of Interest Rates* (Princeton: Princeton University Press, 1966).

Some Topics That Didn't Make It into the 1972 Edition

7. Martin L. Leibowitz, "The Many Facets of Yield to Maturity," reprinted in *Investing: The Collected Works of Martin L. Leibowitz,* ed. Frank J. Fabozzi (Chicago: Probus Professional, 1992), Chapter III B-1.

8. F. R. Macaulay, *Some Theoretical Problems Suggested by the Movements of Interest Rates, Bond Yields and Stock Prices in the U.S. Since 1856* (New York: National Bureau of Economic Research, 1938).

9. Martin L. Leibowitz, "How Financial Theory Evolves Into the Real World—Or Not: The Case of Duration and Immunization," in *Investing: The Collected Works of Martin L. Leibowitz,* ed. Frank J. Fabozzi (Chicago: Probus Professional, 1992), 727–736. The paper is based on a speech given by Martin Leibowitz at the Eastern Finance Association Meeting, New York, NY, April 22, 1983.

10. Robert W. Kopprasch, *Understanding Duration and Volatility* (New York: Salomon Brothers, Inc., Bond Portfolio Analysis Group, September, 1985).

11. Martin L. Leibowitz, "Horizon Analysis for Managed Bond Portfolios," *Journal of Portfolio Management* 1, no. 3 (Spring 1975): 23–34.

12. Gil Babcock, *Duration as a Link* (Cambridge, MA: Ballinger Publishing, 1997); Gerald O. Bierwag, *Duration Analysis* (Cambridge, MA: Ballinger Publishing, 1997).

13. F. M. Redington, "Review of the Principles of Life-Office Valuations," *Journal of the Institute of Actuaries* 78, no. 3 (1952).

14. Martin L. Leibowitz, "Liability Returns: A New Look at Asset Allocation," *Journal of Portfolio Management* 13, no. 2 (Winter 1987): 11–18.

15. Terence C. Langetieg, Lawrence L. Bader, Alfred Weinberger, and Martin L. Leibowitz, "Measuring the Effective Duration of Pension Liabilities," in *Investing: The Collected Works of Martin L. Leibowitz,* ed. Frank J. Fabozzi (Chicago: Probus Professional, 1992), 99–127. Originally published by Salomon Brothers, Inc., 1986.

16. Martin L. Leibowitz and Alfred Weinberger, "Optimal Cash Flow Matching: Minimum Risk Bond Portfolios for Fulfilling Prescribed Schedules of Liabilities," in *Investing: The Collected Works of Martin L. Leibowitz,* ed. Frank J. Fabozzi (Chicago: Probus Professional, 1992), 739–752. Originally published by Salomon Brothers, Inc., 1981.

17. Martin L. Leibowitz, "An Introduction to Bond Immunization," from "Pros and Cons of Immunization: Proceedings of a Seminar on Immunization," in *Investing: The Collected Works of Martin L. Leibowitz,* ed. Frank J. Fabozzi (Chicago: Probus Professional, 1992), 731–751.

18. Martin L. Leibowitz, "Bond Immunization: A Procedure for Realizing Target Levels of Return," in *Investing: The Collected Works of Martin L. Leibowitz,* ed. Frank J. Fabozzi (Chicago: Probus Professional, 1992), 753–776. Originally published by Salomon Brothers, Inc., 1979.

19. Martin L. Leibowitz, "Bond Immunization: Theory and Practice," in *Investing: The Collected Works of Martin L. Leibowitz,* ed. Frank J. Fabozzi (Chicago: Probus Professional, 1992), 777–806. Originally published by Salomon Brothers, Inc., 1980.

20. Lawrence Fisher and Martin Leibowitz, "Effects of Yield Curve Behavior on Immunized Portfolios," in *Investing: The Collected Works of Martin L. Leibowitz,* ed. Frank J. Fabozzi (Chicago: Probus Professional, 1992), 901–904. Originally published by Salomon Brothers, 1983.

21. Martin L. Leibowitz, "Horizon Analysis for Managed Bond Portfolios," in *Investing: The Collected Works of Martin L. Leibowitz,* ed. Frank J. Fabozzi (Chicago: Probus Professional, 1992), 569–594. Originally published in *Journal of Portfolio Management,* 1975.

22. Martin L. Leibowitz, "The Rolling Yield," in *Investing: The Collected Works of Martin L. Leibowitz,* ed. Frank J. Fabozzi (Chicago: Probus Professional, 1992), 627–636.

23. Myron J. Gordon, *The Investment Financing and Valuation of the Corporation* (Homewood, IL: Greenwood Press, 1962).

24. John B. Williams, *The Theory of Investment Value* (Amsterdam: North-Holland Publishing, 1938).

25. Martin L. Leibowitz and J. Stanley Kogelman, *Franchise Value and the Price/Earnings Ratio* (Research Foundation of the Institute of Chartered Financial Analysts, 1994).

INSIDE THE YIELD BOOK

New Tools for Bond Market Strategy

Sidney Homer

and

Martin L. Leibowitz, Ph.D.

Preface to the 1972 Edition

The Yield Book can appropriately be called the playing field of the game of bond investment. Its structure and dimensions and the basics of price-yield relationships deserve the closest study. Too often the dollars and cents significance of bond yields is taken for granted and sometimes even is misunderstood. Our book will attempt to explore some of the basic but less obvious relationships between coupon, maturity, price and yield with the aim of aiding the investor in judging and comparing bond values.

In Part I, which is based on a series of our memoranda previously published by Salomon Brothers, we will first describe the great importance of "interest-on-interest," that is to say, the income derived by the fully compounding investor from reinvesting his coupon receipts. For long-term investments, interest-on-interest is apt to be more than half of total interest receipts. The investor will achieve a fully compounded yield equal to the bond's stated yield-to-maturity at the time of purchase only if he can reinvest all coupons at his purchase yield.

Furthermore, we will show that bond issues with low coupons are far less dependent on "interest-on-interest" than are high coupon bonds. Therefore, yield-to-maturity is not a complete guide to relative bond values even where there is no call or credit risk. To meet this difficulty, we have developed the concept of "realized compound yield" which provides the total prospective yield from all components of return from a given bond investment: principal, interest, and interest-on-interest at various assumed reinvestment rates (and in some cases capital gain or loss). This concept makes it much easier to compare the real prospective return from each of a field of bond issues of widely diverse coupons, maturities, and prices and yields.

Next we explore the volatility of bond prices. This turns out to be far from uniform even in the case of prime bond issues with the same long maturity. Indeed we show why some low coupon medium-term bonds are more volatile than the longest term high coupon bonds. We also show why bond prices are far more volatile in high yield periods than they are for the same yield change in low yield periods. We explore in detail the causes for these differences in volatility.

As a result of studying these wide differences in volatility and in realized compound yield and in other structural and mathematical characteristics, we show how the investor can select his bond purchases according to his individual preferences, either for maximum yield in the long run or for maximum immediate yield or for maximum or minimum volatility or stability. In this connection, we analyze in detail the different characteristics of seasoned premium bonds, new issues and seasoned discount bonds—three categories which frequently perform very differently in the market.

Finally we review the principal types of bond swaps and set up mathematical standards for judging the merit of each swap and what its rewards and risks might be. Here again yield-to-maturity can be a misleading guide while the concept of realized compound yield tells a more accurate story of comparative values.

These tools for bond portfolio management are all set out in Part I. However, for those who wish to go further and explore the mathematics of bond yields and bond prices, that is to say, the mathematical formulae on which our conclusions are based, we have provided in Part II a discussion of the mathematics of bond yields, including the Future Value and the Present Value of a cash flow, the yield-to-maturity concept, dollar pricing, yield-to-call, and realized compound yield.

With the aid of Part II and the general formulae in the Appendix, those with computers can quickly analyze the essential yield and price advantages and disadvantages of each high-grade bond offering.

For their careful reading and criticism of early drafts of this book, the authors are indebted to Dr. Louise Curley, Vice-President of Scudder, Stevens & Clark, Mr. Gordon Crook, President of Lesta Research, Inc. and Professor Martin Gruber of New York University Graduate School of Business Administration. We wish to thank Miss Therese Shay for her work in preparing this manuscript. We especially wish to thank the firm of Salomon Brothers for the strong support they gave to this and many other research projects over the years.

Sidney Homer
Martin L. Leibowitz, Ph.D.

Contents of the 1972 Edition

Part I
BOND YIELDS, BOND PRICES, AND BOND INVESTMENT

Tables

Part I

BOND YIELDS, BOND PRICES, AND BOND INVESTMENT

Part II

THE MATHEMATICS OF BOND YIELDS

PART 1

Bond Yields, Bond Prices, and Bond Investment

CHAPTER 1

Interest on Interest

The recent high level of bond yields and the uncertainty whether yields will be high in the years ahead emphasizes the importance of interest-on-interest, that is to say, the rate at which receipts from coupons can be reinvested in the future. An original investment compounds automatically at the purchase yield only until the funds are paid back in the form of coupons and finally of principal. However, some investors mistakenly expect that a bond purchased at a given yield will always produce that rate as a realized compound yield over the whole life of the bond. If future reinvestment rates during the life of the bond are less than the purchase yield, then the realized compound yield for the whole life of the bond will be less than the purchase yield; if future rates are higher than the purchase yield, then the realized compound yield will be more than the purchase yield.

Long-Term Par Bonds

For most long-term bonds, the interest-on-interest is a surprisingly important part of the total compounded return to the bondholder: typically over half.

Table 1 shows that for an 8% 20-year bond bought at 100 to yield 8% the total return over the twenty-year period may vary from $1,600 per $1,000 invested (4.84%) to $4,832 (9.01%) depending upon whether the interest-on-interest is 0% (interest spent–in a financially non-productive way–as coupons are paid) or 10%. When the reinvestment rate is also 8%, the coupons over the twenty years will total $1,600 per $1,000 invested and the interest on this interest will total $2,201 or 58% of the total return of $3,801. If the rate of interest-on-interest is 6%, the interest-on-interest will decline to $1,416, and the total return to $3,016 per $1,000 invested, bringing the total realized compound yield to the purchaser down from the original 8% to 7.07%. On the other hand, if the rate of interest-on-interest rises to 10%, interest-on-interest will rise to $3,232 and total return to $4,832 per $1,000 invested bringing the total realized compound yield to the purchaser up to 9.01%.

TABLE 1

An 8% Non-Callable 20-Year Bond Bought at 100 to Yield 8%

Interest-on-Interest						
Reinvestment Rate	% of Total Return	Amount	Coupon Income	Discount	Total Return	Total Realized Compound Yield
0%	0%	$ 0	$1,600	0	$1,600	4.84%
5	41	1,096	1,600	0	2,696	6.64
6	47	1,416	1,600	0	3,016	7.07
7	53	1,782	1,600	0	3,382	7.53
8*	58*	2,201*	1,600*	0	3,801*	8.00*
9	63	2,681	1,600	0	4,281	8.50
10	67	3,232	1,600	0	4,832	9.01

*Yield from Yield Book.

It follows that a present purchaser of a long-term 8% non-callable bond at 100 is by no means assured of a realized yield of 8% for the life of his investment if by yield is meant interest compounded on the entire original investment for the entire life of the bond: it might turn out to be 6.64% or 9.01% or more or less, depending on the future trend of bond yields. The uncertainty is entirely confined to the compounding factor. In terms of simple interest, the investor is sure to get 8% from this 8% bond, i.e., $80 a year per $1,000 if the bond is not called or defaulted.

The Yield Book

The Yield Book serves the essential function of providing a uniform basis for comparing the market values of bonds having different coupons, maturities, dollar prices and, consequently, different cash flows over their life. To achieve this uniformity, the Yield Book in essence refers every dollar of every bond's cash flow to the standard of an initial investment allowed to accumulate compound interest semiannually at the Yield Book rate until it is paid off in the form of coupon or principal. For example, suppose one has two 20-year bonds, one with a coupon of 8% and the other with a 4% coupon, both priced "to yield 8%." This 8% figure can be taken to mean that both bonds are equivalent to the standard of an 8% semiannually compounded investment, which would realize a return of $3,801 per $1,000 invested over the twenty-year period.

It is not so well known that to obtain this objective it is necessary that the bonds' coupon income be reinvested so as to gather "interest-on-interest" at a rate exactly equal to the yield-to-maturity itself. The two 8% yield-to-maturity bonds in the above example would realize the standardized 8% return of $3,801 per $1,000 invested only if each and every coupon were itself reinvested at an exact 8% rate. If the coupons cannot be reinvested at the Yield Book rate, then the realized compound yield over the bond's life of the dollars originally invested may vary widely from the Yield Book figure. For this reason, when facing future periods involving possible major swings in yield levels, it becomes vitally important to distinguish between the yield-to-maturity (as stated in the Yield Book) and the realized compound yield that will actually be obtained if the bond is held to maturity.

Simple Interest vs. Compound Interest

Many investors, like university endowment funds and foundations and private investors, simply collect and spend their coupons. They tend to ignore the variability of compound interest. Others, like pension funds, accumulate interest receipts, merge them with principal and reinvest them; these are vitally affected by the future rate of interest and ordinarily cannot, when they invest, obtain any assurance as to just what their total return will be.*

Maturity

As maturity is reduced, the importance of interest-on-interest declines sharply. This is illustrated by Table 2 which shows that for a 1-year 8% bond at 100, interest-on-interest will account for only 2% of total return, while for a 40-year 8% bond it will account for 86% of total return. The uncertainty can be said to be basic only for longer maturities.

TABLE 2

Effect of Maturity on the Importance of Interest-on-Interest

(Assuming Reinvestment at Yield Rate)

	% of Total Return Represented by Interest-on-Interest	
Maturity	**8% Bonds Bought at 100 to Yield 8%**	**4% Bonds Bought at 100 to Yield 4%**
1 Year	2%	1%
5 Years	17	9
10 "	33	18
20 "	58	34
30 "	75	47
40 "	86	59

*It would be possible to design a bond issue that would guarantee a rate of compound interest by paying coupons in debt rather than cash, but it has rarely if ever been done. Savings bonds do provide guaranteed compound interest.

It is obvious, however, that shorter maturities, while reducing or almost eliminating the uncertainty of the rate of interest-on-interest do not solve the problems of maintaining future income. Indeed, the uncertainty is larger with shorter term bonds because in the reinvestment of shorts at maturity the coupon, in addition to the compounding factor, is uncertain. Thus, the old rule will usually hold: if future rates are to rise, shorts bought now will be better than longs; if rates decline, longs will be better than shorts.

Long-Term Discount Bonds

Table 3 shows the same calculation for a deep discount bond, a 20-year 4% bond selling at about 60⅜ to yield 8%. The top panel shows total return in dollars from one bond, and the bottom panel translates the same figures on the basis of each $1,000 invested, so that the returns can be compared with the 20-year 8% bond in Table 1. Here we find that the variation of total return based on changes in interest-on-interest is also large, but not as large as in the case of the par bonds. This is because the discount (eventual capital gain) is a fixed component of total return that does not vary with future interest rates. When coupon income is a smaller proportion of total return, interest-on-interest must also be a smaller portion of total return. The difference, however, between the par bond and the discount bond is not so large as to provide an absolute guide for selection. If interest-on-interest varies, between 6% and 10%, the total realized compound yield of the 8% bond will vary between 7.07% and 9.01%, while that of the 4% bond will vary between 7.25% and 8.85%. At lower future rates, the 4% bond will yield more than the 8% bond because the fixed discount substitutes for some variable interest; at higher future rates the 8% bond will yield more than the 4% bond because interest-on-interest is a larger component of total return and there is no discount.

TABLE 3
A 4% 20-Year Bond Bought at 60.414 to Yield 8%

Interest-on-Interest Reinvest-ment Rate	% of Total Return	Amount	Coupon Income	Discount	Total Return	Total Realized Compound Yield
			A: Per Bond			
0%	0%	$ 0	$ 800	$ 396	$1,196	5.53%
5	31	548	800	396	1,744	6.90
6	37	708	800	396	1,904	7.25
7	43	891	800	396	2,087	7.61
8*	48*	1,100*	800*	396*	2,296*	8.00*
9	53	1,341	800	396	2,536	8.41
10	57	1,616	800	396	2,812	8.85
		B: Per $1,000 Invested				
0	0	0	1,325	655	1,980	5.53
5	31	907	1,325	655	2,877	6.90
6	37	1,172	1,325	655	3,152	7.25
7	43	1,474	1,325	655	3,454	7.61
8*	48*	1,820*	1,325*	655*	3,800*	8.00*
9	53	2,218	1,325	655	4,198	8.41
10	57	2,674	1,325	655	4,654	8.85

*Yield from Yield Book.

Another way of viewing this effect is to compare the different Yield Book values giving rise to the same realized compound yield under the same reinvestment assumption. For example, the 8% par bond (Table 1) with coupons reinvested at 6% results in a realized compound yield of 7.07%. To obtain this same realized compound yield of 7.07% under the same reinvestment assumption (6%), the 4% coupon bond (Table 3) would have to be priced to yield 7.70% by the Yield Book. In other words, one could "give up" as much as 30 basis points in yield at cost, and the 4% discount bond would still prove to be as good a buy from the standpoint of realized compound yield. This comparison would, of course, not be valid in case of stable or rising interest rates.

Long-Term Bonds at Lower Yields

These considerations show that long-term bonds bought a few years ago at yields of 4% to 5% are actually permitting the purchasers to receive a much higher compound yield than the expected rate if the purchasers have been reinvesting their coupons. This is because those lower yields at cost assumed future reinvestment rates of 4% to 5%, while their coupons have recently been reinvested at rates as high as 8% to 9%. Table 4 below is comparable to Table 1 except that the original investment is in a 4% bond at 100 to yield 4%. Discount rates are tabulated all the way from 0 to 10%. It will be seen that the proportion of total return depending on interest-on-interest is exactly the same as that of the 8% bond in Table 1 if the reinvestment rates are the same while, of course, the total returns and yields are very much less.

TABLE 4

A 4% Non-Callable 20-year Bond Bought at 100 to Yield 4%

Interest-on-Interest						
Reinvest-ment Rate	% of Total Return	Amount	Coupon Income	Discount	Total Return	Total Realized Compound Yield
0%	0%	$ 0	$ 800	0	$ 800	2.96%
1	9	83	800	0	883	3.19
2	18	178	800	0	978	3.44
3	26	285	800	0	1,085	3.71
4*	34*	408*	800*	0	1,208*	4.00*
5	41	548	800	0	1,348	4.31
6	47	708	800	0	1,508	4.65
7	53	891	800	0	1,691	5.01
8	58	1,101	800	0	1,901	5.40
9	63	1,341	800	0	2,141	5.80
10	67	1,616	800	0	2,416	6.24

*Yield from Yield Book.

Timing of Rate Changes

In all of the above tables, the future rate of interest-on-interest is stated as one figure which might seem like an average for the twenty-year period, but it is not: It is an artificially fixed rate of reinvestment for all coupons from first to last at the indicated rate assumed by the tables. In real life, rates vary widely from year to year, and a simple average would be fallacious because of the time factor. A low reinvestment rate a year or two after investment followed by higher rates would bring much bigger total interest-on-interest than an early period of high rates followed by low rates. This is because the high reinvestment rate later would earn much more interest from the larger accumulation of funds being reinvested. Thus, the maximum income benefit to today's purchaser would accrue from a rapid rise in interest rates soon after his purchase and thereafter sustained high rates. This, of course, is just the opposite to his profits or losses from principal fluctuations.

Investment Implications

(1) The purchaser of long-term bonds who plans to compound his return has not achieved a certainty as to just what his total compounded realized yield will be even if the bonds are non-callable. The area of doubt is perhaps a yield range of 2%.

(2) Conversely, the purchaser of non-callable long-term bonds who plans to spend his income can count on a predetermined rate of return provided only that the bonds remain in good standing.

(3) For the compounding investor who expects interest rates to average lower over a long period of years than at time of purchase, there is a structural advantage in discount bonds over par bonds because that part of his return represented by the discount is fixed and cannot decline with interest rates. This advantage is supplementary to other advantages such as superior call protection and (for taxpayers) a lower tax rate. However, these advantages are often offset when discount bonds yield substantially less than high coupon bonds.

(4) Conversely, for those who expect high or higher interest rates in the years ahead but who are constrained to stay with long-term bonds, there is a structural advantage in

par or premium bonds because their total return will rise more rapidly with rising rates. Also, they usually yield more at time of purchase.

(5) Short-term bonds provide much greater certainty of the compounded rate of return than do long-term bonds, but only for limited periods corresponding to the short-term maturities. Thereafter, because their entire principal amount must be reinvested at the then prevailing rates, the area of uncertainty is very much larger than in the case of long-term bonds.

CHAPTER 2

The Power of Compound Interest, Perpetual Bonds and Discount Bonds

Compound interest at high rates is one of the most potent growth forces in our investment markets. The rate of compounding, of course, is crucial. Capital left at semiannual compound interest of 4% (tax free) will double every 17.5 years, at 6% every 11.7 years, at 8% every 8.8 years and at 10% every 7.1 years.

Compounding occurs not only in fixed income investments, but also in the compounding of retained earnings by business enterprises. The key uncertainty in both types of investment is the rate at which future coupon receipts or future retained earnings can be reinvested. The business concern has to expand rapidly and profitably in order to compound large retained earnings at a good rate. The bond investor, as we have seen in Chapter 1, is to a large extent at the mercy of future interest rates for the rate at which his investment will compound over long periods. However, some types of bonds, such as deep discount bonds, promise to compound at going rates for a much longer period of years than do other types of bonds such as high coupon par bonds even for the same maturity.

Table 5 illustrates the dynamic effect of compounding over very long periods of time.

TABLE 5

The Power of Compound Interest

At 8% Compounded Semiannually:

$1,000 will grow to	$2,000+	in 9 years
" " " "	7,106	in 25 years
" " " "	50,504	in 50 years
" " " "	2,550,749	in 100 years

For those interested in the long pull, $1,000 at 8% will grow to over 42 quadrillion dollars in four hundred years. Evidently the first hundred years are the hardest.

Why then is our very old world not much richer than it is? Aside from the destructive effects of wars, revolutions and inflations, and the incidence of taxes, there is a very human propensity to consume. Furthermore, a sustained assured 8% compound interest rate has never been available over long periods of history, and even 6% has been exceptional.

Types of Investment Funds

For the purposes of this analysis, there are two types of investment funds: those that can fully compound, and those that cannot. Typical of those that cannot regularly compound is the private investor living off of investment income, or the college endowment fund that is pressed to distribute all its income and is not growing. Typical of those that can compound are pension and retirement funds.

In between these types of funds are those like life insurance companies and growing endowment funds whose need for current income requires them to pay out a good part of their investment income. However, since they are growing, they can and often should invest as though they were fully compounding since current non-investment receipts take care of current disbursements.

These chapters will attempt to differentiate between these two types of bond funds. They will point out the types of bonds which are best suited to maximize current income and to other types of bonds which are best suited to maximize the rate of compounding.

Two Eccentric Types of Bonds

For purposes of Yield Book analysis, bonds can be classified along three scales: maturity (short to medium to long-term), coupon (low coupon to high coupon) and price (deep discount bonds to par bonds to premium bonds). At the extremes of these scales are two eccentric types of bonds which are rarely met with in real life, but which are worth examining carefully because they illustrate basic price-yield relationships which influence all customary types of bonds. These two extreme types of bonds are: 1) non-callable perpetual bonds with no maturity (including non-callable preferred stocks), and 2) pure discount bonds with 0 coupons (for example, Series E savings bonds).

Perpetuals

Perpetual bonds are the grandfathers of all modern long-term bonds. They appeared hundreds of years ago in Europe under the name "perpetual annuities." They were usually redeemable at par after a specified future date, but only at the option of the borrower.

They were not then considered to be loans at interest, which were condemned as immoral and were often illegal, but rather they were looked upon as income contracts which could be bought and sold with complete legality. They were sold by the governments of nations, states and cities, and by private land owners. They became a very popular medium of investment and often enjoyed an active secondary market.

In the 18th century, the English Government's new funded debt took this form, i.e., the Consols which are still outstanding. The first American funded debt was all in the form of perpetuals which our Government redeemed as soon as it could under the bond contracts. It was in the course of the 19th century that specific maturities became popular. Actually many of these late 19th century bond issues which often had 100-year maturities and were non-callable were, in effect, longer term loans than the old perpetuals because the latter usually could be redeemed sooner.

The negligible difference between the Present Value of perpetuals and of very long-term bonds is illustrated by the following calculation of the Present Value of a 100-year 8% bond at par:

The Present Value of a stream of $40 semiannual coupons for 100 years discounted at 8%	=	$ 999.60
The Present Value of $1,000 payable in 100 years discounted at 8%	=	.40
Total Present Value of 8% 100-year bond at 8%	=	$1,000.00

The Present Value of a perpetual is, of course, merely the Present Value of the coupon stream to infinity at the stated yield and the difference in Present Value between 100 years and infinity is negligible. Thus, very long-term bonds are much like perpetuals and should follow almost the same pattern of market fluctuations.

The calculation of the yields or prices of perpetuals does not require a Yield Book. The yield (in terms of decimals) is simply the coupon divided by the price. The price (% of par) is simply the coupon divided by the (decimal) yield. The following scoreboard shows the prices and yields of perpetuals at all unit coupons between 2% and 8%.

TABLE 6
Price of Perpetuals

	Coupon						
Yield	2%	3%	4%	5%	6%	7%	8%
2%	100	150	200	250	300	350	400
3%	66 2/3	100	133 1/3	166 2/3	200	233 1/3	266 2/3
4%	50	75	100	125	150	175	200
5%	40	60	80	100	120	140	160
6%	33 1/3	50	66 2/3	83 1/3	100	116 2/3	133 1/3
7%	28 1/2 +	42 7/8 +	57 1/8 +	71 3/8 +	85 3/4	100	114 1/4 +
8%	25	37 1/2	50	62 1/2	75	87 1/2	100

The Volatility of Perpetuals

One of the principal objectives of these studies will be to measure and compare the potential price volatility of many kinds of bond contracts. Price volatility can be measured in two ways: 1) by percentage changes in price caused by *basis point* changes in yield and 2) by percentage changes in price caused by *percentage* changes in yield.

It will be seen that the volatility of perpetuals per 100 basis point change in yield is not stable but decreases progressively and proportionately as yields rise. This, of course, means that a 100 basis point change in a low yield range is a larger percentage yield change and so leads to a larger percentage price change than a 100 basis point change in a high yield range. It seems logical to expect that larger or smaller percentage yield changes will always lead to larger or smaller percentage bond price changes. However, as we shall see, this relationship does not apply to many other types of bonds.

TABLE 7

Volatility of Perpetuals by Basis Point Change in Yield

100 Basis Point Yield Increases	% Yield Change*	% Price Change*
2% to 3%	+50%	-33.33%
3% to 4%	+33.33	-25
4% to 5%	+25	-20
5% to 6%	+20	-16.67
6% to 7%	+16.67	-14.29
7% to 8%	+14.29	-12.50

**NOTE:* The reason why these two percentage columns are not identical for any given yield change is that the prices are declining and hence their percentage is based on the top of a range while the yields are rising and hence their percentage is based on the bottom of the related range. This is the same statistical quirk which sometimes afflicts portfolio managers when they find that a 50% loss can be offset only by a 100% gain. Throughout this study, the percentage pluses (yield or price) will, therefore, always be larger than the equivalent minuses measuring the same absolute change. If the above table were presented in terms of falling yields and rising prices, the two percentage columns would simply be reversed, i.e., 3% to 2% = −33.33% yield change = +50% price change.

TABLE 8

Volatility of Perpetuals by Percentage Change in Yields

33 1/3% Yield Increases	% Yield Change	% Price Change
2.25 to 3%	+33.33%	-25%
3 to 4%	+33.33	-25
4 to 5.33+%	+33.33	-25
5.33+ to 7.11+%	+33.33	-25
7.11+ to 9.48+%	+33.33	-25

Table 8 illustrates the fact that for perpetuals a given percent yield change at any part of the yield scale will cause a constant percentage price change. This is because the formula for computing the Present Value of an infinite stream of coupon payments reduces to a very simple formula:

$$\text{Present Value} = \frac{\text{Coupon Amount in \$}}{\text{Yield (in decimals)}}$$

$$\text{e.g., Present Value} = \frac{\$60}{.06} = \$1000$$

$$\text{or } \frac{\$60}{.08} = \$750 \text{ etc.}$$

Regardless of the coupon any given percentage change in the divisor (the yield) at any rate level will give a constant percentage change in the quotient (the Present Value). However, as we shall see below, this direct simple relationship between yield change and price change applies only to perpetuals (and to nearly the same extent to near perpetuals), but does not apply to most other forms of bond contracts.

Discount Bonds With 0 Coupons

At another eccentric extreme there are the pure discount bonds with no coupon payments (e.g., Series E Savings Bonds). In sharp contrast to other types of bond contracts, these offer fully compounded interest at the promised rate throughout the life of the bond, and therefore, no reinvestment of coupons is required.* The importance and uncertainty of reinvesting coupons was emphasized in Chapter 1. The entire return of these discount bonds is derived from the discount, i.e., the difference between the cost price and the redemption price at maturity. It is useful to analyze such bonds here (although in real life they rarely exist) because they reveal in extreme and readily understandable ways certain characteristics of all conventional low coupon discount bonds.

Because the entire return of 0 coupon discount bonds is derived

*Press reports last year suggested that AT&T was considering this type of bond. It has obvious advantages both for compounding institutions and for certain private investors and it would relieve the company of new cash interest disbursements for a period of years.

from the discount, and because the return is fully compounded, the hypothetical discounts must be very large, much larger than in the case of any conventional coupon bond with the same maturity and yield. Thus, as Table 9 below shows, a 20-year maturity would have to be priced as low as 20⅞ to yield 8% compounded, 37¼ to yield 5% and 55⅛ to yield 3%.

TABLE 9
The Hypothetical Prices of 0 Coupon Discount Bonds of Various Maturities

Rate	1 Year	10 Years	20 Years	30 Years
2%	98.03	81.95	67.17	55.04
3	97.07	74.25	55.13	40.93
4	96.12	67.30	45.29	30.48
5	95.18	61.03	37.24	22.73
6	94.26	55.37	30.66	16.97
7	93.35	50.26	25.26	12.69
8	92.46	45.64	20.83	9.51

These prices are derived entirely from compound interest tables and are merely the Present Value of a $100 lump sum payable at a stated future date discounted at a stated rate of interest. The Present Value of a future principal payment is an ingredient of all bond price calculations with the sole exception of perpetuals, but it is usually one of two ingredients, the other being the Present Value of a coupon stream. With the perpetuals, the price consists only of the value of the coupon stream. With 0 coupon discount bonds, we have only to evaluate a future lump sum payment.

The Volatility of 0 Coupon Discount Bonds

0 coupon discount bonds, if they were marketable, would be the most volatile type of straight high-grade bond. Their volatility would often considerably exceed that of perpetuals. This is because the entire income is discounted from a distant date, i.e., maturity, whereas for coupon bonds including perpetuals a large part of the income is

discounted from near coupon dates. For example, in the case of any 8% coupon bond at par, payments receivable in the first ten years are equal to 80% of the original investment.

In a sense, 0 coupon discount bonds are roughly analogous to 0 dividend growth stocks (or low dividend growth stocks) except that the discount factor is part of the contract in the case of the bond and in the case of the stock it depends on the future rate of return on retained earnings. This structural similarity helps in part to explain why growth stocks are also highly volatile. Any reduction or increase in the expected discount factor can have a very large effect on a price which fluctuates without the self-correcting mechanism created for income stocks by the change in current yield.

Table 10 shows that 0 coupon discount bonds fluctuate in price almost directly according to *basis point* changes in yield regardless of whether yields are high or low, that is to say, almost regardless of the percentage changes in yield. This is because the entire return is in the form of an eventual principal payment and each *basis point* change in the discount factor has an almost identical percentage effect on the price. This is just the opposite of the volatility of perpetuals (see Tables 7 and 8) where the percentage yield change completely determines the volatility.

TABLE 10

The Volatility of 0 Coupon Discount Bonds by Basis Point Change in Yield

100 Basis Point Yield Increases	% Yield Change	% Price Change by Maturity — 0 Coupon Discount Bonds: 1 Year	10 Years	20 Years	30 Years	Any Coupon Perpetuals
2 to 3%	+50%	-.98	-9.40	-17.92	-25.64	-33.33%
3 to 4%	+33.33	-.98	-9.36	-17.85	-25.54	-25.00
4 to 5%	+25.00	-.97	-9.32	-17.77	-25.43	-20.00
5 to 6%	+20.00	-.97	-9.27	-17.69	-25.32	-16.67
6 to 7%	+16.67	-.96	-9.23	-17.61	-25.22	-14.29
7 to 8%	+14.29	-.96	-9.19	-17.53	-25.11	-12.50

The table above shows the very rapid increase in volatility of discount bonds as maturity lengthens in a manner almost proportionate to the increase in maturity. It shows that 30-year discounts are more volatile even than perpetuals per 100 basis point change in yield at all yield ranges except the very lowest, and that even 20-year discounts are more volatile than perpetuals in yield ranges of 5% and up.

Table 11 below shows, conversely, that 0 coupon discount bonds, if measured according to *percentage changes* to yield, become rapidly more volatile as yields rise. This is because they fluctuate almost proportionately to basis point changes in yields and there are more basis points in, for example, a 10% yield change at high yield levels than at lower yield levels. This again is very different from perpetuals which fluctuate strictly according to percentage yield changes.

TABLE 11
The Volatility of 0 Coupon Discount Bonds
By Percentage Change in Yield

33 1/3% Yield		% Price Change By Maturity				
		0 Coupon Discount Bonds				Any Coupon
Increases	% Yield Change	1 Year	10 Years	20 Years	30 Years	Perpetuals
2.25 to 3.00%	+33.33%	- .74	- 7.14	-13.76	-19.91	-25%
3.00 to 4.00%	"	- .98	- 9.36	-17.85	-25.54	-25
4.00 to 5.33+%	"	-1.29	-12.22	-22.94	-32.36	-25
5.33+ to 7.11+%	"	-1.71	-15.84	-29.16	-40.38	-25
7.11+ to 9.48+%	"	-2.25	-20.36	-36.57	-49.48	-25

The formula for computing the Present Value of a single lump sum future payment is as follows (for a more detailed explanation of all yield formulae, see Part II.):

$$\text{Present Value} = \frac{\text{Principal amount}}{\text{(1 plus semiannual yield in decimal) raised to a power equal to the number of compounding periods.}}$$

e.g., for a lump sum payment of $1,000 30 years hence at 6% compounded semiannually,

$$\text{Present Value} = \frac{\$1,000}{(1.03)^{60}} = \frac{\$1,000}{5.89} = \$169.73$$

In this equation, the denominator rises with yield as follows:

Yield Increases	Denominator Increases	% Growth in Denominator
2% to 3%	1.82 to 2.44	+34.5%
3% to 4%	2.44 to 3.28	34.3
4% to 5%	3.28 to 4.40	34.1
5% to 6%	4.40 to 5.89	33.9

Thus each 100 basis points change in yield creates almost the same constant percentage change in the denominator and hence also in the Present Value. However, the changes do decelerate very slightly as yields rise, as is evident from Table 10.

Table 11 above shows: 1) How rapidly the volatility of the discount bonds increases with maturity and 2) How rapidly the volatility of the discount bonds increases with rising yields if the latter are measured by a fixed percentage yield change. This is important because percentage yield change is a much more realistic way to measure actual yield volatility in the market than basis point yield change. In other words, basis point swings in yields are apt to be larger at high yield levels than they are at low yield levels. In combination, these two factors, which increase the volatility of discount bonds, i.e., longer maturity and higher yield levels, result in extremely high rates of volatility.

The importance of these somewhat theoretical calculations, as we shall spell out in later chapters, lies in the fact that most conventional coupon bonds partake partly of the characteristics of perpetuals and partly of the characteristics of 0 coupon discounts in varying degrees. The next chapter, which will analyze the yields and prices of conventional coupon bonds, will find some interesting and useful standards of volatility that are understandable best in terms of a combination of these two components.

Investment Implications

All long-term conventional coupon bond issues combine in varying degrees the volatility characteristics of perpetuals and the very different and often greater volatility characteristics of 0 coupon discount bonds. This is because they all have a stream of coupon payments plus a lump sum payment at maturity. In some bonds, however, the coupon stream is relatively more important and in others the lump sum payment is relatively more important. Therefore, longer maturity and lower quality are by no means the only causes of greater volatility. Furthermore, as we saw in Chapter 1, some coupon issues of a given maturity compound the yield at the predetermined rate over much longer periods than do others of the same maturity, while conversely some provide much larger current income than others bought at the same yield.

Subsequent chapters will attempt to analyze these combined effects on different types of conventional coupon bonds. It will be seen that specific types of bonds are most suitable to meet specific types of investment objectives. Some provide maximum volatility for a given maturity, others provide minimum volatility for the same maturity at the same yield, others provide maximum current income for a given yield and maturity, others provide maximum assured long range total return at the expense of current income. In actual investment, all of these structural advantages and disadvantages, of course, have to be weighed against differences in the yields at which the bonds can be bought.

CHAPTER 3

The Volatility of Bond Prices

It is sometimes erroneously supposed that the volatility of high-grade bond prices in response to a given change in yield is entirely a function of maturity. This is only partly true. There are two other factors which affect volatility importantly: the coupon rate and the general level of yields. *All things else being equal,* with the same percentage change in yield, the volatility of the price of a bond increases:

(1) As maturity lengthens, (the longer the maturity, the greater the price volatility).
(2) As coupon rate declines, (the lower the coupon, the greater the price volatility).
(3) As yields rise, (the higher the yield level from which a yield fluctuation starts, the greater the price volatility).

Since these three determinants of volatility sometimes act in opposite directions on one issue, we frequently find eccentric volatilities such as shorter term low coupon bonds which are more volatile in price than otherwise identical higher coupon longer term bonds (see Table 12).

Before attempting to explore the structural forces which create these three determinants of volatility, we will present three empirical tables which illustrate in summary form the volatility effect of these three variables: maturity, coupon and the starting level of yields.

Table 12 shows the well known increase in volatility with maturity. It also shows that this rule does not always hold. It traces just two coupons, 3's and 8's, and it covers a 33⅓% yield increase in a high yield range selected to coincide with data presented in the tables in Chapter 2. While the volatility almost always increases progressively with maturity, the incremental increases in volatility provided by one more year of maturity become steadily less as maturity lengthens. For example, volatility increases much more between one year and ten year maturities than it does between eleven years and twenty years, while the increase in volatility between twenty years and thirty years is small. The exceptions are noteworthy: perpetuals are less volatile than low coupon maturities of over twenty years, and twenty year 3's are more volatile than thirty year 8's.

TABLE 12
Increase in Price Volatility by Increase in Maturity
Yield Increase 7.11% to 9.48% or by 1/3rd

	Price Volatility	
Maturity	3% Coupon	8% Coupon
1 Year	- 2.23%	- 2.21%
5 Years	-10.00	- 9.14
10 "	-17.23	-14.79
20 "	-25.00	-20.64
30 "	-27.20	-23.09
Perpetuals	-25.00	-25.00

Table 13 shows the less well known increase in volatility as coupon declines. The increase in volatility is particularly rapid with coupons below 3%. In real life coupons below 2% rarely exist except for a few deep discount municipal issues, some of which have fractional coupons under 1%; such issues approach the extreme volatility of theoretical 0 coupon discount bonds which promise only one lump sum payment at maturity. The table is confined to only twenty and thirty-year maturities at the same high yield range employed in Table 12, i.e., a yield increase of one third from 7.11% to 9.48%. However, the same increase in volatility occurs when the coupon rate declines in every ordinary maturity and yield range.

TABLE 13
Increase in Price Volatility by Decrease in Coupon
Yield Increase 7.11% to 9.48% or by 1/3rd

	Price Volatility	
Coupon	20 Years	30 Years
8	-20.64%	-23.09%
7	-21.14	-23.50
6	-21.76	-24.03
5	-22.54	-24.73
4	-23.58	-25.72
3	-25.00	-27.20
2	-27.07	-29.69
1	-30.40	-34.61
0	-36.57	-49.48

Finally Table 14 shows that as the general level of yields increases, volatility, if measured by the same percentage yield change, also increases. It is sometimes erroneously supposed that all things else being equal volatility is a function of percentage changes in yield, i.e., that a 33⅓% yield increase at low yield levels, such as 3% to 4%, will produce a similar percentage price decline as a 33⅓% yield increase at a high yield level such as 7.11% to 9.48%. This is only true of perpetuals. The table shows that for a 33⅓% increase in yields, the volatility increases rapidly as the general level of yields rises. While the table contains just two coupons, 3's and 8's, and just one maturity, 30 years, this increase in volatility per percentage change in yield occurs in all ordinary maturities and for all conventional coupons as yields rise.

TABLE 14
Increase in Price Volatility as Yields Rise
(30 Year Maturity)

	Price Volatility of	
33 1/3% Yield Increases	3% Coupon	8% Coupon
2.25 to 3%	-14.01%	-11.78%
3 to 4%	-17.38	-14.58
4 to 5.33%	-21.00	-17.60
5.33 to 7.11%	-24.48	-20.57
7.11 to 9.48%	-27.20	-23.09

The Causes of Volatility

The increase in bond price volatility with increases in maturity (Table 12 above) needs very little mathematical explanation. The current yield from the stream of coupon payments is increased by the amortization of a discount or reduced by the amortization of a premium and these amortizations are semiannual affairs. Therefore, the more years to maturity, the larger the premium or discount for a given yield difference away from the coupon rate, and also the larger the change in the premium or discount when yields change.

The reason why the <u>increase</u> in volatility becomes progressively less as maturity lengthens is that the less volatile coupon stream accounts for more and more of a bond's Present Value as maturity lengthens (see Table 16) while the more volatile lump sum payment at maturity accounts for less and less of a bond's Present Value. Eventually in fact, at very long maturities, the overall volatility of a bond decreases with maturity. The maximum volatility of an 8% bond is at 109 years maturity and of a 3% coupon is at 34 years maturity in the yield range 7.11% to 9.41% (see Table 12).

The increase in bond price volatility as the coupon rate declines is due to the same factors. The lower the coupon (at the same yield and maturity) the larger part of the total yield is provided by the lump sum payment of the discount. And since the lump sum payment is more distant in time than all but one of the coupon payments, its Present Value is more volatile than that of all but one of the coupon payments.

Finally, the increase in bond price volatility as yields rise (if measured by percentage changes in yield) is explained by the fact that at higher yields there are more basis points in a given percentage change in yield. Since the Present Value of the lump sum portion of the cash flow fluctuates roughly proportionately to basis point yield change rather than percentage yield change, its Present Value changes much more rapidly in high yield areas than in low yield areas.

The Two Eccentric Types of Bonds

In Chapter 2 we tabulated and explained the volatility characteristics of two extreme types of bond contracts, neither of which are often found in real life: 1) the perpetual bonds with no maturity and hence no lump sum payment at maturity (like non-callable preferred stocks); and 2) 0 coupon discount bonds which offer only one lump sum payment which includes principal and interest (like savings bonds). We found that the volatility characteristics of these two types of bonds were very different, almost opposite, as follows:

(1) The price volatility of perpetuals is exactly proportionate to percentage changes in yield at any level of yields (see Table 15 below). Thus, a 33⅓% yield increase, whether it be from 3% to 4% or from 7.11% to 9.48%, will always produce a 25% price decline for perpetuals. (It would follow that if yield change were measured not by percentages of yield, but by basis points, the volatility of perpetuals would decline sharply as yields rise.)

(2) The volatility of discount bonds with only a lump sum payment is not proportionate to percentage changes in yield (see Table 15), but rather more nearly proportionate to basis point changes in yield. Therefore, their volatility rises sharply as yields rise, if yield fluctuations are measured in percentages of the starting yields, because more basis points of change occur at higher yields.

The effect of these two conflicting standards of volatility, i.e., percentage change in yield and basis points change in yield, are compared as follows:

TABLE 15

Volatility of Perpetuals and of 0 Coupon Discount Bonds Compared

Yield Change by Percentage (+33 1/3%)	Price Change: Perpetuals Any Coupon	Price Change: Discount Bonds 30 Years	100 Basis Points Yield Change	Price Change: Perpetuals Any Coupon	Price Change: Discount Bonds 30 Years
2.25 to 3%	-25%	-19.91%	2 to 3%	-33.33%	-25.64%
3 to 4%	-25	-25.54	3 to 4	-25	-25.54
4 to 5.33%	-25	-32.36	4 to 5	-20	-25.43
5.33 to 7.11+%	-25	-40.38	5 to 6	-16.67	-25.32
7.11+ to 9.48+%	-25	-49.48	6 to 7	-14.29	-25.22
			7 to 8	-12.50	-25.11

(Derived from Chapter 2, Tables 7, 8, 10 and 11.)

Coupon Bonds in Real Life

In real life almost all bonds are coupon bonds which combine a stream of coupon payments with a lump sum payment at maturity. Therefore, their volatility is determined by a combination of the volatility characteristics of perpetuals and the very different volatility characteristics of the lump sum payment. In the case of long par or premium bonds, the coupon stream plays a greater role in determining the bonds' Present Value than in the case of discount bonds and, therefore, their volatility tends more to resemble that of perpetuals. In the case of deep discount low coupon bonds, the coupon stream is relatively less and the lump sum payment is relatively more, and, therefore, the volatility tends somewhat more to resemble that of the 0 coupon discount bonds. The relative weight of these two different standards of volatility is illustrated by the comparisons in Table 16 which shows Present Value broken down into coupon stream and lump sum payment.

This table indicates that with all conventional coupon bonds of reasonably long maturity the Present Value and hence the changes in the Present Value of the coupon stream outweighs the lump sum payment at maturity. Also, the longer the maturity, the closer the bond's coupon stream approaches the volatility characteristic of a perpetual. Consequently, in such cases, the volatility of the bond itself will come closer to that of perpetuals than to that of pure

TABLE 16
Present Value of Par and Discount Bonds
(Yield 8% Compounded Semiannually)

Coupon	Maturity	Price	Present Value of		
8%	10	100	20 $40 Coupons	$543.61	54%
			$1,000 Principal	456.39	46%
			Total	$1,000.00	
8%	30	100	60 $40 Coupons	$904.94	90%
			$1,000 Principal	95.06	10%
			Total	$1,000.00	
5%	30	66.06	60 $25 Coupons	$565.59	86%
			$1,000 Principal	95.06	14%
			Total	$660.65	
3%	30	43.44	60 $15 Coupons	$339.35	78%
			$1,000 Principal	95.06	22%
			Total	$434.41	

discount bonds. The longer the maturity, the greater the weight of the coupon stream. Nevertheless, as coupons decline, if yield and maturity stays the same, the lump sum payment becomes more important and volatility standards will be modified and will contain a larger ingredient of the higher volatility characteristics of pure discount bonds. This also implies increased volatility as yields rise.

The Volatility of Yields

Heretofore we have used and compared two ways of measuring the volatility of yields: 1) by percentage change (+33⅓%); and 2) by basis point change (+100 basis points). We have found that the valuation of a pure coupon stream exactly follows percentage changes in yield and that the valuation of a pure lump sum payment loosely follows basis point changes in yield (see Table 15). Which standard of yield volatility is true to real life?

Common sense says that yields fluctuate according to percentages of starting yields; that is to say, a yield change from 6% to 8% (or vice versa) is as likely in a high yield market as a yield change from

3% to 4% (or vice versa) is in a low yield market, or that a yield change by 100 basis points between 8% and 9% is less significant and more common in a high yield market than is a change by 100 basis points from 3% to 4% in a low yield market. As we are attempting to estimate price volatility as yields change, it is an essential first step to determine whether percentage yield changes or basis point yield changes should provide our standards of volatility.

Common sense is right. Table 17 shows that in the postwar years in periods of high yields there were usually greater basis points ranges of yield fluctuations. High or low percentage yield fluctuations merely reflected dynamic periods and stable periods. Indeed, the percentage average annual range in the disastrous years of 1966-70 when the total range was 4.87-9.35% was exactly the same as in the also dynamic years 1956-60 when the range of yields was 3.15-5.15%. The percentage fluctuations certainly did not fall as yields rose, which they must have done if basis points were the right standard of fluctuation.

TABLE 17
Yield Fluctuations, New Aa Utility Bonds

	Range of Yields	Average Annual Yield Range in Basis Points	Average Annual Range in %
1951-55	2.80 to 3.78%	41	13
1956-60	3.15 to 5.15	84	19
1961-65	4.19 to 4.80	32	7
1966-70	4.87 to 9.35	129	19

Therefore, from this point on in our analysis we will assume that in real life percentage yield changes are a sound standard for measuring yield and price volatility. It is against this standard that we tabulated the volatility increases that occur as coupons decline and the volatility increases that occur as yields rise.

In summary, we have seen that volatility of a pure coupon stream is always proportionate to a percentage yield change, but the volatility of the lump sum payment at maturity is not only greater than for the coupon stream but increases rapidly as yields rise.

Therefore, high coupon bonds are less volatile than are lower coupon bonds with the same maturity, and, furthermore, the volatility of all bonds with a reasonable maturity rises rapidly as yields rise, so that, for example, a 10% yield increase around the 8% yield level creates a much larger price fluctuation than a 10% yield increase around the 4% yield level. The volatility of any conventional high-grade bond thus results from the interactions of three factors: maturity, coupon and the starting level of yields. The first two are matters of choice to the portfolio manager. The third is beyond his control, but he can take it into account in planning his portfolio.

Summary of Bond Price Volatility

Table 18 below lists the volatility of all bonds with rounded coupons of 0% to 9% and all the most common maturities from 1 year to perpetuity. These are calculated on two yield assumptions: a 25% decline in yields from 9.48% to 7.11% and a 25% decline in yields from 7.11% to 5.33%.* All three of the sometimes puzzling and conflicting trends of volatility which we have discussed are visible in this table.

All the volatilities in the higher yield range are larger than the comparable volatilities in the lower yield range except for perpetuals.

All of the volatilities decline as coupon increases if yield change and maturity is the same, again with the exception of perpetuals.

All of the volatilities increase with maturity if coupon and yield are the same. Here perpetuals are an exception only in the case of lower coupons.

The combination of these three volatility factors creates some unconventional comparisons. For example:

> 10-year 1's, 2's and 3's are more volatile or almost as volatile as 15-year 9's.

*Since all tables heretofore were based on rising yields, we thought for variety's sake and for reader morale, we should base these summary tables on comparable falling yields. The 25% decline in yields covers exactly the same ground as the previously assumed inverse 33 1/3% rise in yields (see discussion in Chapter 2, page 36). These yield ranges were selected because they were used in Chapter 2 and thus the tables are comparable.

15-year 1's are more volatile than 30-year 9's, while the 15-year 2's and 3's are almost as volatile.

20-year 1's, 2's, 3's and 4's are more volatile than 30-year 9's in the highest yield range.

In the highest yield range, 25-year 1's, 2's, 3's and 4's are more volatile than perpetuals, as are all 30-year coupons up to 5's.

TABLE 18

SUMMARY OF BOND PRICE VOLATILITY

Coupon	Maturity 1 Yr.	2 Yrs.	3 Yrs.	4 Yrs.	5 Yrs.	10 Yrs.	15 Yrs.	20 Yrs.	25 Yrs.	30 Yrs.	Perpetuals
	% Price Increases as Yields Decline by 25% from 9.48% to 7.11%										
0	2.30	4.66	7.07	9.53	12.05	25.55	40.68	57.64	76.64	97.92	-
1	2.30	4.62	6.96	9.33	11.70	23.54	34.57	43.67	49.90	52.93	33.33
2	2.29	4.58	6.87	9.14	11.39	22.01	30.83	37.13	40.76	42.19	33.33
3	2.28	4.55	6.78	8.97	11.11	20.81	28.31	33.33	36.15	37.36	33.33
4	2.28	4.51	6.69	8.81	10.86	19.85	26.49	30.85	33.37	34.62	33.33
5	2.27	4.48	6.61	8.66	10.63	19.06	25.12	29.10	31.51	32.86	33.33
6	2.27	4.45	6.54	8.53	10.42	18.40	24.05	27.81	30.18	31.62	33.33
7	2.26	4.42	6.46	8.40	10.23	17.84	23.19	26.80	29.18	30.71	33.33
8	2.26	4.39	6.40	8.29	10.06	17.36	22.48	26.01	28.40	30.02	33.33
9	2.25	4.36	6.33	8.18	9.90	16.94	21.89	25.36	27.78	29.46	33.33
	% Price Increases as Yields Decline by 25% from 7.11% to 5.33%										
0	1.74	3.51	5.31	7.14	9.00	18.81	29.51	41.17	53.87	67.73	-
1	1.73	3.48	5.23	6.99	8.76	17.53	25.91	33.41	39.60	44.16	33.33
2	1.73	3.45	5.16	6.86	8.54	16.53	23.54	29.24	33.48	36.32	33.33
3	1.73	3.43	5.10	6.74	8.35	15.74	21.87	26.62	30.08	32.41	33.33
4	1.72	3.40	5.04	6.63	8.17	15.08	20.62	24.84	27.91	30.06	33.33
5	1.72	3.38	4.98	6.52	8.01	14.54	19.65	23.54	26.41	28.49	33.33
6	1.71	3.35	4.93	6.43	7.86	14.08	18.88	22.55	25.31	27.38	33.33
7	1.71	3.33	4.87	6.34	7.73	13.68	18.26	21.77	24.47	26.54	33.33
8	1.71	3.31	4.82	6.25	7.60	13.34	17.74	21.15	23.81	25.89	33.33
9	1.70	3.29	4.78	6.17	7.49	13.04	17.30	20.63	23.27	25.36	33.33

(0 coupon and perpetual bonds are largely theoretical. They are included in these tables to illustrate the mathematical extremes.)

Finally Table 19 shows the increases in volatility obtained by lengthening maturity according to the volatilities calculated in Table 18. It uses two coupons, 3% and 8%, for the yield range 9.48% to 7.11%+ and one coupon, 8%, for the yield range 7.11% to 5.33%. It shows, for example, that an increase in maturity from 1 year to 2 years will about double volatility, while an extension from 1 to 10 years will increase volatility 9.2 times for 3's and 7.6-7.7 times for 8's. However, an extension from 10 years to 30 years will increase volatility by only 1.7 to 1.9 times. It shows that the increase in volatility by extending maturity is faster with lower coupons than with higher coupons. It also shows that in the lower yield range, although volatility is less than in the higher yield range, the increase in volatility by an extension of maturity is greater than in the higher yield range.

TABLE 19
CHANGE IN RELATIVE VOLATILITY AS MATURITY IS INCREASED

	Years									
To:	1	2	3	4	5	10	15	20	25	30
	3% Coupon									
From:	Yields Decline by 25% from 9.48% to 7.11%									
1 Year	1.0	2.0	3.0	3.9	4.9	9.2	12.4	14.6	15.8	16.4
2 "	-	1.0	1.5	2.0	2.5	4.6	6.2	7.3	7.9	8.2
3 "	-	-	1.0	1.3	1.7	3.1	4.2	4.9	5.3	5.5
4 "	-	-	-	1.0	1.2	2.3	3.2	3.7	4.0	4.2
5 "	-	-	-	-	1.0	1.9	2.5	3.0	3.2	3.4
10 "	-	-	-	-	-	1.0	1.4	1.6	1.7	1.8
15 "	-	-	-	-	-	-	1.0	1.2	1.3	1.3
20 "	-	-	-	-	-	-	-	1.0	1.1	1.1
25 "	-	-	-	-	-	-	-	-	1.0	1.0
30 "	-	-	-	-	-	-	-	-	-	1.0
	8% Coupon									
From:	Yields Decline by 25% from 9.48% to 7.11%									
1 Year	1.0	1.9	2.8	3.7	4.5	7.6	9.9	11.5	12.5	13.2
2 "	-	1.0	1.5	1.9	2.3	3.9	5.1	6.0	6.5	6.9
3 "	-	-	1.0	1.3	1.6	2.7	3.5	4.1	4.5	4.7
4 "	-	-	-	1.0	1.2	2.1	2.7	3.2	3.4	3.6
5 "	-	-	-	-	1.0	1.7	2.2	2.6	2.8	3.0
10 "	-	-	-	-	-	1.0	1.3	1.5	1.6	1.7
15 "	-	-	-	-	-	-	1.0	1.2	1.3	1.3
20 "	-	-	-	-	-	-	-	1.0	1.1	1.1
25 "	-	-	-	-	-	-	-	-	1.0	1.1
30 "	-	-	-	-	-	-	-	-	-	1.0
	8% Coupon									
From:	Yields Decline by 25% from 7.11% to 5.33%									
1 Year	1.0	1.9	2.8	3.7	4.5	7.7	10.2	12.6	13.9	15.1
2 "	-	1.0	1.4	1.9	2.3	4.0	5.3	6.5	7.2	7.8
3 "	-	-	1.0	1.3	1.6	2.7	3.6	4.5	5.0	5.4
4 "	-	-	-	1.0	1.2	2.1	2.8	3.4	3.8	4.2
5 "	-	-	-	-	1.0	1.7	2.3	2.8	3.1	3.4
10 "	-	-	-	-	-	1.0	1.3	1.6	1.8	1.9
15 "	-	-	-	-	-	-	1.0	1.2	1.4	1.4
20 "	-	-	-	-	-	-	-	1.0	1.1	1.2
25 "	-	-	-	-	-	-	-	-	1.0	1.1
30 "	-	-	-	-	-	-	-	-	-	1.0

Investment Implications

Many of the structural advantages and disadvantages of the different types of bond contracts revealed by these studies can be offset by differences in the yields on these different types of bonds as we stated earlier. Therefore, the purpose of these analyses is not to provide the portfolio manager with a rounded program of action, but rather to inform him of some of the technical yield and price advantages and disadvantages of different types of bond contracts which he can weigh against price.

Nevertheless, a few partial guides to investment policy can be derived from this study of bond price volatility. For example:

(1) Since volatility increases rapidly as yields rise for all coupons and maturities (except perpetuals), both the risks and rewards from bond investment were much larger in recent high yield markets than they ever were in the lower yield markets which prevailed prior to 1969. Table 14 suggests that the price volatility was nearly 50% greater in 1971 than it was ten years earlier when yields were in the 3% to 5% range. This greater risk was, of course, compensated by a yield which had doubled and by the greater opportunity for price appreciation. Nevertheless, maturity and coupon selection was far more important than it was before 1969.

(2) Volatility for all bonds of maturity over 1 or 2 years is very large in higher yield ranges regardless of coupon. It is, furthermore, relatively larger for medium maturity bonds than Table 18 suggests because the yields of medium and short maturities usually fluctuate much more than the yields of long maturities. For example, if the yields of 10-year maturities rise or fall 50% more than the yields of 30-year maturities, which is not uncommon, the price volatility of 10-year bonds could approach the volatility of 20-30-year bonds of the same coupon. It

follows that so-called medium maturities, i.e., 5 to 10 years, are often a poor compromise between long and short if the investor seeks some measure of price stability and especially if he expects to sell out before maturity either to buy long bonds more cheaply or to invest elsewhere. For portfolio managers seeking to profit by the cyclical fluctuations of bonds, these tables suggest that a portfolio mix shifting between very shorts and very longs is usually better than a compromise consisting of medium maturities.

(3) Many investors seek to avoid or minimize prospective volatility because they expect higher yields. If this preference is very strong, then they should invest in shorts and plan to reinvest later on in the higher yielding longs they anticipate. The danger in this policy is, of course, the high risk of yield loss if yields turn counter to one's prediction and move downward.

(4) On the other hand, some investors may expect moderately higher yields, but may not be able to accept either the long-term yield risks or the lower current yields entailed in buying short. Such investors can consider high coupon premium bonds having several years of remaining call protection. These bonds often provide solid yield advantages, both to call and to maturity, which together with their lower volatility makes them a fair price and yield hedge against moderate yield increases. On the other hand, if yields drop, the investor will have purchased a handsome yield over at least the period of call protection.

(5) Those who expect substantially lower yields over the long-term should, of course, seek maximum volatility, and maximum yield protection. For both these reasons, they should favor long-term low coupon bonds provided the yield sacrifice is not too large.

(6) If in a bear bond market medium maturities are selling to

yield more than long maturities, these medium maturities could enjoy a price recovery just as large as long maturity bonds with much less downside risk. This is because mediums are in any event very volatile and the yields of mediums should eventually decline more than the yields of longs. In this event, mediums could be attractive for those expecting a medium-term drop in yields, but also wishing to avoid high price risk.

CHAPTER 4

The Yields of Premium Bonds, Par Bonds and Discount Bonds

As a result of the extraordinarily wide two-way fluctuations of bond yields over the last few years and the heavy volume of new corporate bond issues that have come out at different levels of the market, the investor today has available to him a much larger selection of high-grade seasoned corporate bond issues than ever before. Coupons range from 2⅝% up to 9½% for issues of uniform high quality and long maturity. Offering prices recently ranged simultaneously from 60 up to 115. Yields of essentially similar credits ranged from 6.50% up to 8.25%. These differences were attributable largely to difference in coupons. Therefore, the question of whether to buy new issues or seasoned issues and whether to buy high coupon bonds (at premiums), current coupon bonds (at or around par), or low coupon bonds (at significant discounts), has become more pressing than ever before.

In order to simplify the problem of selection, we will here attempt to describe and evaluate the yield and price advantages and disadvantages of three typical (but theoretical) prime corporate bond issues priced at the prevailing yields of February 1, 1971. These are as follows:

Premium Bonds. 8¾'s of 2001 selling at 109¼ to yield 7.94% to maturity and 7.66% to call at 107 in 1976.

Par Bonds. 7's of 2001 selling at 100 to yield 7.00% to maturity, callable at 107 in 1976.

Discount Bonds. 4's of 2001 selling at 67.18 to yield 6.50% to maturity.

If the guide to selection were only maximum yield as conventionally computed, the choice would be simple: the 8¾'s would be much the best buy; the 4's would be much the worst buy, and the 7's would lie in between. There are, however, many other considerations beside conventionally computed yields such as: 1) the effect of potential call on the yield of the 8¾'s and 7's (the 4's are immune from call); 2) the differing incidence of "interest-on-interest" (the rate at which future coupons can be reinvested by those investors who compound) which affects high coupon bonds more than low coupon bonds (see Chapter 1); 3) the higher price volatility of low coupon bonds compared with the lower volatility of high coupon bonds (see Chapter 3); 4) the effect of call risk on future price fluctuations; and 5) the combined effect of yield differences and prospective price changes on overall return.

The Effect of Potential Call on Yield

Let us assume that by the time the 8¾'s and the 7's are callable the going rate for new corporate issues of the same quality and maturity is 6%. If so, the 8¾'s would certainly be called and the 7's might be called. Let us assume that both are called and the proceeds reinvested in new issues are to yield 6% and to mature in 2001. Table 20 shows the yields at cost of the 8¾'s and the 7's if called and if not called, and also the yield of the 4's.

TABLE 20

A Comparison of Yields

	30-Year Yields
8 3/4's of 2001 @ 109 1/4 if not called	7.94%
7's of 2001 @ 100 if not called	7.00
4's of 2001 @ 67.18	6.50
8 3/4's 2001 @ 109 1/4 if called and reinvested @ 6%	6.23
7's of 2001 @ 100 if called and reinvested @ 6%	6.31

If not called, these yields for full compounding assume reinvestment of coupons at purchase yield up to maturity. If called, these yields assume reinvestment of all coupons and call proceeds at 6% fully compounded (for method, see Table 22). No sinking funds.

The lower part of this table reveals a very different line-up of potential yields. If the higher coupon bonds are called and refunded at 6%, the 4's promise the highest yield for a full thirty-year period and the 8¾'s promise the lowest yield but the differences are not great. However, there are other factors which should influence selection which will be discussed later. First, we will analyze yield-to-call.

Yield-to-Call and the Minimum Yield

The calculation of yield-to-call has become a standard procedure for evaluating high premium bonds although, as we shall see, it is deficient in several respects. For the yield-to-call, the pertinent cash flow is the coupon stream to the call date ending with the redemption payment at the bond's call price. For example, the 8¾ 30-year bond selling at 109¼ and callable in five years at 107 has a yield-to-maturity of 7.94% and a yield-to-call of 7.66%. This means that the cash flow to maturity discounted at 7.94% and to call discounted at 7.66% both lead to the same Present Value of 109¼.

Since the option to exercise the call lies with the issuer, the conservative investor can only count on receiving the smaller of these two yields. This has led to the common practice of evaluating such premium bonds in terms of their "minimum yield," i.e., the smaller of the yield-to-maturity and the yield-to-call. Thus, the "minimum yield" on the 8¾'s of 2001 at 109¼ would be 7.66%, based on the yield-to-call.

As the market price changes, the yield-to-maturity and yield-to-call will both move in the same direction, but with the yield-to-call always moving faster.

Because of the need to determine the minimum yield, investors in premium bonds often find their days further enriched by the job of performing yield-to-call computations. In the following section, we present an alternative way to follow the minimum yield of premium bonds as the market price changes. This method would seem to be more practical, more informative, and easier than the conventional procedure.

The Cross-Over Yield

Table 21 shows that high coupon bonds with 5-year call protection can command sizeable price premiums and still give potentially reasonable yields-to-call. At high premiums, however, the yield-to-call, which is the limiting yield, should be well above short or medium-term market yields to compensate for the risk of non-call.

While at all prices below call price the yield-to-maturity is always the minimum yield, as the price level rises to and above call price the yield-to-call drops more rapidly and soon becomes the smaller or minimum yield. More precisely, when the price of the 8¾'s exceeds 107.37 (or ⅜ths points above call price) the minimum yield "crosses over" from the yield-to-maturity to the yield-to-call.

There is a "cross-over price" (to coin a phrase) for all bonds with deferred call features. Above the cross-over price, the yield-to-call

TABLE 21
Yield to Call and to Maturity - 8 3/4% - 30-Year Bond Callable at 107 in Five Years

Dollar Price	Yield to Maturity	Yield to Call	Minimum Yield Based on
100.00	8.750%	9.866%	Maturity
101.00	8.656	9.616	"
102.00	8.564	9.369	"
103.00	8.473	9.125	"
104.00	8.384	8.884	"
105.00	8.296	8.646	"
106.00	8.209	8.410	"
107.00	8.124	8.178	"
107.37 *(1)*	8.093 *(2)*	8.093	Either
108.00	8.040	7.947	Call
109.00	7.958	7.720	"
110.00	7.876	7.495	"
111.00	7.796	7.272	"
112.00	7.717	7.052	"
113.00	7.640	6.835	"
114.00	7.563	6.619	"
115.00	7.488	6.406	"
120.00	7.126	5.374	"
125.00	6.788	4.393	"

(1) Cross-over price.
(2) Cross-over yield.

will *always* be the minimum yield. Below the cross-over price, the yield-to-maturity will *always* provide the minimum yield. At the cross-over price, both yields are equal at what might be termed the "cross-over yield."

In the example in Table 21 the cross-over price for the 8¾'s of 2001 is 107.37 and corresponds to a cross-over yield of 8.09%. In other words, at 107.37 the yield-to-maturity and the yield-to-call are both equal to 8.09%. In this example, as always, the cross-over price exceeds the call price (107) but only by a small amount. For longer periods to the call date, this premium becomes more substantial. The cross-over price would be 108 if the 8¾'s were not callable for ten years and then at 107.

Knowing the cross-over yield can often help the investor. As long as a bond trades at a yield-to-maturity *above* its cross-over yield, the yield-to-maturity will be the minimum yield. Only when the bond's yield-to-maturity drops below the cross-over yield, must the investor bother to compute the yield-to-call which will then provide the minimum yield. Furthermore, the yield-to-call does not achieve real significance as a means of evaluation until it drops substantially below the yield-to-maturity.

One convenient feature of the cross-over *yield* is that the same yield figure holds during the entire period up to the call date. The cross-over price does not quite share this constancy, but will decline very slightly with time until it reaches the call price on the call date.

The cross-over yield can be determined very easily. One simply uses the Yield Book to find the yield-to-maturity of the bond selling at the *call price* with a maturity *shortened* by the period to deferred call. For the 30-year 8¾'s of 2001, the term is shortened to 25 years by subtracting the five years to the first call. For the resulting 8¾%, 25-year bond selling at 107 (the call price), the Yield Book then gives a yield-to-maturity of 8.09%. This figure will be the cross-over yield for the entire five years.

The cross-over yield has two other interesting interpretations, both relating to the point where the cash flow determining the bond's value at minimum yield "crosses over" from the flow to maturity to the flow to call.

First, the cross-over yield is the "gross cost" to the issuer of calling the bond, not counting transaction costs in the refunding process. In other words, if, on the call date, the issuer could refund at a net rate lower than the cross-over yield, then he would reduce his gross borrowing costs.

The second interpretation has to do with average reinvestment rates throughout the bond's life. Suppose the investor over the years could reinvest his coupon income plus (if the bond is called) the principal and call premium at a rate exceeding the cross-over yield. He will then obtain a better realized compound yield (see Chapter 1) if the bond is called than if he were able to hold it to maturity.

Conversely, if his reinvestment rates are below the cross-over yield, which will usually be the case, he will obtain a better realized compound yield if the bonds were not called.*

Problems with the Conventionally Computed Minimum Yield

The "minimum yield," as explained earlier, is the conventional procedure for allowing for the "threat of call" in evaluating premium bond investments. Unfortunately, there are several flaws in this procedure which have serious implications.

The most obvious problem is that the minimum yield figure tends to obscure the all important question of contract duration. A yield of 7.66% (minimum yield of the 8¾'s) over five years has very different investment implications from a yield of 7.00% over 30 years (yield-to-maturity) of the 7's. These two figures are certainly *not directly* comparable, nor is it a simple matter to decide just how they can be made comparable.

A second problem with the minimum yield concept relates to the question of "interest-on-interest" which was discussed in Chapter 1. In some ways, the uncertainty is magnified with premium bonds because the yield-to-maturity and the yield-to-call can imply two possibly widely different reinvestment rates for the same coupon dollars.

A third and more subtle problem has to do with investor reaction to the uncertainty arising out of the call feature, an uncertainty which is always present but is more poignant in the case of premium bonds. Thus, a long-term investor tends to view premium bonds with a certain distaste since he must face the possibility that his bond might be called after only a few years. This threat is present even

*The cross-over yield can prove useful in yet another context. The call feature of most bonds is structured in terms of a sequence of declining call prices, each of which becomes operative at a specified later date. Yield to first call, i.e., the one immediately following the period of call protection, usually is the lowest yield-to-call along the entire sequence of step-downs in the call price. When this is not the case, the cross-over yield approach provides a simple technique for determining the most stringently limiting call price.

when the minimum yield is given by the yield-to-maturity. Similarly, the intermediate-term investor, operating on the yield-to-call as the minimum yield, must always keep in the back of his mind the possibility that the call might never materialize. Because of these uncertainties, the minimum yield (whether based on yield-to-maturity or to call) is always going to be a somewhat suspect figure to at least one class of investors.

Because of these problems, it is no surprise that the minimum yield fails on the most fundamental count of all—it does not really help to explain the actual market price relationship between premium bonds and par bonds.

In defense of the minimum yield, it should be reiterated that it *is* the conventional method for evaluation and the investor would be well advised, if for no other reason than this, to become thoroughly versed in its usage and implications.

However, for purposes of analyzing and understanding the character of premium bonds, we clearly need a more powerful tool which can overcome the problems cited above. In the next section, we shall take the concept of total realized compound yield which was described in Chapter 1 and which assumes that all coupons and other payments received are reinvested at a variety of assumed discount rates, and show how this approach can be extended to deal with premium bonds so as to overcome many of these comparability problems.

Realized Compound Yields to Maturity

In Chapter 1, the term "realized compound yield" was used to describe the total effective compound yield obtained from a bond purchased at a given price when the coupon income is reinvested and thus compounded at a specified "reinvestment rate" over the entire life of the bond. Only when the reinvestment rate equals the yield-to-maturity at purchase, does the realized compound yield coincide with the Yield Book's yield-to-maturity. However, for reinvestment rates differing from the purchase yield-to-maturity, it was shown that the realized compound yield figures could differ widely. Moreover, it was shown that the magnitude of this uncertainty varied with coupon rates, e.g., deep discount bonds would be relatively less sensitive to reinvestment rate levels because the discount does not require reinvestment, while current coupon and premium bonds, because of their greater interim cash flow, would be much more sensitive.

In computing realized compound yields, the key question is what reinvestment rate to use. For purposes of illustration, we use the current new issue rate of 7% (February 1, 1971). Taking this as a

TABLE 22

Realized Compound Yields to Maturity
30 Year 8 3/4's Priced at 109 1/4 to Yield 7.94% to Maturity and Callable at 107 in 5 Years

Assumed Reinvestment Rate = 7%
(Semiannual Compounding Throughout)

	Not Called	Called
Original Investment Per Bond	$1,092.50	$1,092.50
First 5 Years		
10 Coupons During 5 Years	437.50	437.50
Compound Interest on Coupons @ 7%	75.75	75.75
Coupon Cash Available for Reinvestment at End of 5th Year	513.25	513.25
Next 25 Years		
Compound Interest on Reinvesting This Coupon Cash @ 7%	2,353.20	2,353.20
50 Coupons During 25 Years	2,187.50	1,872.50 (1)
Compound Interest on Reinvesting Coupons @ 7%	3,543.66	3,033.37
Principal Repaid at Maturity	1,000.00	1,070.00
Total $ Accrued	$9,597.61	$8,842.32
Effective Yield on Original Investment to Achieve $ Accrued at Maturity	7.38%	7.09%

[1] 1.07 (number of bonds bought with proceeds of call) × $35 (semiannual coupon on a 7% bond) = $37.45 per coupon.

standard reinvestment rate, the new 7% par bonds would have a realized compound yield of 7.00% which equals its present yield-to-maturity. However, the 8¾'s premium bond would have a realized compound yield of 7.38% (assuming no call) instead of 7.94% as given in the Yield Book. The 4's would yield 6.76% against 6.50% in the Yield Book. The method of computation for the 8¾'s, both called and not called, is shown in Table 22.

If the 8¾ bond were called at the end of the fifth year, the coupon flow and the compound interest over the first five years would be identical with the "not-called" case. At the end of the fifth year, however, the call price of $1,070 per bond would suddenly become available for reinvestment at 7%. As shown in the table, this would lead to an accrual of $8,842.32 at maturity, corresponding to a realized compound yield of 7.09%.

Thus, the realized compound yield over the 30 years to maturity for the 8¾'s would be 7.09%, if called, as against 7.38%, if not called. In other words, the *minimum* realized compound yield would be 7.09%. This compares with a realized compound yield for new 7's over the same period of 7.00%. These yields are remarkably close together even though we are comparing 8¾'s with 7's.

All the realized compound yield figures cover the same 30-year period. All are based on the same 7% reinvestment rate. The yield spread between the premium bond and the new issue shrinks from 66

TABLE 23

Realized Compound Yields Over a 30-Year Period

Reinvestment Rate	8 3/4's Not Called	8 3/4's Called	7's Not Called	7's Called	4's
9%	8.60%		8.20%		7.86%
8	7.98	7.95%	7.58		7.29
7.94	7.94*	7.90	7.55		7.26
7.66	7.77	7.66*	7.38		7.11
7	7.38	7.09	7.00*	7.17%	6.76
6.50	7.09	6.66	6.72′	6.74	6.50*
6	6.80	6.23	6.45	6.31	6.25
5	6.26	5.37	5.92	5.45	5.79

*Purchase yields.

basis points to only 9 basis points in terms of minimum realized compound yields. This would seem to imply that the minimum realized compound yield more accurately reflects the price relationships between premium bonds and par bonds as determined in the marketplace. The realized compound yield figures thus overcome many of the difficulties inherent in the conventional minimum yield approach.

Table 23 shows the 30-year realized compound yields for all three bonds at various reinvestment rate levels. Several interesting results emerge. First of all, at reinvestment rate levels of 7% of above, the 8¾'s guarantee (call or no call) a better realized compound yield than either the new issue 7's or the discount 4's. At 8% or above, the advantage of the premium bonds is sizeable, at least 37 basis points over the 7's and 66 basis points over the 4's. At the other extreme, at a 5% reinvestment rate, the 8¾'s premium bonds would yield as much as 42 basis points *less* than the 4's and 8 basis points *less* than the 7's.

Table 23 also shows that the loss in yield incurred by the call of the 8¾'s is not large unless rates decline substantially; it is less than 29 basis points at reinvestment rates of above 7%.

For the long-term holder, these results indicate that, from the point of view of yield alone, the premium bonds at these yield differentials have attractiveness provided the reinvestment rate stays above 6%. If this proviso holds, the premium bond will at the very worst cost the investor 8 basis points relative to other assured opportunities. On the other hand, if the bond is not called and higher rates prevail, the premium bond may enjoy an advantage of as much as 40 basis points over the purchase of the 7% new issue and 74 basis points over the 4's.

CHAPTER 5

The Price Volatility of Premium Bonds, Par Bonds and Discount Bonds

The yield analysis in Chapter 4 will suffice to guide that very special investor who feels the need to check his bond market values only once every few years. However, few investors now cling to this rigidly long-term orientation. In fact, most bond portfolio managers pay close attention to interim movements in interest rates and the corresponding bond price reactions. In the context of this discussion, this means that the intermediate term price potentials of premium, par and discount bonds are an integral consideration in selecting the best instrument for a given portfolio. Since the price potentials of these three issues are very different, they serve to qualify any selection based solely on yield.

Premium bonds, because of their high current yield (always greater than their yield-to-maturity) and potentially short life, are considered by some short-term investors as high payoff, but risky alternatives to short instruments. For such investors, the consideration of price volatility may be all important, especially since upward moves in interest rates could suddenly transform a premium bond from a soon-to-be-called short into a long-term instrument.

At first blush, premium bonds appear to behave strangely in the market under changes in interest rates. As prices advance, there often appears to be a temporary ceiling which for a while obstructs their price advances in response to generally declining yields. On the other hand, when yields are rising, the premium bonds seem to take their own, sometimes rather casual, delayed course towards lower price levels.

In fact, premium bonds are often referred to as "cushion bonds" to indicate that they have a built-in safety cushion to soften the pain of generally falling prices because of their advantageous yield-to-maturity level. For example, the 8¾'s of 2001, priced at 109¼, have a yield-to-maturity of 7.94% or 94 basis points above the new issue rate of 7.00%. If new issue rates were to move to, say, 8% or 9%, this 94 basis point spread would naturally narrow and this narrowing would reduce the price decline of the 8¾'s as compared with that of lower coupon issues.

A certain portion of this more stable behavior is also explained by the purely mathematical properties of high coupon bonds which make them the least volatile long-term bonds for a given move in yield (see Chapter 3). However, these purely mathematical properties do not account for most of the "ceiling and cushion" effects. These are largely due to the call feature.

Suppose that the new issue rate moves from 7% to 5%, 6%, 7%, 8%, or 9% over the course of a one-year period. How will these three issues behave? Because of the much higher current yields on premium bonds, a fair comparison requires that coupon income be considered along with and added to the percentage price changes. The realized compound yield provides an ideal method for doing this. A sample calculation is shown in Table 24.

TABLE 24
Sample Computation of Realized Compound Yield Including Price Changes Over One Year Period

8 3/4's Priced at 109.25 (7.94 YTM) Moving to 104.91 (8.30 YTM)	
Original Investment Per Bond	$1,092.50
2 Coupons During Year	87.50
Interest on 1 Coupon @ 7%	1.53
Principal Value at End of Year @ 8.30 YTM	1,049.10
Total $ Accrued	$1,138.13
Total $ Gain	$45.63
Realized Compound Yield (for 2 Semiannual Compounding Periods) Required to Obtain Gain of $.04176 per dollar invested (45.63 ÷ 1092.50) after 2 periods (From Compound Interest Tables)	4.13%

Table 25 combines price changes over one year with coupon yield and interest-on-interest to obtain a total compound yield for one year if the new issue rate moves from 7% to 5%, 6%, 7%, 8%, or 9%. It clearly shows the "ceiling and cushion" effects of premium bonds. If new issue rates rise from 7% to 8% or 9%, the 8¾'s far outperform the 7's and the 4's. This is partly due to the cushion. If rates remain unchanged at the 7% level, then the yield advantage of the 8¾'s also results in the best one year performance. However, if new issue rates drop, the discount bond enjoys a very big advantage.

TABLE 25
Total Realized Compound Yields: Interest Plus Price Change Over 1-Year Period

New Issue Rate One Year Later	Bond	Cost	Yield-to-Maturity at Cost	Current Yield at Cost	Estimates One Year Later: Yield Maturity	To Call	Price	Change in Price %	Total Realized Compound Yield Per Annum
5%	8 3/4s	109 1/4	7.94%	8.01%	6.98%	4.35%	121.89	+11.57%	18.83
	7s	100	7.00	7.00	5.90	4.43	115.19	+15.19	21.19
	4s	67.18	6.50	5.95	4.70		88.98	+32.45	35.37
6%	8 3/4s	109 1/4	7.94	8.01	7.66	6.66	112.62	+ 3.08	10.94
	7s	100	7.00	7.00	6.50	6.68	106.49	+ 6.49	13.18
	4s	67.18	6.50	5.95	5.50		78.38	+16.67	21.57
7%	8 3/4s	109 1/4	7.94	8.01	7.94	7.59	109.13	- .11	7.89
	7s	100	7.00	7.00	7.00		100.00	0	7.00
	4s	67.18	6.50	5.95	6.50		67.56	+ .51	6.51
8%	8 3/4s	109 1/4	7.94	8.01	8.30		104.91	- 3.97	4.13
	7s	100	7.00	7.00	7.50		94.12	- 5.88	1.24
	4s	67.18	6.50	5.95	7.40		59.64	-11.22	- 5.24
9%	8 3/4s	109 1/4	7.94	8.01	8.80		99.48	- 8.94	- .80
	7s	100	7.00	7.00	8.00		88.79	-11.21	- 4.16
	4s	67.18	6.50	5.95	8.00		55.14	-17.92	-12.14

TABLE 26

Total Realized Compound Yields Over a 5-Year Period

New Issue Rate and Average Reinvestment Rate	Bond	Cost	Yield-to-Maturity at Cost	Current Yield at Cost	Estimates Five Years Later: Yield Maturity	Estimates Five Years Later: Price	Change in Price %	Total Realized Compound Yield Per Annum
5%	8 3/4s	109 1/4	7.94%	8.01%	Called	107	- 2.06%	7.26%
	7s	100	7.00	7.00	"	107	+ 7.00	7.74
	4s	67.18	6.50	5.95	4.70%	89.77	+33.62	10.52
6%	8 3/4s	109 1/4	7.94	8.01	Called	107	- 2.06	7.41
	7s	100	7.00	7.00	6.50	106.14	+ 6.14	7.75
	4s	67.18	6.50	5.95	5.50	79.75	+18.71	8.67
7%	8 3/4s	109 1/4	7.94	8.01	Called	107	- 2.06	7.56
	7s	100	7.00	7.00	7.00	100	0	7.00
	4s	67.18	6.50	5.95	6.50	69.31	+ 3.17	6.56
8%	8 3/4s	109 1/4	7.94	8.01	8.30	104.71	- 4.16	7.42
	7s	100	7.00	7.00	7.50	94.39	- 5.61	6.31
	4s	67.18	6.50	5.95	7.40	61.52	- 8.43	4.89
9%	8 3/4s	109 1/4	7.94	8.01	8.80	99.50	- 8.92	6.89
	7s	100	7.00	7.00	8.00	89.26	-10.79	5.67
	4s	67.18	6.50	5.95	8.00	57.04	-15.09	3.93

Table 25 also shows that the premium bond provides the least volatile return over the one year period. This would itself be a major point of interest for certain classes of investors, e.g., those who are essentially short-term oriented but who would like to take advantage of high long rates.

In Table 26 the time period is extended over the five years to the first call date on the premium bond. The accrual of coupon and compound interest over the longer time span is relatively much greater; since similar price fluctuations occur over a five-year period, they have a milder impact on the annual total of realized compound yields. Also, the imminence of the call suppresses the price fluctuations of the premium bonds.

Nevertheless, the same general ceiling and cushion pattern emerges. The premium bonds present an extremely stable return—a range in realized compound yield of only 67 basis points while the new issue rates range from 5.00% to 9.00%. The discount bonds give the highest return if rates decline. The advantages and disadvantages, which are often very large, are summarized in Table 27.

TABLE 27

Basis Point Advantage of Minimum Realized Compound Yield
8 3/4's over 7's

Assumed Future Reinvestment Rate	Over a Period of 1 Year	5 Years	30 Years
5%	- 236	- 48	- 8
6	- 224	- 34	- 8
7	89	56	9
8	289	111	37
9	336	122	40

Basis Point Advantage of Minimum Realized Compound Yield
8 3/4's over 4's

Assumed Future Reinvestment Rate	1 Year	5 Years	30 Years
5%	-1654	- 326	- 42
6	-1063	- 126	- 2
7	138	100	33
8	937	253	66
9	1134	296	74

(From Tables 23, 25 and 26.)

Summary and Investment Implications

All of these methods of calculating the rate of return, both with and without price fluctuations and with and without full compounding by coupon reinvestment, are summarized on Table 28. Lines 1, 2, and 3 are simple conventional yield calculations without considering either potential price changes or changes in the discount rate for reinvesting coupon income. Lines 5, 8, 11, 14 and 17 ignore price fluctuations, but modify the standard yield calculations by allowing for various reinvestment rates from 5% to 9%. The other lines (in bold type) add in potential price changes corresponding to the assumed reinvestment rates in either the first year after purchase or the fifth year.

It is evident that no one issue shows up best under all these calculations. To use such figures constructively, the portfolio manager must first clarify his objectives. Given the February 1, 1971 yield relationships used in the table, some conclusions may be summarized as follows:

(1) The investor who seeks primarily to maximize immediate current coupon income and who ignores price changes should be guided by line 3. He would certainly select the 8¾'s first and the 4's last.

(2) The investor who is seeking a high yield medium-term investment, who believes the 8¾'s will be called, or at least will hold up at call price, and who doubts that there will be a large rise or large fall in yields, would be guided by lines 3 and 13 and thus would pick the 8¾'s.

(3) The investor who spends his income and who seeks maximum assured yield in the conventional sense for a full thirty-year period and without regard to price fluctuations, should be guided by lines 1 and 4. Line 4 gives him his probable minimum yield and line 1 gives him a likely maximum yield. Since the differences in line 4 are small, he would probably be guided by line 1 where the differences are large, and buy the 8¾'s.

TABLE 28
Summary of Yield Calculations

		8¾s 2001 at 109¼	7s 2001 at 100	4s 2001 at 67.18
1	Yield-to-Maturity (1)	7.94	7.00	6.50
2	Yield-to-Call (1)	7.66		
3	Current Yield (1)	8.01	7.00	5.95
4	Yield to Mat. if 8¾s + 7s are called and Reinvested at 6%	6.23	6.31	6.50
	9% Reinvestment Rate:			
5	Fully Compounded Yield to Mat.	8.60	8.20	7.86
6	**Principal & Interest 1 year**	**– .80**	**–4.16**	**–12.14**
7	**Principal & Interest 5 years**	**6.89**	**5.67**	**3.93**
	8% Reinvestment Rate:			
8	Fully Compounded Yield to Mat.	7.98	7.58	7.29
9	**Principal & Interest 1 year**	**4.13**	**1.24**	**–5.24**
10	**Principal & Interest 5 years**	**7.42**	**6.31**	**4.89**
	7% Reinvestment Rate:			
11	Fully Compounded Yield to Mat.	7.09*	7.00	6.76
12	**Principal & Interest 1 year**	**7.89**	**7.00**	**6.51**
13	**Principal & Interest 5 years**	**7.56***	**7.00**	**6.56**
	6% Reinvestment Rate:			
14	Fully Compounded Yield to Mat.	6.23*	6.31*	6.25
15	**Principal & Interest 1 year**	**10.94**	**13.18**	**21.57**
16	**Principal & Interest 5 years**	**7.41***	**7.75**	**8.67**
	5% Reinvestment Rate:			
17	Fully Compounded Yield to Mat.	5.37*	5.45*	5.79
18	**Principal & Interest 1 year**	**18.83**	**21.19**	**35.37**
19	**Principal & Interest 5 years**	**7.26***	**7.74***	**10.52**

* Called and reinvested.
(1) Conventionally calculated.

(4) The investor who seeks maximum fully compounded yield for 30 years, and is relatively indifferent to interim price fluctuations, would be guided by lines 5, 8, 11, 14 and 17. These show a large advantage for the 8¾'s in 9% and 8% markets, a slight advantage in a 7% market, a moderate advantage for the 7's in a 6% market, and an advantage for the 4's in a 5% market. This choice between the 8¾'s and the 7's would not be clearcut but the 4's would have little appeal except if very low rates are anticipated.

(5) The investor who seeks high compounded yield combined with maximum price stability would be guided by all of the **principal and interest** lines. He would select the 8¾'s as combining the smallest price range with an income which is close to the highest or the highest in most of the markets analyzed.

(6) The investor who seeks maximum *performance*, i.e., principal plus fully compounded interest, would have to formulate a market projection for one year ahead or for five years ahead. He would be guided by all the **principal and interest** lines and would ignore all other yield calculations.

a. If he is bearish on bonds for the next year but still wants the yield of long-term bonds, his first choice would obviously be the 8¾'s and his second choice would be the 7's.

b. If he is bullish for the next year, his obvious choice would be the 4's.

c. If he is bearish for the next five years but still wants the yield of long-term bonds, his first choice would be the 8¾'s and his second choice the 7's. However, for this five-year period, the differences are much smaller than in the case of the one year period.

d. If he is bullish for the next five years, his first choice would be the 4's.

It should be noted that yield-to-call calculations play a secondary role in all of these judgments. If the objective is pure yield over the long-term, the fully compounded yield to maturity (if called and if not called) is a much better guide to values than yield-to-call.

All of these calculations are from the point of view of a non-taxpayer. In the case of taxpayers, the income advantage of the 4's would, of course, increase because of the capital gain. However, tax-exempt bonds ordinarily provide better net yields than discount corporate bonds to full corporate taxpayers.

Finally all of these yield and performance statistics are based on the yield spreads which prevailed February 1, 1971. Such yield spreads change dynamically from month to month and from issue to issue and such changes would naturally alter these calculations and preferences. Any one group or issue can be overpriced or underpriced and can thereby change its rank in the schedules. For example, in these tables the discount 4's are priced 50 basis points below the 7% new issue level. This spread in recent years has varied between 100 basis points and 27 basis points for Aa utility bonds. A study of the history of such yield spreads would help the investor to evaluate the significance of present yield spreads.

CHAPTER 6

Evaluating Bond Portfolio Swaps

If all bond swaps were good bond swaps, we would use a more constructive title for this chapter and call it EVALUATING BOND PORTFOLIO IMPROVEMENTS. Alas, however, there are as many bad swaps as good, so we have chosen the conventional and neutral term "swap." The purpose of this chapter and the next is to present a comprehensive method of evaluating several types of swaps. This method combines in one figure most of the advantages and disadvantages of each specific swap in a way that permits an overall measurement of possible loss or gain.

A Classification of Bond Swaps

These chapters will limit their consideration to four important types of swaps which depend for their validity on correct mathematical comparisons. These we will call:

I. Substitution Swaps.
II. Intermarket Spread Swaps.
III. Rate Anticipation Swaps.
IV. Pure Yield Pickup Swaps.

The Substitution Swap is the simplest of all. The investor now holds a particular bond. For conciseness, we shall refer to this bond as the "H-bond" (H for now held). He is offered a bond for proposed purchase which we shall refer to as the "P-bond" (P for purchase). Except for price, the P-bond is essentially identical to the H-bond in all pertinent characteristics–coupon, maturity, quality, call features, marketability, sinking fund provisions, etc. In other words, the P-bond is theoretically a perfect *substitute* for the H-bond.

As an example, suppose the investor holds a 30-year Aa utility 7% coupon bond (the H-bond) which is currently priced at par.* He is offered, on swap, another 30-year Aa utility 7% coupon bond (the P-bond) at a yield-to-maturity of 7.10%. The proposed swap seems to provide a pickup of 10 basis points. Transient factors inherent in any marketplace will always lead to such temporary price discrepancies between bonds of equal value. When these discrepancies are in the right direction, i.e., the H-bond priced above the P-bond, then they constitute a swap opportunity.

The Intermarket Spread Swap is the second category. Here, the offered P-bond is essentially a different bond from the investor's H-bond, and the yield spread between the two bonds is largely determined by the yield spread between two segments of the bond market itself. The investor believes that this "intermarket" yield spread is temporarily out-of-line, and he executes the swap in the hope of profiting (on a comparative basis) when the discrepancy in this spread is resolved.

As an example, suppose the H-bond is a 30-year Aa utility with a 7% coupon priced at par. (For purposes of comparability, most of the bonds in these examples have been selected and priced to correspond to the three representative bonds discussed in Chapter 4.) For the P-bond, consider another Aa utility, the discount 30-year 4's priced at 67.18 to yield 6.50% to maturity. The present spread between these two bonds is an adverse 50 basis points. Suppose our hypothetical investor believes that the present 50 basis point spread is far too low and that the markets should work their way towards a 60 basis point spread or higher. If he executes the swap by selling the 7's and buying the 4's and his expectations are realized, then the 4's

*Prices in all of these examples are typical of the February 1971 market.

will do substantially better in the market than the 7's, and he can reverse the swap with a "pickup" of 1.35 points in price at the expense of 50 basis points less yield for a limited period.

The Rate Anticipation Swap is the third category. Here the investor feels that the overall level of interest rates is going to change, and he wants to effect a swap which will net him a relative gain if this happens. Presumably he shortens or lengthens maturity, but there are other ways to profit by rate expectations within the long-term market: for example, premium bonds do better than discount bonds when yields rise and vice versa.

The Pure Yield Pickup Swap is the fourth category. Here there are no expectations of market changes but a simple attempt to increase yield. A good example would be the reverse of the swap described above, out of the 4's into the 7's, motivated purely by the higher yield of the 7's without expectation of a capital gain due to a shift in yield spread.

There is a wide variety of other swap situations which are beyond the scope of this analysis. These include tax swaps, multibond swaps, swaps for improved liquidity, for improved quality, to increase or reduce volatility, etc.

The Workout Time

In many of the swap situations described herewith, the investor is counting on a realignment of values to take place over a period of time. We shall refer to this period as the "workout time." For example, in the Substitution Swap, the investor knows that the H-bond (the bond now held) and the P-bond (the proposed purchase) will certainly coincide in price at maturity. This then is the longest possible "workout time" for the Substitution Swap. If the two bonds are indeed perfect substitutes in the marketplace, aside from the momentary aberration which provided the swap opportunity, then the workout time should be fairly short, perhaps a few months. The sooner the swap works out, i.e., the sooner the momentarily underpriced P-bond recovers its anticipated equality with the H-bond price, the quicker the investor can if he wishes pick up his anticipated capital gain. This in turn serves to improve his rate of return over the workout period of the swap.

It should be emphasized, however, that to realize the full advantage from such swaps there is no need at all of actually reversing them. Provided only that the discount on the P-bond, which caused its purchase, has been eliminated, the investor can retain the full advantage of his gain by simply holding the P-bond or by swapping it at the end of the workout period into a third issue which is then underpriced.

Measuring the Value of a Swap

Suppose a swap works out precisely as anticipated. By what yardstick should its value be measured?

One hears many standards applied to swapping. Some of these standards capture only one or two of the several facets of total return. For example, an "improved annual income" is an inadequate standard because it may be offset by larger capital sacrifice and, hence, a long run sacrifice in income. A "pickup in basis points" may be offset by the H-bond's better interest-on-interest or capital performance at the prevailing reinvestment rates (see Chapter 1). A "take out of dollars" for equal par amounts might be at the expense of investing those dollars at a lower reinvestment rate. All of these measures fail to encompass the totality of values in any swap.

A proper swap yardstick must take into account all of the components of return over the workout period—coupon income, capital gain, principal amortization and reinvestment of the respective cash flows at some prevailing rate. In addition, a good yardstick should be sensitive to the impact of the workout time, accurately revealing the effect of different workout times.

Actually constructing such a yardstick for swaps is surprisingly simple. If the swap is executed, then the accumulated dollar return in the workout period will consist of the P-bond's coupon income, interest-on-interest, and capital gain. The sum total of these elements divided by the P-bond's purchase cost will provide a net gain per invested dollar. One can then find that annual interest rate which, when compounded semiannually, would realize this same gain per invested dollar over the workout period. As readers of our earlier chapters will recognize, this is just what we have referred to as the "realized compound yield." Table 24 of Chapter 5 shows the details of a sample computation of realized compound yield. This yield figure provides a comprehensive and readily understood measure of the P-bond's total return under various assumed workouts and of the H-bond's total return under the same workouts if it had been held.

The per annum difference in the realized compound yield of the P-bond over that of the H-bond provides an ideal measure of the value or dangers of the swap. It meets all the criteria specified above, and can also be readily compared with the conventional yield-to-maturity figures.

The Substitution Swap

The Substitution Swap is simple in concept. Both the H-bond and the P-bond are equivalent in quality, coupon and maturity. The swap is executed at a basis point pickup which is expected to be eradicated by the end of the workout period.

It will prove very revealing to determine the value of a concrete Substitution Swap in terms of improved realized compound yield. For this example, take as the H-bond 30-year 7's priced at par to yield 7.00%. The P-bonds are, of course, then also 30-year 7's but suppose they are priced to yield 7.10% for a modest 10 basis point pickup. For the purposes of the example, assume that the workout period is one year. During this period, the prevailing reinvestment rate for coupons remains unchanged at 7%. At the end of the workout period, both the H-bond and the P-bond are priced at par to yield 7.00%.

The realized compound yield of the H-bond is 7.00%, as we would naturally expect. However, the P-bond has a realized compound yield of 8.29% over the one year workout period. The steps in the computation are shown in Table 29.

In other words, this 10 basis point Substitution Swap with a one year workout period results in a 129 basis point improvement in realized compound yield—but only for one year.

TABLE 29

Evaluating a Sample Substitution Swap

H-Bond: 30-Year 7's @ 7.00% P-Bond: 30-Year 7's @ 7.10%
Workout Time: 1 Year
Reinvestment Rate : 7%

	H-Bond	P-Bond
Original Investment Per Bond	$1,000.00	$ 987.70
Two Coupons During Year	70.00	70.00
Interest on 1 Coupon @ 7% for One Half Year	1.23	1.23
Principal Value at End of Year @ 7.00 YTM	1,000.00	1,000.00
Total $ Accrued	1,071.23	1,071.23
Total $ Gain	71.23	83.53
Gain Per Invested Dollar	.07123	.08458
Realized Compound Yield	7.00%	8.29%
Value of Swap	129 Basis Points in One Year	

To put these results in a properly qualified perspective, it must be realized that this gain of 129 basis points in realized compound yield is achieved only during the single year of the workout period. To obtain such a realized compound yield over the extended 30-year period, the investor must continue to swap an average of once a year, picking up 10 basis points each time or at least averaging such a pickup on balance.

At the very worst, the swap will not "workout" until both bonds reach their common maturity, i.e., 30 years hence. In that case, the realized compound yield gain would be 4.3 basis points. This is even less than the 10 basis point pickup in yield-to-maturity. (See page 98 below for an explanation of this difference.) However, as the workout time is reduced, the relative gain in realized compound yield over the workout period rises dramatically. The following figures assume that the H-bond's price remains stable at par—i.e., no overall change in rate levels is assumed.

TABLE 30

Effect of Workout Time on Substitution Swap
30-Year 7's Swapped from 7.00% YTM to 7.10% YTM
(7% Reinvestment Rate)

Workout Time	Realized Compound Yield Gain
30 Years	4.3 Basis Points Per Year
20 "	6.4 " " " "
10 "	12.9 " " " "
5 "	25.7 " " " "
2 "	64.4 " " " "
1 "	129.0 " " " "
6 Months	258.8 " " " "
3 "	527.2 " " " "

Table 30 shows that the gain in realized compound yield is approximately inversely proportional to the workout time. For example, if we shorten the workout time from thirty years to one year, i.e., by a factor of 30, then the annual gain jumps from 4.3 to 129 basis points, i.e., increases by the same 30 factor.

TABLE 31

Effect of Initial YTM Pickup on Substitution Swap
30-Year 7's Swapped from 7.00% YTM
(7% Reinvestment Rate)

Initital Pickup in YTM	Basis Point Gain in Realized Compound Yield	
	1-Year Workout	30-Year Workout
5 Basis Points	64.6	2.2
10 " "	129.0	4.3
15 " "	193.4	6.4
20 " "	257.9	8.6
25 " "	322.2	10.7
30 " "	386.5	12.8

Table 31 shows how the gain in effective yield grows with additional pickups in basis points of yield-to-maturity on the initial swap. For example, if the P-bond can be picked up at 7.20% rather than at 7.10%, the resulting gain in realized compound yield in one year increases from 129 to 258 basis points. In this case, doubling the initial yield pickup doubles the gain. This rule of proportionality holds to a very close approximation, as Table 31 demonstrates, for both the 1-year and the 30-year workout times.

Up to this point, we have been assuming that our Substitution Swap worked out exactly as anticipated, with the P-bond realigning itself with the H-bond's price (assumed constant) at the end of the workout period. This will often not be the case and there are, of course, various risks present even in this simple swap category.

The risks arise from four sources: 1) a slower workout time than anticipated; 2) adverse interim spreads; 3) adverse changes in overall rates; and 4) the P-bond not being a true substitute.

Major changes in overall market yields will, of course, significantly affect the price and the reinvestment components of both the H-bond and the P-bond. The resulting changes in the realized compound yields will vary greatly depending on the workout period. Thus, an upward movement in rates may lead to a low total realized yield (principal plus interest) over the first year because of the sudden price drop while the same higher rate will result in an increased yield over life because of the greater reinvestment component. However, in the Substitution Swap, these effects tend to run in parallel for both the H-bond and the P-bond. For this reason, the *relative* gain from the swap is insensitive to even major rate changes. In Table 32, a sudden yield move is assumed, and (for purposes of simplicity) the bonds are priced and the coupons are reinvested at the same specified new rate. For the 30-year workout period, the swap provides the same gain of 4.3 basis points for reinvestment rates ranging from 5% to 9%. Over shorter workout periods, the P-bond–because of its slight discount–is slightly more volatile than the H-bond and so performs better than the H-bond as rates drop. However, even if the yield-to-maturity on both bonds surged to 9.00% by the end of one year, the investor could still obtain a relative gain of 116 basis points by having executed the swap. This is, of course, a *relative* gain only, as the table shows. Obviously, on an absolute basis, the investor with hindsight would have preferred not to be holding any 30-year bonds at all.

TABLE 32

Effect of Major Rate Changes on the Substitution Swap
(30-Year 7's Swapped from 7.00% to 7.10%)

Reinvestment Rate and YTM at End of Workout Period	Realized Compound Yields-Principal Plus Interest: 1-Year Workout H-Bond	1-Year Workout P-Bond	1-Year Workout B.P. Gain	30-Year Workout H-Bond	30-Year Workout P-Bond	30-Year Workout B.P. Gain
5%	34.551	36.013	146.2	5.922	5.965	4.3
6	19.791	21.161	137.0	6.445	6.488	4.3
7	7.00	8.29	129.0	7.000	7.043	4.3
8	- 4.117	- 2.896	122.1	7.584	7.627	4.3
9	-13.811	-12.651	116.0	8.196	8.239	4.3

The Intermarket Spread Swap

The Intermarket Spread Swap is really a swap from one department of the bond market to another. The motivation is the investor's belief that the yield spreads between the two market components are out of line for one reason or another, so that a better value is afforded by the P-bond. The swap is executed so that the anticipated realignment will provide a relative capital advantage or a better yield with at least an equal capital performance.

For clarity, we will at first pin the H-bond to a constant yield-to-maturity level during the workout period, and assume that the yield changes are concentrated in the P-bond.

The Intermarket Spread Swap can be executed in two directions. First, the swap can be made into a P-bond having a greater yield-to-maturity than the H-bond. This is done either for the extra yield in the belief that the spread will not widen or in the belief that the intermarket spread will narrow, resulting in a lower relative yield-to-maturity for the P-bond and, consequently, a higher relative price for the P-bond.

The second direction for this type of swap is when the P-bond has a lower yield-to-maturity than the H-bond. Here the investor will profit only if the yield spread enlarges leading to relatively lower P-bond yields and consequently relatively higher P-bond prices which would more than offset the yield loss.

As a concrete example in the "yield give-up" direction, suppose the H-bond is again the 30-year 7's at par. The P-bond is the 30-year 4's priced at 67.18 to yield 6.50%. The investor believes that the present 50 basis point spread is too narrow, and will widen. For purposes of analysis, we shall first assume that the spread does in fact enlarge from 50 to 60 basis points by the end of a one-year workout period. The reinvestment rate for coupons is taken to be 7.00%. Under the initial assumptions, the value of the swap in terms of realized compound yield can be computed as shown in Table 33. The 10 basis point spread gain, assumed in the example, is rather small for this type of swap, but does create a significant gain of 91.4 basis points for one year.

TABLE 33

The Value of a Sample Intermarket Spread Swap in Yield Give-Up Direction

	H-Bond: 30-Year 7's @ 7.00%	P-Bond: 30-Year 4's @ 6.50%
Initial Yield-to-Maturity	7.00%	6.50%
Yield-to-Maturity at Workout	7.00	6.40
Spread Growth 10 basis points from 50 basis points to 60 basis points		
Workout Time : 1 Year		
Reinvestment Rate: 7%		
Original Investment Per Bond	$1,000.00	$671.82
Two Coupons During Year	70.00	40.00
Interest on One Coupon @ 7.00% for 6 Months	1.23	.70
Principal Value at End of Year	1,000.00	685.34
Total $ Accrued	1,071.23	726.04
Total $ Gain	71.23	54.22
Gain Per Invested Dollar	.0712	.0807
Realized Compound Yield	7.000%	7.914%
Value of Swap	91.4 Basis Points in One Year	

Table 34 demonstrates the effect of various workout times and spread growths on this swap. One immediately notices that the yield give-up works against the investor over time. Consequently, when a swap involves a loss in yield, which many of the best swaps do, there is a high premium to be placed on a favorable spread change being achieved within a relatively short workout period. This "workout time risk" also tends to aggravate the risk of adverse spread moves since the passage of time does not work in the investor's favor.

TABLE 34

Effect of Various Spread Realignments and Workout Times on a "Yield Give-Up" Intermarket Swap

H-Bond: 30-Year 7's @ 7.00% P-Bond: 30-Year 4's @ 6.50%
Initial Yield Give-Up: 50 Basis Points
Reinvestment Rate: 7%

Basis Point Gain in Realized Compound Yields
(Annual Rate)

Spread Growth (Basis Points)	Workout Time				
	6 Months	1 Year	2 Years	5 Years	30 Years
40	1,157.6	525.9	218.8	41.9	-24.5
30	845.7	378.9	150.9	20.1	-24.5
20	540.5	234.0	83.9	- 1.5	-24.5
10*	241.9	91.4*	17.6	-22.9	-24.5
0	- 49.8	- 49.3	- 47.8	-44.0	-24.5
-10	-335.3	-187.7	-112.6	-64.9	-24.5
-20	-614.9	-324.1	-176.4	-85.6	-24.5
-30	-888.2	-458.4	-239.7	-106.0	-24.5
-40	-1,155.5	-590.8	-302.1	-126.3	-24.5

* *Assumed in Table 33.*

*Assumed in Table 33.

General market moves over the short-term would have little effect on this swap's value provided the spread changes as originally anticipated. However, in the marketplace a major move in rates is often accompanied by a significant realignment of spread relationships among many market components. The powerful opportunity and risk potential of this swap can only be appreciated in the context of changes in overall rate levels.

Turning to an example of an Intermarket Spread Swap in the direction of yield pickup, suppose the investor holds the 30-year 4's at 6.50% and takes the 30-year 7's at par as the P-bond. This investor's views on the spread are the opposite from that described above. He feels that the 50 basis points spread is excessive and anticipates a *shrinkage* of 10 basis points over the coming year. Once again keeping the price of the H-bond (the 4's) constant for purposes of analysis, the value of this yield pickup swap, if it works out as expected, turns out to be 169.2 basis points in one year. The computational procedure is shown in Table 35.

TABLE 35

The Value of a Sample Intermarket Spread Swap in a Yield Pickup Direction

	H-Bond: 30-Year 4's @ 6.50%	P-Bond: 30-Year 7's @ 7.00%
Initial Yield-to-Maturity	6.50%	7.00%
Yield-to-Maturity at Workout	6.50	6.90
Spread Narrows 10 basis points from 50 basis points to 40 basis points		
Workout Time: 1 Year		
Reinvestment Rate: 7%		
Original Investment Per Bond	$ 671.82	$1,000.00
Two Coupons During Year	40.00	70.00
Interest on One Coupon @ 7% for 6 Months	.70	1.23
Principal Value at End of Year	675.55	1,012.46
Total $ Accrued	$ 716.25	$1,083.69
Total $ Gain	44.43	83.69
Gain Per Invested Dollar	.0661	.0837
Realized Compound Yield	6.508%	8.200%
Value of Swap	169.2 Basis Points in One Year	

This high value reflects the impact of a 10 basis point capital gain from the decline in spread on top of the 50 basis point advantage from the initial yield pickup. This yield advantage reduces the riskiness of the yield pickup swap. Table 36 demonstrates that the passage of time tends to work in this investor's favor in the event of adverse interim spread moves. In fact, by maturity, the investor is always assured of a gain of 24.5 basis points (not 50) regardless of how much the spread rises or falls. The figure of 24.5 basis points represents the initial 50 basis point advantage "deflated" by reinvestment at the common rate of 7.00%, which is above the yield-to-maturity of the 4's and hence increases their total return above their yield-to-maturity.

TABLE 36

Effect of Various Spread Realignments and Workout Times on a "Yield Pickup" Intermarket Swap

H-Bond: 30-Year 4's @ 6.50% P-Bond: 30-Year 7's @ 7.00%
Initial Yield Pickup: 50 Basis Points
Reinvestment Rate: 7%

Spread Shrinkage (Basis Points)	Basis Point Gain in Realized Compound Yields (Annual Rate) Workout Time: 6 Months	1 Year	2 Years	5 Years	30 Years
40	1,083.4	539.9	273.0	114.3	24.5
30	817.0	414.6	215.8	96.4	24.5
20	556.2	291.1	159.1	78.8	24.5
10	300.4	169.2*	103.1	61.3	24.5
0	49.8	49.3	47.8	44.0	24.5
-10	-196.0	- 69.3	- 6.9	26.8	24.5
-20	-437.0	-186.0	- 61.0	9.9	24.5
-30	-673.0	-301.2	-114.5	- 6.9	24.5
-40	-904.6	-414.8	-167.4	- 23.4	24.5

*Assumed in Table 35.

It is, of course, possible at times to combine a "Substitution Swap" with an "Intermarket Spread Swap." This would mean that the investor sells a fully valued or overvalued component of overvalued "Market A" and buys an undervalued component of undervalued "Market B."

The Rate Anticipation Swap

When portfolio managers anticipate an important change in the level or structure of interest rates they often make swaps designed to protect or benefit their portfolios. Most commonly these *Rate Anticipation Swaps* consist of shortening maturities if higher long yields are expected or lengthening maturities if lower long yields are expected.

It should be noted that the decisive factor is the expected long rate; the change in the long rate will almost always be the chief determinant of the value of the swap, much more so than changes in the short rate. Both long and short rates usually move in the same direction and an expected change in the short rate will usually be taken as a clue to a change in the long rate. However, a change in short rates, without a corresponding change in long rates, will generally have very little effect on the near term value of a maturity swap.

These maturity swaps are highly speculative. There is often a large penalty if yields do not rise or fall as expected in a short period of time. This is especially true because such maturity swaps often involve an immediate loss of yield. This is due to the cyclical behavior of the yield curve which is usually positive. It is always so in periods of low yields so that moving from long to short then involves a large yield loss. Conversely, the curve is sometimes flat or negative in periods of very tight money so that moving from short to long often involves little or no yield pickup and sometimes a yield loss. Nevertheless, these periods of maximum yield loss are usually the best times to make maturity swaps in both directions.

When the swap involves a loss in yield, time works heavily against the swapper. A prompt realignment of yields in the expected direction is often essential for the swap to work out profitably. If this occurs, the realized gains are usually very large.

In evaluating maturity swaps, capital gains or losses will be critical over the first year or so. If extended time periods are involved, coupon income and interest-on-interest will also be important, all of which add up to realized compound yield.

Table 37 lists the total realized compound yield from 30-year 7's @ 100, 10-year 6½'s @ 100, and 5-year 6's @ 100, if held for one year or for five years with a wide variety of terminal yields. It also compares these total returns with that of 5% one year bills rolled over at 5%. In all cases, any interim coupons are assumed to be reinvested at a 7% rate.

The table vividly illustrates the importance of the passage of time. In the case of the 30-year 7's, if the market moves from 7% to 8% in one year the 7's provide a total return of minus 4.14% or 914 basis points less than the bills. If the same yield increase takes 5 years, the 7's—in spite of their large price decline—provide a yield of 5.37% or 37 basis points better total return per year than the bills. Again, if the market moves in one year from 7% to 6%, the 7's will provide a spectacular gain of 1,481 basis points over the bills, but if this same yield decline takes five years the gain will be reduced to a still excellent 381 basis points a year, that is to say, an average return of 8.81% vs. 5% from the bills.

The table also shows that if the yield of the 10-year 6½'s in one year moves from 6½% to 9% they will yield 1,378 basis points less than bills, but if the time span is five years they will actually yield a trifle more than bills.

The five year columns in the table represent a special case: the five year calculations are based on the assumption that the 5% bills are rolled over at 5% each year. This implies that the entire yield change takes place in the fifth year. If the long yields rose or fell gradually during this period the bill yields would probably also rise or fall gradually thus reducing the yield advantage of all the bonds as yields rose and increasing them as yields fell. The one year calculation,

TABLE 37

Evaluating Maturity Swaps If Yields Change
5, 10 and 30-year Bonds vs. 1 Year-Bills
(Fully Compounded Interest Plus Price Change)

If Future Bond Yields to Maturity Move to	One Year Hence: Return of Bonds	One Year Hence: Return of Bonds vs. Bills	Five Years Hence: Return of Bonds	Five Years Hence: Return of Bonds vs. Bills
	30-Year 7's @ 100 and Bills at 5% Rolled			
9%	-13.85%	-1,885 BP	3.90%	- 110 BP
8	- 4.14	- 914	5.37	+ 37
7.50	1.24	- 376	6.16	+ 116
7.00*	7.00	+ 200	7.00	+ 200
6.50	13.18	+ 818	7.88	+ 288
6.00	19.81	+1,481	8.81	+ 381
	10-Year 6 1/2's @ 100 and Bills at 5% Rolled			
9%	- 8.78%	-1,378 BP	5.04%	+ 4 BP
7.50	.15	- 485	5.94	+ 94
7.00	3.29	- 171	6.25	+ 125
6.50*	6.51	+ 151	6.57	+ 157
6.00	9.81	+ 481	6.88	+ 188
5.50	13.20	+ 820	7.20	+ 220
	5-Year 6's @ 100 and Bills at 5% Rolled			
9%	- 3.83%	- 883 BP	6.12%	+ 112 BP
7.25	1.82	- 318	6.12	+ 112
6.50	4.32	- 68	6.12	+ 112
6.00*	6.01	+ 101	6.12	+ 112
5.50	7.73	+ 273	6.12	+ 112
5.00	9.47	+ 447	6.12	+ 112

*Purchase yields to maturity.

however, is realistic since 1-year bills are bought or sold at the switch date.

This type of calculation provides a good measure of the opportunity and risk involved in a "maturity swap." The portfolio manager who shortens maturity drastically at a loss in yield of 200 basis points must expect a substantial increase in yields within a year or two because otherwise his yield loss will soon overtake his superior principal performance. The swapper into longs at a big yield increase has time in his favor but over the near-term he can fare very badly if long yields rise further. Finally, the swapper from short to long at a yield loss also has time against him.

Another way to evaluate a maturity swap is spelled out in Table 38. It also compares 30-year 7's at 100 with 5% 1-year bills. The table shows the terminal breakeven prices and yields-to-maturity of the 7's which will equate their total return to that of the 5% bills at the end of 1 year, 2 years, 3 years, 4 years and 5 years. These breakeven prices can be viewed as the limits of price decline beyond which the bills would outperform the bonds.

Thus, if the 7's in one year decline in price by 2.06 points (to a price of 97.94 to yield 7.17%) their total realized compound yield if sold would be exactly equal to that of the bills. Similarly in five years if the 7's decline to 86.90 to yield 8.25% points, their total realized compound yield if sold would be exactly equal that of the bills if rolled over at 5%. Of course, if bill yields rose to 6% early in this span the breakeven price of the 7's would be higher. Consequently, the swapper out of the 7's into the bills expects a yield rise in one year of more than 17 basis points.

TABLE 38

Breakeven Prices and Yields of a Maturity Reduction Swap
30-Year 7's @ 100 into 5% Bills Rolled at 5%

Time Period	Breakeven Price Decline of 7's	Future Equating Price of 7's	Future Yield to Maturity of 7's
1 Year Hence	2.06 Points	97.94	7.17%
2 Years Hence	4.36 "	95.64	7.37
3 " "	7.00 "	93.00	7.61
4 " "	9.87 "	90.13	7.90
5 " "	13.10 "	86.90	8.25

From this table it is apparent that a swap out of 7's into bills will gain importantly from even a moderate bond market decline if it occurs soon but not if it is long deferred. Conversely, the swapper into the 7's will lose his entire yield advantage if there is only a small decline in the bond market in the first year, but his yield advantage will offset a much larger price decline provided it is spaced over a longer period of time.

Apart from maturity swaps there are other types of Rate Anticipation Swaps. Thus, within the long-term market, we have seen in Chapter 5 that discount bonds are much more volatile than premium bonds. If lower yields are anticipated, the portfolio manager can switch from long-term par bonds or premium bonds into similar long-term discount bonds. Since this usually involves a yield give-up, the passage of time is against him, but the possible gain in principal is very large. If higher yields are anticipated, he can swap into premium bonds which are much less volatile; in the event of a bond market decline, premium bonds should decline much less than par bonds and very much less than discount bonds. Furthermore, a swap into premium bonds usually entails a large yield increase so that time in this case would work in favor of the premium bonds.

CHAPTER 7

Yield Pickup Swaps and Realized Losses

The Pure Yield Pickup Swap

Probably a majority of institutional bond swaps are done purely for the purpose of achieving an immediate gain in return, either in terms of current coupon income or in terms of yield-to-maturity or both. These swaps can be made and often are made without reference to substitutions or to yield spreads, interest rate trends, or overvaluation or undervaluation of the issues involved. For example, suppose the investor swaps from the 30-year 4's at 67.18 to yield 6.50% into the 30-year 7's at 100 to yield 7.00%, just as in the earlier example, but this time for the sole purpose of picking up the additional 105 basis points in current income or the 50 basis points in yield-to-maturity. He is not motivated by a judgment that the intermarket spread will shrink or that yields will rise or fall. He has no explicit concept of a workout period–he intends (at least at this point) to hold the 7's to maturity. As far as this investor is concerned, he is making a "portfolio improvement" leading only to improved yield in a long-term high-grade investment vehicle. Hence, the name we have assigned.

It is not uncommon that this is the *only* type of swap that pension fund managers are allowed to consider. Even then, the portfolio manager's freedom to evaluate and carry out these swaps is frequently constrained by rigid, sometimes arbitrary rules, occasionally inconsistent formulae, and often unnecessary inhibitions against realizing losses (see below).

The evaluation of the benefits of such a seemingly simple swap is not as simple as it looks and in practice it is sometimes computed fallaciously. Obviously the increase in the current yield from 5.95% to 7% vastly overstates the benefit from the swap because it ignores the guaranteed 48.8% appreciation of the 4's when they are paid off at maturity. But even the 50 basis points Yield Book increase in yield, which takes full account of the prospective appreciation of the 4's, is an overstatement of the basis point benefits of the swap. We shall see below that the true guaranteed gain from the swap (if the 7's are held to maturity and are not called) will not be 50 basis points but may range between 20 basis points per year (if the reinvestment rate is 6%) to 29 basis points per year (if the reinvestment rate is 8%). These gains, however, are very worthwhile.

This narrowing of the yield gain from that suggested by "yield-to-maturity" occurs over an extended holding period because the same reinvestment rate will prevail for reinvesting the coupons of both the H-bond and the P-bond, and this reinvestment rate naturally benefits the bond with the lower starting yield relative to the bond with the higher starting yield. Thus, it pulls the total returns together. The relative benefit of the reinvestment rate to the lower yielding of two issues will be greater at low future reinvestment rates and less at high future rates.

A proper evaluation of a swap of this sort, which is based on holding the P-bond to maturity, must take account of three factors for both issues (see Table 39): 1) the coupon income; 2) the interest-on-interest (which varies with the assumed common reinvestment rate); and 3) the amortization to par. A fourth factor, which is so dominant in many other sorts of swaps, namely, interim market price changes, may here be ignored. A simple addition of the above three money flows, divided by the dollars invested, will give a total return in dollars which, with the aid of Compound Interest Tables, will give the total realized compound yield as a percent of each dollar invested.

In Table 39, this switch from 4's to 7's is evaluated in this way. It

TABLE 39

Evaluating a Pure Yield Pickup Swap

Sell: H-bond 30-Year 4's @ 67.182 to Yield 6.50%
Buy: $671.82 par of P-bond 30-Year 7's @ 100 to Yield 7.00%

4's (One Bond)	
Coupon Income Over 30 Years	$1,200.00
Interest-on-Interest at 7%	2,730.34
Amortization	328.18
Total Return $	$4,258.52
Realized Compound Yield	6.76%
7's (.67182 of One Bond)	
Coupon Income Over 30 Years	$1,410.82
Interest-on-Interest @ 7%	3,210.02
Amortization	0
Total Return $	$4,620.84
Realized Compound Yield	7.00%
Gain in $	$ 362.32
Gain in Basis Points at 7% Reinvestment Rate	24 Basis Points Per Annum
Gain @ 6% Reinvestment Rate	20 Basis Points Per Annum
Gain @ 8% Reinvestment Rate	29 Basis Points Per Annum

will be seen that although the principal invested in both issues is only $671.82 per bond (the price of the H-bond) the switch over a period of thirty years results in a gain of $210.82 per bond in coupon income, a much more important gain of $479.68 per bond in interest-on-interest (at a common assumed reinvestment rate of 7%) and a loss of the $328.18 per bond in capital gain to maturity which the H-bond will enjoy while the P-bond will not. These three factors add up to a net gain from the switch of a large $362.32 per bond which amounts to 54% of the investment. This is a net gain of 24 basis points per year, i.e., total return rises from 6.76% for the 4's to 7% for the 7's.

The true yield of the 4's rises above the Yield Book yield of 6.50% to a fully compounded yield of 6.76% because the assumed reinvestment rate of 7% is above the 4's implicit reinvestment rate of 6.50%. For the 7's, the 7% assumed reinvestment rate is identical to their yield-to-maturity and hence full compounding does not change this rate.

Alternatively, as the table shows, at a 6% future reinvestment rate the advantage of the switch shrinks to 20 basis points per year or $244.63, while at an 8% reinvestment rate the advantage of the switch rises to 29 basis point per year or $508.49. It seems evident that efforts to evaluate such switches without reference to an assumed reinvestment rate are apt to be misleading.

The table shows that if we ignore interim price changes and the possibility that the 7's will be called this is a valuable swap at any reasonable reinvestment rate. It will be worth something between $244.63 and $508.49 per bond depending on the reinvestment rate. Even if the 7's are called in a 6% market, the switch will be worth at least $75.24 per bond to maturity.

Why then do such riskless spreads exist in the market and indeed are often exceeded (doubled!)? Why do not holders of lower yielding issues who are relatively indifferent to interim price movements generally switch for yield pick ups even of 10 basis points or 20 basis points, which are common and often are safe from call risk and from unfavorable relative market fluctuations?

Realized Losses from Swaps

The answer unfortunately often lies in generally accepted accounting practices which make an artificial distinction between realized profits or losses and book profits or losses and between coupon income and amortized capital gains or losses. The result is that many funds with large book losses are frozen and are thus prevented from realizing large risk-free gains in both principal and interest. It can be estimated that many tax-free funds could be earning at least 1% more than they are, and from the same type of investments, if they were free to make even obvious risk-free swaps.

Any well-considered "yield pickup swap" pays a net gain to the swapper regardless of the cost of the H-bond. The profit from the swap is the same whether the H-bond is sold at a profit or at a loss. The net gains from the swap detailed in Table 39 are over and above recovery of the whole book loss incurred in selling the H-bond, whatever that might be. In this case the gains are after subtracting the $328.18 per bond loss if these H-bonds were purchased at 100. This book loss is equivalent to the amortization gain which the holder of the H-bond will automatically receive and the seller lose—regardless of his cost.

Nevertheless, on the books of this swapper, if conventionally kept, this swap would show a loss of $328.18 per bond in the year of the swap and an offsetting income gain of only $7.03 per bond that year. Some accountants would even charge this realized loss to the fund's income account for the year of the swap and this could lead to an increase in required contribution in spite of the fact that the fund's cash flow and ability to pay benefits has increased as a result of the swap. Indeed if through some market aberration the P-bond were identical with the H-bond, but priced 5 points lower (an immediate clear gain of $50 per bond or 7.4%) the books would show a loss which might well force the portfolio manager to decline what is in effect a free and valuable accession of assets. Funds which value at market are often free to ignore costs and, therefore, to make profitable portfolio improvements. However, many funds carry their bonds at amortized cost and as a result are inhibited from making portfolio improvements if they involve realizing large losses.*

One unsound accounting practice leads to others. For example, it has become fashionable to evaluate bond swaps by computing the number of years which will be required for the additional cash flow from the P-bond to recoup the book loss from the swap.

Even if we are forced by convention to accept this artificial and unsound "time test" for evaluating swaps, we should consider the wide differences in the methods by which the loss-recovery period is computed. Since interest-on-interest is a large component of total

*Note that the authors of this book are, or have been, bond dealers and hence have a vested interest in encouraging bond market activity.

return, it should be considered in comparing the cash flows of the P-bond with the cash flow of the H-bond. Often, however, it is overlooked.

Returning to our original example of the 30-year 4's at 6.50% into the 30-year 7's at par, let us see how this recovery time may be computed. For every H-bond sold at 67.182, the dollar amount of $671.82 is used to purchase the 7's at 100. The annual coupon payment from this .67182 fraction of a 7% P-bond is just .67182 of $70 or $47.03. Subtracting the H-bond annual coupon of $40, we obtain a net annual coupon gain of $7.03 per H-bond sold.

This cash flow can be reinvested and compounded at some interest rate. Depending on the assumed average reinvestment rate, the dollars accrued from the added cash flow, including the interest-on-interest, grow from year to year as shown in Table 40. When the extra dollars accumulated reach the point of equalling the book loss, then it is argued the book loss will have been recouped and the time to that point will define the recovery time. After the recovery time, the additional cash flow is considered to be all profit.

As Table 40 demonstrates, the recovery time is critically dependent on the unknown reinvestment rate. At a 6% rate, the recovery time for this swap is twenty-three years. At an 8.00% rate, it drops to twenty years. These are long and discouraging time spans for a transaction which in fact is immediately profitable, and they seem to illustrate the unsoundness of this guide.

One common error is to compute the recovery time by simply dividing the book loss by the annual coupon gain. This ignores the all-important compounding of "interest-on-interest." In this example, this method would lead to $328.18 ÷ ($7.03 per year) = 46.68 years, a dismally excessive time by any standard, indeed exceeding the 30-year life of both bonds. This is equivalent to taking the first year's gain of $7.03 as representative of all future gains when in fact due to compounding it will always be the smallest gain of any future year. From Table 40, one sees that this method also corresponds to an implied 0% reinvestment rate.

Many "pure yield swaps" are more complex than the above example, involving P-bond amortization and differing maturities.

TABLE 40

Timing of Additional Cash Flow from a Pure Yield Pickup Swap

Sell: 30-Year 4's @ 67.182 to Yield 6.50%   Buy: 30-Year 7's @ 100 to Yield 7%

Additional Cash Flow at Various Reinvestment Rates

Elapsed Years	0%	6.00%	6.50%	7.00%	7.50%	8.00%
.5	$ 3.51	$ 3.51	$ 3.51	$ 3.51	$ 3.51	$ 3.51
1.0	7.03	7.13	7.14	7.15	7.16	7.17
20.0	140.55	264.92	280.45	297.08	314.85	333.88
20.5	144.06	276.39	293.08	310.99	330.17	350.73
21.0	147.58	288.19	306.12	325.39	346.05	
21.5	151.09	300.35	319.58	340.29		
22.0	154.60	312.87	333.48	355.70		
22.5	158.12	325.77	347.82			
23.0	161.63	339.06				
23.5	165.14	352.73				
46.5	326.77					
47.0	330.29					

Recovery Time for Book Loss of $328.18 Indicated by [box]

These require some extension of the recovery time computation. The preceding example did not touch on these factors since it involved a swap into a P-bond priced at par and having the same maturity as the H-bond.

As a new example, let us keep the 30-year 4's as the H-bond at 67.18 to yield 6.50%, but now consider a swap into a P-bond consisting of 20-year 5's priced at 81.418 to yield 6.70%. The book loss per H-bond is, of course, unchanged at $328.18. For each H-bond sold, the manager could purchase $671.82 ÷ $814.18 = .8251 of the 5's, i.e., the P-bonds. If so, he picks up an annual coupon of .8251 × $50 = $41.26, or a coupon gain of only $1.26 per year over the H-bond coupon. Thus, per H-bond sold, an additional $.63 becomes available every six months for reinvestment–until the twentieth year. At that point the P-bond matures, the principal is redeemed, and the P-bond's coupon flow terminates. Thus, the swapper has deliberately incurred an interest rate risk for the period beyond the maturity of the P-bond. However, the principal payment will be reinvested in some manner and, therefore, contingent calculations are possible. The simplest and most consistent approach is to assume that at maturity of the P-bond the $1,000 principal will be used to purchase a par bond having a coupon equal to the assumed reinvestment rate, maturing ten years later at the maturity of the H-bond. This is equivalent to letting all accrued dollars continue to compound at the same reinvestment rate as before maturity.

For example, assuming a 7.00% reinvestment rate, then twenty years hence for each .8251 fraction of the matured P-bond, one can buy .8251 of an annual $70 coupon, or $57.76 per year. This is an annual coupon gain of $17.76 over the H-bond. Why does the coupon gain rise from $1.26 per year per H-bond to $17.76 per year?

This brings up the second factor–amortization of the P-bond's discount. The P-bond has also accrued a capital gain of $185.82 per P-bond or .8251 × $185.82 = $153.32 per H-bond sold. This gain in book value will often be accrued on a straightline basis, so that 1/20th of the overall gain, or $7.67 per H-bond will be added each year to the investment return of the P-bond. A better technique which seems to be gaining in favor is the so-called "scientific amortization." This entails treating the bond as maintaining the purchase yield-to-maturity throughout its life. Whatever amortization technique is used, the book value gain so achieved by the P-bond must be included in the computation of the swap's recovery time.

Table 41 shows the total accumulation from the accrued book value gain under scientific amortization of both the H-bond and the P-bond plus accrual of additional reinvested cash flow up to and beyond the twenty year maturity date. The recovery time for this swap is 25 years at a 7.00% reinvestment rate, and 28.5 years at a 6.00% rate. At the erroneous 0% reinvestment rate, the manager would never even come close to recovering the book loss.

Let us repeat at this point that this type of time computation is a highly artificial product of an accounting system which misstates the status of a portfolio. In fact, any well-considered swap which promises a higher overall yield for the life of the H-bond is a net gain from the day that the swap is executed. In such swaps, however, care must be taken to recognize possible losses due to differences in maturity, call risk, credit rating and sinking funds. Switches involving such risks can be entirely sound if the risks are fully evaluated, but such swaps are not pure riskless yield swaps. On the other hand, differences in coupon are often unimportant, if offset by differences in principal amortization, because most true tax-free long-term funds—like pension funds—should be indifferent to the source of income accruals, whether from coupon or from interest-on-interest or from capital gain.

Finally many funds are unfortunately limited to swaps where the P-bond is priced close to the price of the H-bond. This costly limitation is often motivated by a desire to keep par values (i.e., maturity value) intact. This ignores the fact that (in a tax-free fund) accumulated income is just as valuable a component of future principal as is capital amortization to maturity and indeed potentially more valuable since it is received sooner and can be reinvested.

TABLE 41

Timing of Additional Cash Flow and Amortization From a Pure Yield Pickup Swap

Sell: 30-Year 4's @ 67.182 to Yield 6.50%   Buy: 20-Year 5's @ 81.418 to Yield 6.70%

Elapsed Years	P-Bond Value @ 6.70%	Additional Cash Flow at Various Reinvestment Rates Plus Amortization of P-Bond		
		0%	6%	7%
0	81.418	0	0	0
.5	81.646	2.51	2.51	2.51
1.0	81.881	5.07	5.09	5.10
1.5	82.124	7.71	7.78	7.79
19.5	99.178	171.04	191.93	197.27
20.0	100.00	178.45	200.71	206.46
P-Bond Matures and Proceeds Reinvested at Reinvestment Rate				
20.5		178.45	206.88	217.20
21.0		178.45	213.25	228.32
24.5		178.45	263.45	317.82
25.0		178 45	271.51	[332.45]
28.0		178.45	325.20	431.68
28.5		178.45	[335.12]	450.30

Recovery Time for Book Loss of $328.18 Indicated by [ ]

Summary and Investment Implications

In these chapters we have discussed four important types of bond swaps: the Substitution Swap, the Intermarket Spread Swap, the Interest Rate Anticipation Swap and the Pure Yield Pickup Swap. The Substitution Swap is very elementary. It merely substitutes an almost identical bond for a pickup in price (a higher yield-to-maturity). The Intermarket Spread Swap depends on a yield spread judgment that one department of the market is overpriced compared with another. The Interest Rate Anticipation Swap seeks to profit by expected changes in the level of bond yields. The Pure Yield Pickup Swap ignores relative values and the market outlook and simply seeks to increase yield-to-maturity.

In practice two or more of these types of swaps can be combined in one transaction although, if so, the investor would be well advised to separate out in his own mind the multiple judgments involved. In fact, it is sometimes not enough to make sure that any one proposed swap will all by itself be valuable: a relevant question is whether at the time there may not be a better swap available for the H-bond or another more overvalued H-bond. It is too much to expect the portfolio manager to always be selling the one most overvalued item in his portfolio and to use the proceeds to buy the one best value available in the market, but this ideal can be kept in mind.

The central purpose of these chapters has been to clarify the nature of different types of swaps and to discover sound methods for evaluating each type. Its importance lies in the fact that too often swaps are evaluated by mathematical formulae which are incomplete. For example, a swap based on a mere increase in yield-to-maturity could cost money because it does not take account of the interest-on-interest, or of interim principal fluctuations, or of differences in maturity, or of differences in coupon and thus of the timing and size of the two money flows. A mere increase in coupon or current yield may be entirely misleading if it does not also take account of differences in amortization to maturity or in price change or in interest-on-interest.

We have proposed that to evaluate every swap the total realized compound yield of both the H-bond and the P-bond should be calculated and compared including coupon, interest-on-interest, amortization and, where pertinent, interim market fluctuations. This calculation cannot be independent of future reinvestment rates and hence the results must be stated in a range of probabilities rather than as one single figure. Furthermore, for most swaps the workout time will be a crucial consideration greatly enhancing or reducing the value of the swap.

Substitution Swaps, if true substitution is involved, are almost foolproof, but is this a suitable criterion for a portfolio manager? The gains from them are usually significant for only limited periods and hence they must be repeated at least annually to be really worthwhile.

Intermarket Spread Swaps require judgments of future market relationship (yield spreads). Therefore, they can lead to both large permanent gains or losses depending on the soundness of these spread judgments. If a yield loss is involved, the crucial question then becomes how soon the markets will realign as expected.

Rate Anticipation Swaps are highly speculative whether they involve shortening maturity or lengthening maturity. They depend primarily on a realignment of yields within a year or so of the date of the swap and in the anticipated direction.

Pure Yield Pickup Swaps, because they are designed to pay off over a long period of years, require careful attention to interest-on-interest, amortization and, of course, to quality and call protection.

Given this wide variety of swaps (and there are many other kinds not analyzed in this book), there are at most times a wide variety of sound swaps available to the manager of any widely diversified portfolio, including some which involve no speculative risk at all. These frequent and obvious market discrepancies, some of which are very large, exist partly because many institutions are inhibited from realizing book losses. This is particularly true because extreme market distortions most often occur in bear bond markets and this is just when many portfolios suffer their largest book losses. For this reason, institutions which are uninhibited by book loss considerations enjoy an important advantage over other institutions.

For many long-term investment funds, like pension funds, which normally hold some long-term bonds, the norm for judging their bond performance should not be cash but rather the level (price and yield) of the long-term bond market itself. A profitable swap gains against the market whether the latter is advancing or declining. In summary, for a tax-free fund which, to meet its own liabilities, is normally invested in some long-term bonds, relative performance in terms of principal plus fully compounded income is the best norm for good management.

PART II

The Mathematics of Bond Yields

CHAPTER 8

Simple and Compound Interest

Simple Interest

Suppose $1.00 were loaned today for one year at simple interest of 7% payable at maturity. One year hence the creditor would receive the following:

Principal	$1.00
Plus Interest @ 7%	.07
Total	$1.07

The generalized formula for this total repayment is extremely simple. If P (principal) is invested today at simple interest rate R (expressed as a decimal, e.g., not 7% but .07), then the payment received T years hence (number of interest periods which, in this case, equals the number of years) will be:

$$P + (T \times R \times P)$$

which can be usefully simplified to be

$$P\,(1 + TR)$$

or as in the above example,

$$\$1\,(1 + 1 \times .07) = \$1\,(1 + .07) = \$1.07$$

The annual growth factor at 7% is 1.07 regardless of the principal amount P.

This calculation can lead to two conclusions:

The value one year hence of $1 loaned today at 7% simple interest will be $1.07.

A $1.07 payment received in one year has a value today of $1 under a 7% simple interest rate assumption. Or more usefully, dividing both the value today and the value in one year by 1.07, we can say that $1 to be received 1 year hence has a value today of $.93458.

In these examples there is only one interest payment and that takes place at maturity. If we assume a two-year loan of $1 at 7%, the above formula P (1 + TR) would tell us that the following payment will be received at maturity:

$$\begin{aligned}\$1\ (1 + 2 \times .07) &= \$1\ (1 + .14)\\ &= \$1\ (1.14) = \$1.14\end{aligned}$$

This is an accurate simple interest calculation if all of the interest were payable at maturity, but in real life the first $.07 of interest would probably be payable at the end of the first year and the second $.07 of interest would be payable at the end of the second year. It makes a great deal of difference when the interest on such a loan is payable because if interest payments are made before maturity, e.g., monthly or quarterly, semiannually, or annually, then the creditor has the option of reinvesting them or spending them when received. The first $.07 received one year hence is worth more than if it were received two years hence.

Compound Interest

This leads us to compound interest calculations which assume one or a series of interest payments before maturity and add in the reinvestment income from these earlier payments on the assumption that they are reinvested (interest-on-interest) or at least that the creditor has the option of spending them or reinvesting them.

Suppose the same $1 were loaned for two years at 7% per annum compound interest payable at the end of the first and second years, with the first interest payment reinvested (compounded) at 7%. In this case the calculation is more complex.

Of course, we do not know at what rates the creditor can actually invest his interim interest payments, but for purposes of this simple illustration, we have assumed it to be the same rate that he received on his original loan contract. Note that the borrower is not responsible for providing interest-on-interest.

One year hence the creditor receives $.07 as the first year's interest payment on $1 at 7%.

Two years hence the creditor, if he has reinvested this first $.07 payment at 7%, will receive the following:

Second year's interest @ 7% on original $1 principal	$ .07
Second year's interest @ 7% on reinvesting first year's interest payment of $.07	$ .0049
Total interest earned in second year	$ .0749
Plus return of original $1 principal	1.00
Plus return of reinvested first year's interest payment	.07
Total receipts at end of second year	$1.1449

At simple interest he would have received $1.14 at the end of two years. At interest compounded annually, he receives $1.1449. And although the difference in one year appears small,we saw in Chapter 1 that this bonus, this "interest-on-interest," accumulates so rapidly that for a 20-year bond at 8%, interest-on-interest often amounts to more than the total of all the coupon payments themselves.

The formula for compounding is slightly more complex:

P = Principal = $1

T = Number of interest periods which, in this case, equals the number of years = 2

R = Interest rate as a decimal per interest period = .07

At the end of the first year, the $1 invested would have grown to

\$1.07. At the end of the second year, this \$1.07 would have grown further by a multiple of 1.07, i.e.,

$$\$1.07 \times 1.07 = \$(1.07)^2 = \$1.1449$$

This gives us the formula for the total receipts from compound interest at the end of T interest periods:

$$P(1+R)^T$$

or as in the example,

$$\$1\ (1+.07)^2 = \$1\ (1.07)^2 = \$1\ (1.1449) = \$1.1449$$

Correspondingly, if there are to be three years of annual compounding at 7%, the growth factor will be raised to the third power, $(1.07)^3$; if four years, the growth factor will be $(1.07)^4$, etc., etc.

Semiannual Compounding

While the above calculations are all for annual interest payments, in real life most bond issues pay interest semiannually. Semiannual interest payments are, of course, worth more than annual interest payments at level rates of reinvestment because half of the year's interest is received six months sooner and hence can be reinvested sooner and earn more interest-on-interest. Let us assume the same transaction that we analyzed above, i.e., \$1 invested for 2 years at 7% compound interest, but with interest payable semiannually, that is, 3½% of the principal payable as interest to the investor each six months.

Here we use exactly the same formula used above, i.e., total receipts will be $P(1+R)^T$ (principal times one plus the rate of interest as a decimal multiplied by itself as many times as there are interest periods). The principal P stays the same, \$1 invested. The rate R becomes .035 (half of the annual rate of .07) and T becomes 4 for a two year period (4 interest payments at 3½% each),

$$\begin{aligned} P(1+R)^T &= \$1\ (1+.035)^4 \\ &= \$1\ (1.035)^4 \\ &= \$1.1475 \end{aligned}$$

Thus, by moving from annual compounding to semiannual compounding, the total value of $1 invested today rises two years hence from $1.1449 if compounded annually (see previous example) to $1.1475 if compounded semiannually. Throughout the rest of this book we will assume semiannual compounding.

We will discuss first the time value of money, that is to say, the manner in which it grows at compound interest. This will lead us to the Future Value of a cash flow (i.e., a flow of coupon payments) and the effect of reinvestment of this cash flow (interest-on-interest). We will then consider the Present Value of this cash flow under various reinvestment assumptions. We will then discuss the Present Value of a bond, i.e., of the cash flow plus the principal payment. We will show how a bond's Present Value relates to its yield-to-maturity and yield-to-call. We will illustrate the computation of total realized compound yield. This is the result of regular reinvestment of all coupons as received at various assumed reinvestment rates and is often a basic value factor in comparing one bond with another.

CHAPTER 9

The Time Value of Money

In evaluating any investment where money is paid today in order to purchase future returns, the impact of time itself on both the Present Value and the Future Value of expected payments must be considered. One dollar received today is worth more from either point of view than one dollar received one year from now. The dollar received today can be put to work right away. It can be reinvested so as to return more than one dollar one year from now. Even in the case of the investor who spends all his income as it is received, the dollar which can be spent today is still potentially worth more than the future dollar. In a sense, the spender places an implicit time value on his money by foregoing the return from potential reinvestment of his money. The concept of the potential reinvestability of funds lies at the heart of any effort to measure this time value of money.

The Future Value of $1 Today

Taking the specific example cited at the end of Chapter 8, suppose income can be reinvested at an annual rate of 7% compounded semiannually, i.e., at a rate of 3½% per semiannual period. Then $1 today, as we saw, would become

$$\$1 \times (1.035) = \$1.035$$

at the end of six months. Compounding this amount for a second six month period, one obtains

$$\$1.035 \times (1.035) = \$1.071$$

at the end of the first year. This figure is equivalent to

$$\$1.00 \times (1.035) \times (1.035) = \$1.00 \times (1.035)^2,$$

i.e., to our original dollar multiplied by the second power of the "growth factor" of (1.035).

Continuing to compound the investment for a third period, we would end up with

$$\$1.00 \times (1.035)^3 = \$1.109$$

after 1½ years, and

$$\$1.00 \times (1.035)^4 = \$1.148$$

after 2 years (four interest payments). After 3½ years (7 semiannual compounding periods), the initial \$1 will have grown to

$$\$1 \times (1.035)^7 = \$1.272$$

This is 27.2% more than our original \$1 investment. This amount of \$1.272 is called the "3½-year Future Value of \$1 Today" (at 7% compounded semiannually).

While these examples so far all involve the initial investment of only \$1, the Future Value of any principal sum invested today is, of course, just that sum multiplied by the corresponding Future Value of \$1 at the assumed terms. For example, \$3 million invested for 3½ years at 7% compounded semiannually would have a Future Value of

$$\begin{aligned} &\$3 \text{ million} \times (1.035)^7 = \\ &\quad = \$3 \text{ million} \times 1.272 + \\ &\quad = \$3{,}816{,}837.79 \end{aligned}$$

Using simple algebra, the formula for the Future Value of a present investment has been generalized in Chapter 8. According to this formula, the Nth-year Future Value of \$1 received or paid today will just be

$$(1 + R)^T,$$

where T is the number of semiannual interest periods (i.e., T = 2N), and R is the interest rate per period, expressed as a decimal.

In Compound Interest Tables (see sample Tables 42A, B and C), the Future Value of $1 today is usually referred to as the "Amount of 1." These tables are arranged in terms of the rate per interest period and the number of compounding interest periods. Thus, as in our earlier example, for the 3½-year Future Value of $1 at 7%, one would use the table for 3½% (the rate of interest per semiannual compounding period), and then look up the value corresponding to 7 half year periods, i.e., 1.272.

TABLE 42A

Compound Interest and Annuity Tables
(Abbreviated Sample)
3 1/2% Per Period
7% Compounded Semiannually

Number of		Future Worth		Present Worth	
Years	Compounding Periods	Amount of 1 How $1 Will Grow	Amount of 1 Per Period How it Will Grow	of $1 Due in the Future	of $1 Payable Periodically
1/2	1	1.035	1.000	.966	.966
1	2	1.071	2.035	.934	1.900
1 1/2	3	1.109	3.106	.902	2.802
2	4	1.148	4.215	.871	3.673
2 1/2	5	1.188	5.362	.842	4.515
3	6	1.229	6.550	.814	5.329
3 1/2	7	1.272	7.779	.786	6.115
5	10	1.411	11.731	.709	8.317
7 1/2	15	1.675	19.296	.597	11.517
10	20	1.990	28.280	.503	14.212
12 1/2	25	2.363	38.950	.423	16.482
15	30	2.807	51.623	.356	18.392
20	40	3.959	84.550	.253	21.355
25	50	5.585	130.998	.179	23.456
30	60	7.878	196.517	.127	24.945

These tables are abbreviations and simplifications of standard Compound Interest Tables such as those published by the Financial Publishing Co. of Boston. While their tables run to 9 decimals, we round the figures to 3 decimals. We use only 15 time periods against their 240 time periods. We illustrate with only 3 discount rates, while they provide data on a very wide range of rates. We omit their calculations on sinking funds.

TABLE 42B

Compound Interest and Annuity Tables
(Abbreviated Sample)
3 1/4% Per Period
6 1/2% Compounded Semiannually

Number of		Future Worth		Present Worth	
Years	Compounding Periods	Amount of 1 How $1 Will Grow	Amount of 1 Per Period How it Will Grow	of $1 Due in the Future	of $1 Payable Periodically
1/2	1	1.033	1.000	.969	.969
1	2	1.066	2.033	.938	1.907
1 1/2	3	1.101	3.099	.909	2.815
2	4	1.136	4.199	.880	3.695
2 1/2	5	1.173	5.336	.852	4.547
3	6	1.212	6.509	.825	5.373
3 1/2	7	1.251	7.721	.799	6.172
5	10	1.377	11.597	.726	8.422
7 1/2	15	1.616	18.943	.618	11.725
10	20	1.896	27.564	.527	14.539
12 1/2	25	2.225	37.680	.450	16.938
15	30	2.610	49.550	.383	18.982
20	40	3.594	79.822	.278	22.208
25	50	4.949	121.503	.202	24.552
30	60	6.814	178.893	.147	26.254

This Future Value concept can be used to measure the time value of money. Suppose the 7% reinvestment rate was a certainty over the next 3½ years. Then an investor faced with a choice between $1.00 today or $1.20 3½ years hence would have an easy decision. The 3½-year Future Value of $1 today is $1.27 while the Future Value of $1.20 paid in 3½ years is, of course, just $1.20. The $1.00 paid today provides the better Future Value if it can be invested at 7%.

Interest on an Interest Payment

Future Value is closely related to and indeed assumes at least the opportunity of earning interest-on-interest. Suppose the investor has just received a $20 interest payment from a 4% coupon bond having 3½ years of remaining life. He reinvests this $20 amount

TABLE 42C

Compounded Interest and Annuity Tables
(Abbreviated Sample)
3% Per Period
6% Compounded Semiannually

Number of		Future Worth		Present Worth	
Years	Compounding Periods	Amount of 1 How $1 Will Grow	Amount of 1 Per Period How it Will Grow	of $1 Due in the Future	of $1 Payable Periodically
1/2	1	1.030	1.000	.971	.971
1	2	1.061	2.030	.943	1.913
1 1/2	3	1.093	3.091	.915	2.829
2	4	1.126	4.184	.888	3.717
2 1/2	5	1.159	5.309	.863	4.580
3	6	1.194	6.468	.837	5.417
3 1/2	7	1.230	7.662	.813	6.230
5	10	1.344	11.464	.744	8.530
7 1/2	15	1.558	18.599	.642	11.938
10	20	1.806	26.870	.554	14.877
12 1/2	25	2.094	36.459	.478	17.413
15	30	2.427	47.575	.412	19.600
20	40	3.262	75.401	.307	23.115
25	50	4.384	112.797	.228	25.730
30	60	5.892	163.053	.170	27.676

at a 7% rate. *Note that this reinvestment rate can be quite different from either the coupon rate or the yield-to-mauturity rate.* After 3½ years (i.e., 7 semiannual periods), the Future Value of $1 is

$1.272 (See Table 42A),

so that the $20 coupon payment will have grown to

$20 × 1.272 = $25.44

Of this amount, interest-on-interest will account for

$5.44,

or all growth beyond the original $20. Note that there is no need to discuss the bond's yield-to-maturity in this example. This is no coincidence. As we shall see more explicitly later, reinvestment rate and yield-to-maturity are very different concepts.

Present Value of $1 Received in the Future

So far we have discussed the Future Value of present dollars. The reverse way of looking at the time value of money is through the concept of the Present Value of future dollars. Under the assumptions made above, $1 would grow to $1.272 in 3½ years. This means that since

$$\frac{\$1}{1.272} = \$.786,$$

the sum $.786 invested today would grow in 3½ years by a factor of 1.272 to precisely $1.

Thus, $.786 is the Present Value of $1 to be received in 3½ years under the assumption of a 7% interest rate compounded semi-annually. Stated another way, $.786 paid today on these terms is equivalent to $1 paid 3½ years hence.

If the terms are the same, the Present Value of $1 paid in the future is the reciprocal of the Future Value of $1 paid today.

More generally, this observation shows that if the T half-year Future Value of $1 at an interest rate R per period is

$(1 + R)^T$, (the standard Future Value formula discussed above)

then the Present Value of $1 to be received in T half-years must just be the reciprocal,

$$\frac{1}{(1 + R)^T}$$

This is the standard Present Value formula.

Generalizing, the Present Value of any amount paid at some future point is just this amount multiplied by the corresponding Present Value of $1. Thus, a $20 payment received in 3½ years would have a Present Value under a 7% interest rate assumption of

$$\$20 \times .786 = \$15.72$$

In Compound Interest Tables, the Present Value of $1 is often referred to as the "Present Worth of $1 Due in the Future." Using the tables to find the Present Value of $1 to be received in 3½ years under a 7% interest rate, we would first turn to the 3½% page (Table 42A), and then look up the value corresponding to 7 periods, .786, i.e., the same value as we computed earlier by taking the reciprocal of the Future Value of $1 at these terms.

Present Values can also be used to solve the problem of the investor forced to choose between accepting $1 today versus, say, $1.20 3½ years hence. The Present Value of $1 today is, of course, just $1, while the Present Value of $1.20 received 3½ years hence is

$$\begin{aligned} \$1.20 \times \frac{1}{(1+.035)^7} &= \$1.20 \times \frac{1}{(1.035)^7} \\ &= \$1.20 \times \frac{1}{1.272} \\ &= \$1.20 \times .786 \\ &= \$\ .943 \end{aligned}$$

Based on its greater Present Value, the investor should choose the $1 payable today.

The Principle of Evaluation at a Common Point in Time

From working out the preceding example, a $1.20 payment 3½ years hence is seen to have a $.94+ Present Value and, of course, a 3½-year Future Value of $1.20. Suppose one wanted to know the 2-year Future Value of this payment? Since we already know its Present Value is $.94+, and since the 2-year Future Value of $.94 is just

$$\begin{aligned} \$.94 \times (1.035)^4 &= \$\ .94 \times (1.148) \\ &= \$1.083\ , \end{aligned}$$

we have the answer at once: $1.20 in 3½ years is equivalent to $.94 now which is equivalent to $1.083 in 2 years.

This demonstrates a key point. A payment made at any point in time can be evaluated as of any other point of time if the rate is assumed. Moreover, when any two alternative payments are to be compared, they must be compared in terms of their values at some *common point in time.* It is usual to take the present as this common time point, and then compare Present Values.

At the same reinvestment rate assumption, a given Present Value completely determines all Future Values. It is also true that any given Future Value determines the Present Value and hence all other Future Values. Whenever one investment has an advantageous Present Value relative to another investment on the same terms, then all Future Values will also be larger and the size of the advantage will grow with time. In subsequent chapters, we shall see that this important evaluation principle applies to a series of payments as well as to a single payment.

CHAPTER 10

The Future Value of a Cash Flow

The Future Value of $1 Per Period

As shown in the preceding chapter, the Future Value of $1 received or paid today, and invested for T semiannual periods at an interest rate R per period, will be

$$(1 + R)^T$$

For example, as we have seen, assuming a 7% rate, $1 today would have a Future Value in 3½ years of

$$\$1 \times (1.035)^7 = \$1.272$$

Now suppose that the payment of $1 were to be made six months from now. What would be its 3½-year Future Value? This $1 would then be subject to 3 years or 6 periods of compounded reinvestment. Consequently, its Future Value 3½ years from today would be

$$\$1 \times (1.035)^6 = \$1.229$$

Similarly, a second payment of $1 made after one year would have a 3½-year from now Future Value of

$$\$1 \times (1.035)^5 = \$1.188$$

and the combined 3½-year Future Value of the \$1 payment in 6 months and the \$1 in one year would be

$$\$1 \times [(1.035)^6 + (1.035)^5] = \$1.229 + \$1.188$$
$$= \$2.417$$

Continuing in this fashion with a \$1 payment every subsequent six months for 7 periods, one would find the 3½-year from now Future Value of this cash flow to be \$7.779, as shown in Table 43.

TABLE 43

Future Value of \$1 Per Period for 7 Periods With Each \$1 Payment Reinvested at 3 1/2% Per Semiannual Period

Payment Made After this Number of Semiannual Periods	Number of Periods Remaining for Compounding the Reinvested Payment	Amount of Payment		Future Value of \$1		Future Value of Payment After 3 1/2 Years*	Interest-on-Interest Component
1	6	\$1	x	$(1.035)^6$	=	\$1.229	\$.229
2	5	1	x	$(1.035)^5$	=	1.188	.188
3	4	1	x	$(1.035)^4$	=	1.148	.148
4	3	1	x	$(1.035)^3$	=	1.109	.109
5	2	1	x	$(1.035)^2$	=	1.071	.071
6	1	1	x	$(1.035)^1$	=	1.035	.035
7	0	1	x	1.000	=	1.000	.000
	Totals	\$7		7.779*		\$7.779*	\$.779*

*Totals have been calculated from values with additional decimal places for accuracy. Consequently, values as presented do not add precisely.

This result of \$7.779 is called the 3½-year Future Value of \$1 Per Period at a 7% interest rate compounded semiannually. As Table 43 shows, it is simply the sum of the Future Values of each \$1 payment reinvested at a rate of 3½% per semiannual period and compounded for the number of periods remaining until the end of the 3½ years.

The Future Value of any series of T \$1 payments received every six months and reinvested at any semiannual interest rate R can be looked up in the Compound Interest Tables or can be computed in a similar manner. This general result is called the Future Value of \$1 Per Period for T periods at the rate R, and its general formula is given in the Appendix (#3).

In Compound Interest Tables, this figure is usually referred to as the "Amount of 1 Per Period" (See Table 42A, B and C). To use the tables for the preceding example, one would first turn to the 3½% rate page and then search down the "Amount of 1 Per Period" column for the value corresponding to 7 interest periods (i.e., 3½ years), and obtain the same value, 7.779, as we found more laboriously in Table 43.

The Future Value of a Level Cash Flow

Now suppose we again have a series of 7 semiannual payments, but of \$20 each instead of \$1 as before. The first \$20 payment is received in six months. It is immediately reinvested at the assumed 7% interest rate, and compounded for the 6 semiannual periods remaining until the end of the 3½ years. The Future Value of this first \$20 payment will be 20 multiplied by the Future Value of \$1 after 6 periods of compounding at 3½% per period, i.e.,

$$\begin{aligned} \$20 \times (1.035)^6 &= \$20 \times 1.229 \\ &= \$24.58 \end{aligned}$$

In other words, the first \$20 payment received six months hence will accumulate an interest-on-interest of \$4.58 from compounded reinvestment over the remaining 3 years. In a similar fashion, the second \$20 payment will accumulate a Future Value of

$$\begin{aligned} \$20 \times 2\tfrac{1}{2}\text{-year Future Value of } \$1 &= \$20 \times (1.035)^5 \\ &= \$20 \times 1.188 \\ &= \$23.76 \end{aligned}$$

Proceeding in this fashion for all 7 $20 payments, we obtain a total Future Value of $155.59 at the end of the 7th period. i.e., after 3½ years (See Table 44).

TABLE 44

Future Value of $20 Per Period
for 7 Periods
With Each $20 Payment Reinvested
at 3 1/2% Per Semiannual Period

Payment Made After This Number of Semiannual Periods	Number of Periods Remaining for Compounding the Reinvested Payment	Amount of Payment		Future Value of $1*		Future Value of Payment After 3½ Years	Interest-on-Interest Component
1	6	$ 20	x	1.229	=	$ 24.58	$ 4.58
2	5	20	x	1.188	=	23.76	3.76
3	4	20	x	1.148	=	22.96	2.96
4	3	20	x	1.109	=	22.18	2.18
5	2	20	x	1.071	=	21.42	1.42
6	1	20	x	1.035	=	20.70	.70
7	0	20	x	1.000	=	20.00	.00
		$140		7.779*		$155.59*	$15.59*

***Values presented are taken from Table 42A, but totals have been calculated using additional decimal places for accuracy.**

This $155.59 is a sum of 7 terms, each being the $20 payment multiplied by the Future Value of $1 over the number of periods remaining for compounding that particular payment. This sum of 7 products is in turn equal to the common $20 factor times the sum of the 7 Future Values of $1 over each of the remaining periods. This latter sum is just the Future Value of $1 Per Period for the 7 periods, (See Tables 43 and 44), i.e., 7.779. In other words, the Future Value of the 7 $20 payments, $155.58, is equal to 20 times the Future Value of $1 Per Period for 7 Periods,

$$\$20 \times 7.779 = \$155.59$$

This method is valid for any series of level payments reinvested at any constant interest rate. A general formula for the Future Value of any such level cash flow is provided in the Appendix (#3).

This method also enables us to use the Compound Interest Tables to quickly find the Future Value of any series of level payments. One first finds the Future Value of $1 Per Period for the appropriate rate and the number of compounding periods, and then multiplies this number by the amount of each level payment.

The Future Value of a Coupon Flow

Suppose an investor purchased a bond with a 4% coupon rate exactly 3½ years prior to its maturity. In six months, the investor would receive his first coupon payment of $20, with subsequent payments every six months until maturity. At maturity in 3½ years (i.e., after 7 semiannual periods), the investor would receive his 7th coupon payment together with the $1000 redemption payment. This series of 7 coupon payments of $20 each corresponds precisely to the level payment cash flow analyzed in Table 44. If we were to again assume a 7% annual reinvestment rate, then the Future Value of the coupon stream at maturity would just be the $155.59 figure computed in Table 44.

In general, any bond purchased for delivery on a date which is an integral number of semiannual periods before its maturity will provide a series of coupon payments, starting at the end of six months, with a payment every six months up to and including the bond's maturity date. The coupon rate is quoted as that percentage of the bond's redemption value which is to be paid annually in two semiannual payments. In the usual case where the redemption value is $1000, a bond will pay an annual dollar amount equal to 10 times its coupon rate stated as a percentage, e.g., 4%, so that each semiannual payment will be 5 times the coupon rate. For example, a 4% bond provides a semiannual interest payment of

$$5 \times 4 = \$20$$

Therefore, in order to use Compound Interest Tables to find the Future Value of a Coupon Flow, we must proceed through the following steps:

(1) Translate the bond's maturity in years into the number of semiannual interest periods, i.e., multiply the remaining life in years by 2.

(2) Use the Compound Interest Tables to find the Future Value of $1 Per Period for the number of interest periods at the desired reinvestment rate per period.

(3) Multiply the bond's coupon rate by 5 to obtain the dollar amount of each coupon payment.

(4) Multiply the coupon payment by the appropriate Future Value of $1 Per Period to obtain the Future Value of the coupon stream.

Tables 45A and 45B provide a simpler procedure for computing the Future Value of a coupon flow for an abbreviated range of reinvestment rates and maturities. In essence, these tables represent the Future Value of the coupon stream from a bond with a coupon rate of 1% per annum. To find the Future Value for any bond with a specified coupon rate and maturity, one finds in that table a value corresponding to the appropriate reinvestment rate and maturity, and then multiplies this value by the bond's coupon rate. For example, with reinvestment at 7%, Table 45B tells us that a 3½-year 1% bond has a coupon stream with a Future Value of $38.897. Multiplying this figure by a factor of 4, we obtain

$$4 \times \$38.897 = \$155.588$$

which is the Future Value of the coupon stream from a 3½-year 4% bond as found in Table 44.

Interest-on-Interest

The Future Value of a bond's coupon flow consists of (1) the sum of the coupon payments, and (2) the accumulated interest-on-interest from the reinvestment of these coupons. For example, our 3½ year 4% bond, reinvested at 7%, provides $140 of coupon payments and $15.59 of interest-on-interest (See Table 44).

TABLE 45A

FUTURE VALUE FACTORS FOR REINVESTED COUPON FLOW

(Future Value of Coupons from 1% Bond of $1,000 Par with Semiannual Payments of $5)

Multiply Factor Below by Coupon % Rate to Obtain Accumulated Dollars Per Bond from Coupons and Interest-on-Interest

Add Principal Value of Bond to this Figure to Obtain Total Future Value

Number of Years of Coupon Flow	Assumed Annual Reinvestment Rate					
	4%	4 1/2%	5%	5 1/2%	6%	6 1/2%
0.5	5.000	5.000	5.000	5.000	5.000	5.000
1.0	10.100	10.112	10.125	10.137	10.150	10.162
1.5	15.302	15.340	15.378	15.416	15.454	15.493
2.0	20.608	20.685	20.763	20.840	20.918	20.996
2.5	26.020	26.151	26.282	26.413	26.546	26.679
3.0	31.541	31.739	31.939	32.140	32.342	32.546
3.5	37.171	37.453	37.737	38.024	38.312	38.603
4.0	42.915	43.296	43.681	44.069	44.462	44.858
4.5	48.773	49.270	49.773	50.281	50.796	51.316
5.0	54.749	55.379	56.017	56.664	57.319	57.984
6.0	67.060	68.011	68.978	69.961	70.960	71.976
7.0	79.870	81.219	82.595	83.999	85.432	86.893
8.0	93.196	95.027	96.901	98.820	100.784	102.796
9.0	107.062	109.464	111.932	114.467	117.072	119.749
10.0	121.487	124.558	127.723	130.987	134.352	137.821
11.0	136.495	140.338	144.314	148.428	152.684	157.088
12.0	152.109	156.837	161.745	166.841	172.132	177.627
13.0	168.355	174.087	180.059	186.281	192.765	199.523
14.0	185.256	192.121	199.299	206.805	214.655	222.865
15.0	202.840	210.976	219.514	228.473	237.877	247.749
16.0	221.135	230.690	240.751	251.349	262.514	274.277
17.0	240.169	251.300	263.064	275.501	288.651	302.557
18.0	259.972	272.848	286.507	301.000	316.380	332.705
19.0	280.575	295.377	311.136	327.920	345.797	364.845
20.0	302.010	318.931	337.013	356.341	377.006	399.108
21.0	324.311	343.557	364.199	386.346	410.116	435.634
22.0	347.513	369.303	392.762	418.025	445.242	474.573
23.0	371.653	396.221	422.770	451.470	482.507	516.084
24.0	396.768	424.364	454.298	486.780	522.042	560.337
25.0	422.897	453.788	487.422	524.059	563.984	607.513
26.0	450.082	484.551	522.222	563.416	608.481	657.806
27.0	478.365	516.713	558.785	604.967	655.687	711.420
28.0	507.791	550.340	597.198	648.835	705.769	768.577
29.0	538.406	585.496	637.557	695.149	758.900	829.508
30.0	570.258	622.252	679.958	744.046	815.267	894.465
35.0	749.890	832.698	926.421	1032.592	1152.970	1289.568
40.0	968.860	1095.588	1241.914	1411.064	1606.815	1833.582
45.0	1235.783	1423.991	1645.771	1907.488	2216.745	2582.633
50.0	1561.162	1834.233	2162.743	2558.622	3036.439	3613.996

TABLE 45B

FUTURE VALUE FACTORS FOR REINVESTED COUPON FLOW

Multiply Factor Below by Coupon % Rate to Obtain
Accumulated Dollars Per Bond from Coupons and Interest-on-Interest
Add Principal Value of Bond to this Figure to Obtain Total Future Value

Number of Years of Coupon Flow	Assumed Annual Reinvestment Rate					
	7%	7 1/2%	8%	8 1/2%	9%	9 1/2%
0.5	5.000	5.000	5.000	5.000	5.000	5.000
1.0	10.175	10.187	10.200	10.212	10.225	10.237
1.5	15.531	15.570	15.608	15.647	15.685	15.724
2.0	21.075	21.153	21.232	21.312	21.391	21.471
2.5	26.812	26.947	27.082	27.217	27.354	27.491
3.0	32.751	32.957	33.165	33.374	33.584	33.796
3.5	38.897	39.193	39.491	39.792	40.096	40.402
4.0	45.258	45.663	46.071	46.484	46.900	47.321
4.5	51.842	52.375	52.914	53.459	54.011	54.568
5.0	58.657	59.339	60.031	60.731	61.441	62.160
6.0	73.010	74.061	75.129	76.215	77.320	78.443
7.0	88.385	89.907	91.460	93.044	94.661	96.310
8.0	104.855	106.964	109.123	111.333	113.597	115.914
9.0	122.498	125.324	128.227	131.210	134.275	137.425
10.0	141.398	145.087	148.890	152.813	156.857	161.028
11.0	161.645	166.360	171.240	176.290	181.517	186.927
12.0	183.333	189.258	195.413	201.806	208.446	215.344
13.0	206.566	213.906	221.559	229.536	237.853	246.525
14.0	231.453	240.438	249.838	259.674	269.967	280.739
15.0	258.113	268.996	280.425	292.428	305.035	318.280
16.0	286.673	299.737	313.507	328.025	343.331	359.472
17.0	317.266	332.826	349.290	366.712	385.151	404.670
18.0	350.038	368.443	387.992	408.757	430.820	454.264
19.0	385.144	406.782	429.852	454.452	480.691	508.682
20.0	422.751	448.051	475.128	504.114	535.152	568.392
21.0	463.037	492.472	524.098	558.087	594.624	633.909
22.0	506.192	540.287	577.064	616.745	659.569	705.798
23.0	552.420	591.756	634.353	680.495	730.491	784.679
24.0	601.941	647.157	696.316	749.778	807.940	871.232
25.0	654.990	706.792	763.335	825.076	892.515	966.202
26.0	711.816	770.983	835.824	906.911	984.874	1070.408
27.0	772.690	840.078	914.227	995.849	1085.732	1184.750
28.0	837.900	914.453	999.028	1092.507	1195.871	1310.212
29.0	907.755	994.510	1090.748	1197.556	1316.146	1447.876
30.0	982.584	1080.684	1189.953	1311.724	1447.490	1598.928
35.0	1444.689	1620.976	1821.452	2049.586	2309.348	2605.294
40.0	2096.534	2401.720	2756.225	3168.342	3647.788	4205.944
45.0	3016.025	3529.931	4139.917	4864.618	5726.345	6751.817
50.0	4313.058	5160.244	6188.119	7436.535	8954.280	10801.090

To find the interest-on-interest contribution from the Compound Interest Tables, one would have to first determine the Future Value of the coupon flow, and then subtract the sum of all direct coupon payments.

To simplify this computation, Tables 46A and 46B provide the interest-on-interest amounts accumulated by a 1% coupon bond. Thus, for our 3½ year 4% bond reinvested at 7%, one first finds the value in Table 46B corresponding to the 3½ year maturity at 7% reinvestment, $3.897. Then one multiplies this value by 4, the coupon % rate, to obtain

$$4 \times \$3.897 = \$15.588,$$

which is the interest-on-interest.

Tables 46A and 46B also demonstrate the rate at which interest-on-interest accumulates with longer maturities and with increasing reinvestment rates.

A general formula for interest-on-interest computations is provided in the Appendix (#4).

Total Future Value of a Bond

In addition to the coupon payments and the interest-on-interest, a bond also provides a cash payment equal to its redemption value, usually $1000, at maturity. If we fix upon the bond's maturity date as the time point for assessing Future Value, then the $1000 redemption payment adds the amount of precisely $1000 to the total Future Value. There is no opportunity for reinvestment of this redemption payment because the time of evaluation coincides with its time of receipt, i.e., maturity.

The total Future Value of a bond's cash flow, evaluated as of its maturity, thus consists of 3 components: (1) the sum of coupon payments, (2) interest-on-interest received from reinvestment of these coupons, and (3) the $1000 redemption payment. For the above example of the 3½ year 4% bond, the total Future Value at maturity would consist of the following component values:

Direct Payments of 7 $20 Coupons	$ 140.00
Interest-on-Interest from Reinvestment of these Coupons @ 7%	15.59
Redemption Payment	1000.00
Total Future Value at Maturity	$1155.59

With the aid of Tables 45A, 45B, 46A and 46B, this analysis can be carried out for any specified bond and any one of the tabulated reinvestment rates. A general formula for the Future Value of a bond at maturity is given in the Appendix (#5).

Notice that in the above discussion, it has not once been necessary to refer to the Dollar Price or the yield-to-maturity of the bond.

Tables 45A and 45B can also be used to determine the Future Value of a bond investment at some future point prior to its maturity if its price is assumed. To illustrate this usage, suppose one wanted to find the total future investment value of a 30 year 4% bond after a holding period of 5 years, assuming the bond at that point will be selling at 80. The computation would proceed as follows:

5-Year Future Value Factor @ 7% Reinvestment Rate (Table 45B)	$ 58.657
X Coupon Percentage Rate	X 4
= 5-Year Future Value of Coupon Flow	$ 234.628
+ Principal Value of Bond at End of 5 Years	+ 800.000
= Total 5-Year Future Value of Investment	$1034.628

These Future Value figures can be used to evaluate alternative bond investments. First, one must standardize the Future Value figures so as to account for today's cost basis of the bond. This can be done through the concept of Future Value Per Dollar Invested Today obtained by simply dividing the Future Value by today's price. For example, if the 30 year 4% bond in the above example were purchased at a Dollar Price of 67.182, then the cost basis would be \$671.82. Using the 5-year Future Value of \$1,034.628 obtained above, the Future Value Per Dollar Invested Today would simply be

$$\frac{1{,}034.628}{671.82} = \$1.54$$

Any alternative bond investment could be evaluated relative to this bond by comparing the corresponding figures for Future Value Per Dollar over equivalent holding periods. In such a comparison, one would naturally want to use the same reinvestment rate assumption for both bonds.

To summarize this procedure, the Future Value Per Dollar Invested Today can be computed as follows:

(1) Find the Future Value Factor from Table 45A or 45B corresponding to the holding period and the assumed reinvestment rate,

(2) Multiply this factor by the coupon rate,

(3) Add the bond's assumed Principal Value at the end of the holding period,

(4) Divide the result by the bond's cost basis at the start of the holding period.

Mathematical formulae are presented in the Appendix for Future Value of a bond prior to its maturity (#6) and for the Future Value Per Dollar Invested Today (#7).

TABLE 46A

INTEREST-ON-INTEREST FACTORS

(Interest-on-Interest Amounts from 1% Bond with Semiannual Payments of $5)

Multiply Factor Below by Coupon % Rate to Obtain Accumulated Dollars Per Bond of Interest-on-Interest

Number of Years of Coupon Flow	Assumed Annual Reinvestment Rate					
	4%	4 1/2%	5%	5 1/2%	6%	6 1/2%
0.5	0.000	0.000	0.000	0.000	0.000	0.000
1.0	0.100	0.112	0.125	0.137	0.150	0.162
1.5	0.302	0.340	0.376	0.416	0.454	0.493
2.0	0.608	0.685	0.763	0.840	0.918	0.996
2.5	1.020	1.151	1.282	1.413	1.546	1.679
3.0	1.541	1.739	1.939	2.140	2.342	2.546
3.5	2.171	2.453	2.737	3.024	3.312	3.603
4.0	2.915	3.296	3.681	4.069	4.462	4.858
4.5	3.773	4.270	4.773	5.281	5.796	6.316
5.0	4.749	5.379	6.017	6.664	7.319	7.984
6.0	7.060	8.011	8.978	9.961	10.960	11.976
7.0	9.870	11.219	12.595	13.999	15.432	16.893
8.0	13.196	15.027	16.901	18.820	20.784	22.796
9.0	17.062	19.464	21.932	24.467	27.072	29.749
10.0	21.487	24.558	27.723	30.987	34.352	37.821
11.0	26.495	30.338	34.314	38.428	42.684	47.088
12.0	32.109	36.837	41.745	46.841	52.132	57.627
13.0	38.355	44.087	50.059	56.281	62.765	69.523
14.0	45.256	52.121	59.299	66.805	74.655	82.865
15.0	52.840	60.976	69.514	78.473	87.877	97.749
16.0	61.135	70.690	80.751	91.349	102.514	114.277
17.0	70.169	81.300	93.064	105.501	118.651	132.557
18.0	79.972	92.848	106.507	121.000	136.380	152.705
19.0	90.575	105.377	121.136	137.920	155.797	174.845
20.0	102.010	118.931	137.013	156.341	177.006	199.108
21.0	114.311	133.557	154.199	176.346	200.116	225.634
22.0	127.513	149.303	172.762	198.025	225.242	254.573
23.0	141.653	166.221	192.770	221.470	252.507	286.084
24.0	156.768	184.364	214.298	246.780	282.042	320.337
25.0	172.897	203.788	237.422	274.059	313.984	357.513
26.0	190.082	224.551	262.222	303.416	348.481	397.806
27.0	208.365	246.713	288.785	334.967	385.687	441.420
28.0	227.791	270.340	317.198	368.835	425.769	488.577
29.0	248.406	295.496	347.557	405.149	468.900	539.508
30.0	270.258	322.252	379.958	444.046	515.267	594.465
35.0	399.890	482.698	576.421	682.592	802.970	939.568
40.0	568.860	695.588	841.914	1011.064	1206.815	1433.582
45.0	785.783	973.991	1195.771	1457.488	1766.745	2132.633
50.0	1061.162	1334.233	1662.743	2058.622	2536.439	3113.996

TABLE 46B

INTEREST-ON-INTEREST FACTORS

Multiply Factor Below by Coupon % Rate to Obtain
Accumulated Dollars Per Bond of Interest-on-Interest

Number of Years of Coupon Flow	Assumed Annual Reinvestment Rate					
	7%	7 1/2%	8%	8 1/2%	9%	9 1/2%
0.5	0.000	0.000	0.000	0.000	0.000	0.000
1.0	0.175	0.187	0.200	0.212	0.225	0.237
1.5	0.531	0.570	0.608	0.647	0.685	0.724
2.0	1.075	1.153	1.232	1.312	1.391	1.471
2.5	1.812	1.947	2.082	2.217	2.354	2.491
3.0	2.751	2.957	3.165	3.374	3.584	3.796
3.5	3.897	4.193	4.491	4.792	5.096	5.402
4.0	5.258	5.663	6.071	6.484	6.900	7.321
4.5	6.842	7.375	7.914	8.459	9.011	9.568
5.0	8.657	9.339	10.031	10.731	11.441	12.160
6.0	13.010	14.061	15.129	16.215	17.320	18.443
7.0	18.385	19.907	21.460	23.044	24.661	26.310
8.0	24.855	26.964	29.123	31.333	33.597	35.914
9.0	32.498	35.324	38.227	41.210	44.275	47.425
10.0	41.398	45.087	48.890	52.813	56.857	61.028
11.0	51.645	56.360	61.240	66.290	71.517	76.927
12.0	63.333	69.258	75.413	81.806	88.446	95.344
13.0	76.566	83.906	91.559	99.536	107.853	116.525
14.0	91.453	100.438	109.838	119.674	129.967	140.739
15.0	108.113	118.996	130.425	142.428	155.035	168.280
16.0	126.673	139.737	153.507	168.025	183.331	199.472
17.0	147.266	162.826	179.290	196.712	215.151	234.670
18.0	170.038	188.443	207.992	228.757	250.820	274.264
19.0	195.144	216.782	239.852	264.452	290.691	318.682
20.0	222.751	248.051	275.128	304.114	335.152	368.392
21.0	253.037	282.472	314.098	348.087	384.624	423.909
22.0	286.192	320.287	357.064	396.745	439.569	485.798
23.0	322.420	361.756	404.353	450.495	500.491	554.679
24.0	361.941	407.157	456.316	509.778	567.940	631.232
25.0	404.990	456.792	513.335	575.076	642.515	716.202
26.0	451.816	510.983	575.824	646.911	724.874	810.408
27.0	502.690	570.078	644.227	725.849	815.732	914.750
28.0	557.900	634.453	719.028	812.507	915.871	1030.212
29.0	617.755	704.510	800.748	907.556	1026.146	1157.876
30.0	682.584	780.684	889.953	1011.724	1147.490	1298.928
35.0	1094.689	1270.976	1471.452	1699.586	1959.348	2255.294
40.0	1696.534	2001.720	2356.225	2768.342	3247.788	3805.944
45.0	2566.025	3079.931	3689.917	4414.618	5276.345	6301.817
50.0	3813.058	4660.244	5688.119	6936.535	8454.280	10301.090

CHAPTER 11

The Present Value of a Cash Flow

The Present Value of $1 Per Period

In Chapter 9, the Present Value of $1 to be received after T semiannual periods was shown to be equal to

$$\frac{1}{(1 + R)^T}$$

when the assumed interest rate is R per period. This corresponds to the fraction of $1 that would have to be invested and compounded at the rate R in order to accumulate the value of $1 at the end of the T periods.

Suppose we have a level cash flow consisting of 7 semiannual payments of $1 each, with payments beginning at the end of the first semiannual period. How would we compute the Present Value of this cash flow assuming a 7% interest rate? Each of the 7 $1 payments has a different Present Value, e.g., the first $1 payment has a Present Value of

$$\frac{\$1}{1.035} = \$.966$$

while the $1 payment received after 2 periods has a Present Value of (see Table 42A),

$$\frac{\$1}{(1.035)^2} = \$.934$$

If the sum of these two Present Value figures,

$$\$.966 + \$.934 = \$1.900$$

were to be invested today at an interest rate of 3½% per semiannual period, then at the end of the first period, the account would have grown by a factor of 1.035 to

$$\$1.90 \times 1.035 = \$1.966$$

After making the scheduled $1 payment, the account balance would become $.966 at the start of the second period. At the end of the second period, this $.966 principal amount would have again grown by a factor of 1.035 to

$$\$.966 \times 1.035 = \$1$$

i.e., just to the right amount to make the second $1 payment. We see that by adding the Present Values of the two future payments, we obtain that dollar amount which must be invested today at the specified rate in order to exactly support these two future payments. In other words, the sum of the two Present Values equals the Present Value of the cash flow consisting of the two $1 payments.

This principle can of course be generalized for any number of payments. Applying it to all 7 $1 payments in our example, we compute that this particular cash flow has a Present Value of $6.115 as shown in Table 47.

This value of $6.115 is called the Present Value of $1 Per Period for 7 periods at a rate of 3½% per period. As we have seen above, it is just the sum of the Present Values of each of the 7 payments.

At a specified interest rate R per period, the Present Value of $1 Per Period for T periods can always be found as the sum of the Present Values for each of the T payments. A general formula for this quantity is provided in the Appendix (#8).

The Compound Interest Tables often refer to the Present Value of

$1 Per Period as the "Present Worth of $1 Payable Periodically." To use the Tables for the above example, one would find the value for 7 periods at 3½% per period, i.e., 6.115, as given in Table 42A.

In the context of Present Values the term "discount rate" is often used in preference to the term "reinvestment rate." Regardless of terminology, the key concept is that of a standard for measuring the time value of money.

TABLE 47

Present Value of $1 Per Period
for 7 Periods
At A Discount Rate of
3 1/2% Per Semiannual Period

Payment Made After This Number of Semiannual Periods	Amount of Payment		Present Value of $1 To Be Received After Indicated Number of Periods*		Present Value of Payment
1	$1	x	.966	=	$ .966
2	1	x	.934	=	.934
3	1	x	.902	=	.902
4	1	x	.871	=	.871
5	1	x	.842	=	.842
6	1	x	.814	=	.814
7	1	x	.786	=	.786
Totals	$7		6.115		$6.115

*From Table 42A.

The Present Value of a Level Cash Flow

Returning to our earlier example of a series of 7 $20 payments under a 7% discount rate assumption, we can again apply the principle that the Present Value of a cash flow equals the sum of the Present Values for each payment. The Present Value of each $20 payment is in turn equal to 20 times the Present Value of $1 to be received at the time of that payment, e.g., the Present Value of the 4th $20 payment is

$$\$20 \times \frac{1}{(1.035)^4} = \$20 \times .871$$

$$= \$17.42$$

Taking out the common $20 factor, the cash flow's Present Value is seen to be 20 times the sum of the Present Values of $1 at each payment time. But this sum is what we have just defined to be the Present Value of 1 Per Period for 7 periods, 6.115 (from Table 47). Consequently, the Present Value of the 7 $20 payments is

$$\$20 \times 6.115 = \$122.30$$

Table 48 demonstrates that this result coincides with the sum of the Present Values of each $20 payment.

TABLE 48

Present Value of $20 Per Period
for 7 Periods
At A Discount Rate of
3 1/2% Per Semiannual Period

Payment Made After This Number of Semiannual Periods	Amount of Payment		Present Value of $1 To Be Received After Indicated Number of Periods		Present Value of Payment
1	$ 20	x	.966	=	$ 19.32
2	20	x	.934	=	18.68
3	20	x	.902	=	18.04
4	20	x	.871	=	17.42
5	20	x	.842	=	16.84
6	20	x	.814	=	16.28
7	20	x	.786	=	15.72
Totals	$140		6.115		$122.30

With the aid of Compound Interest Tables, this technique can be used to quickly find the Present Value of any level cash flow. For the example in Table 48, one would first go to the Compound Interest Tables (see Table 42A), find the factor corresponding to the Present Value of 1 Per Period for the 7 payment periods, 6.115, and then multiply this factor by the amount of each level payment, $20, to obtain the Present Value of the cash flow, $122.30.

The Present Value of a Bond

The level cash flow of 7 $20 payments corresponds, as we know, to the coupon stream from a 3½ year 4% bond. Following the principle that the Present Values of all payments add up to the Present Value of the entire cash flow, we need only add the Present Value of the $1000 redemption payment to the $122.30 Present Value of the bond's coupon stream (Table 48) to obtain the bond's Present Value at a 7% discount rate:

Redemption Payment	$1000.00
X Present Value of $1 to Be Received in 3½ years @ 7% (from Table 42A)	X .786–
= Present Value of Redemption Payment	785.99*
+ Present Value of 7 $20 Coupons at 7% (From Table 48)	+ 122.30*
= Present Value of Bond @ 7%	908.28*
Present Value Expressed as % of $1000 Redemption Value	90.83

*Multiplication and additions carried out with additional decimal places to obtain precise final answer.

This Present Value figure can actually be interpreted in several different ways, all of which are mathematically equivalent. Suppose the investor deposited an amount of $908.28, equal to the bond's Present Value, in a 7% savings account to be compounded semi-annually. The investor could then withdraw a $20 payment every six months, leaving the rest of the interest to be compounded, and after 3½ years, if the rate stayed at 7%, the savings account would contain a principal balance exactly equal to $1,000, the redemption value of the bond. In other words, this interpretation says that the Present Value corresponds to the deposit amount required for a savings account to support a schedule of cash payouts identical to that of the bond itself, including the final principal payment of $1000.

On the other hand, one can equally well view the Present Value of a cash flow in terms of the Present Value of a single amount, namely, the total Future Value accrued as of the last payment date (i.e., the bond's maturity) when all earlier payments have been reinvested and compounded at the specified discount rate. As we saw in the preceding chapter, the Future Value at maturity of a 3½ year 4%

bond at a 7% reinvestment rate is $1,155.59. The Present Value of this lump sum payment 3½ years hence would be, using Table 42A,

Future Value at 3½ Year Maturity @ 7%	$1,155.59
X Present Value of $1 to Be Received in 3½ Years @ 7%	X .786–
= Present Value of Future Value at Maturity	$ 908.28

which is just the bond's Present Value. It is interesting to note that one can also view the Future Value at maturity as the compounded accrual from a single investment today equal in amount to the bond's Present Value. For the above example, the numbers would be as follows:

Present Value of Bond @ 7%	$ 908.28
X Future Value of $1 Invested Today and Compounded Semiannually for 3½ Years at 7%	X 1.272+
= 3½-Year Future Value of Bond's Present Value	$1,155.59

The Appendix provides formulae for the Present Value of a bond's cash flow (#9).

A bond's Present Value will change inversely with changes in the assumed discount rate. The higher the discount rate, the lower the Present Value, and vice versa. As the interest rate increases, a dollar in hand today grows in terms of its earning power to any future point in time. On the other hand, a given bond's cash flow consists of a *fixed* schedule of future payments which do not change in dollar amount with changes in the interest rate. Consequently, this fixed cash flow of a bond becomes less and less attractive relative to *today's* dollars (i.e., Present Value) as the assumed future earning power of today's dollar (i.e., the assumed interest rate) increases. This inverse relationship is illustrated in Table 49 for the case of a 3½ year 4% bond.

TABLE 49

Present Values of A 3 1/2 Year 4% Bond
Under Various Discount Rate Assumptions

Assumed Annual Discount Rate	Present Value of Coupon Stream	Present Value of $1000 Redemption	Total Present Value of Bond
3%	$131.97	$901.02	$1,032.99
3 1/2	130.69	885.64	1,016.33
4	129.44	870.56	1,000.00
4 1/2	128.21	855.76	983.97
5	126.99	841.26	968.25
5 1/2	125.78	827.04	952.82
6	124.60	813.09	937.69
6 1/2	123.44	799.41	922.85
7	122.30	785.99	908.28
7 1/2	121.16	772.82	983.98
8	120.04	759.91	879.95
8 1/2	118.94	747.25	866.19
9	117.86	734.82	852.68

Present Value computations are often used to determine whether or not a particular investment with a specified future cash flow is a good investment, i.e., whether it is worth its cost to the investor. For example, suppose the bond represented in Table 49 were being offered at a net cost of $922.85. Then any investor who based his investment on a discount rate of 7% would find that buying the bond would entail an expenditure of $922.85 in Present Value (cash on hand) to obtain a cash flow having a Present Value to him of only $908.28 at his 7% discount rate. This transaction would result in an expected immediate net loss of $14.57 in Present Value. Consequently, the "7% – discounting" investor would quickly reject the offered bond. On the other hand, an investor who had decided upon a 5% discount rate as being probable would be happy to exhange the $922.85 cost of the bond for the expected $968.25 Present Value of its cash flow.

The investor with a 6½% discount rate would be completely indifferent regarding the bond's purchase. The bond's cost would correspond exactly to his evaluation of the Present Value of the bond's cash flow.

As we shall see in the next chapter, this approach of using Present Value as a basic yardstick for investment decisions lies at the heart of the yield-to-maturity concept.

CHAPTER 12

The Concept of Yield to Maturity

Definition of a Bond's Yield-to-Maturity

There is always one discount rate where the Present Value of a bond's cash flow exactly equals its market value. For the particular example illustrated in Table 49, this "market price matching" discount rate was 6.50% for a price of $922.85. This is precisely how a bond's yield-to-maturity is defined, i.e., it is that discount rate which makes the Present Value of a bond's cash flow equal to its market price.

To further clarify this point, let us review the actual process of how in the absence of a Yield Book one would find the yield-to-maturity for this example of a 3½ year 4% bond with a market value of $922.85. We need to find that discount rate which makes the Present Value of the bond's cash flow equal to its market value. Finding such a special discount rate to match a price always involves a trial and error process. There is no explicit formula that leads directly to the exact number. As a starting point for our example, we know from Chapter 11 that a discount rate of 7% leads to a Present Value of $908.28 for the bond's cash flow. This is below the $922.85 market value. For our next trial, we want to increase the Present Value which means that we must reduce the discount rate.

Accordingly, we might next try a 6% discount rate and so obtain a Present Value of $937.69 (Table 49). This result lies above the bond's market value of $922.85, so we have overshot on our choice of the second trial discount rate. We now know that the yield-to-maturity must lie somewhere between 6% and 7%. If we were to compute all intervening discount rates at intervals of 10 basis points, we would arrive at the tabulation shown in Table 50. This tabulation indicates that the discount rate of 6.50% leads to a Present Value of $922.85. Since this is precisely the bond's market value, it follows that the bond has a yield-to-maturity of 6.50%.

TABLE 50

Present Values of a 4% Bond Maturing in 3 Years and 6 Months and Having a Market Value of $922.85

Annual Discount Rate	Present Values
6.00%	$937.69
6.10	934.70
6.20	931.72
6.30	928.75
6.40	925.79
6.50 Yield-to-Maturity	922.85 Market Value
6.60	919.91
6.70	916.98
6.80	914.07
6.90	911.17
7.00	908.28

Table 50 also demonstrates another important aspect of the yield-to-maturity concept. Suppose we only knew the yield-to-maturity, 6.50%, and we wanted to determine the bond's market value. By using the 6.50% as a discount rate to compute the bond's Present Value, we would, of course, obtain the original market value figure of $922.85. The key point is that the computation procedure (see Table 51) which determines the market value from the 6.50% yield-to-maturity is identical to the computational procedure for finding Present Values.

TABLE 51

Computation of the Market Value at a 6.50% Yield-to-Maturity of a 4% Bond Maturing in 3 Years and 6 Months

Redemption Payment	$1,000.00	
x Present Value of $1.00 (Due at End of 7 Semiannual Periods @ 3.25% Per Period)	x.79941	
= Present Value of Redemption Payment	$ 799.41	$799.41
Coupon Payment	$20.00	
x Present Value of $1.00 Per Period (For 7 Periods @ 3.25% Per Period)	x 6.172	
= Present Value of Coupon Payments	$123.44	$123.44
Bond's Market Value @ 6.50% Yield-to-Maturity		$922.85

TABLE 52

Dollar Prices of a 4% Bond Maturing in 3 Years and 6 Months at Yields from 6% to 7%

Yield-To-Maturity	Dollar Price
6.00%	93.77
6.10	93.47
6.20	93.17
6.30	92.88
6.40	92.58
6.50	92.29
6.60	91.99
6.70	91.70
6.80	91.41
6.90	91.12
7.00	90.83

(Derived from Table 50.)

Pursuing this point from a somewhat different angle, Table 50 can be read as a tabulation of *market values* corresponding to different yield-to-maturity values. Moreover, by presenting these market values as a percentage of the bond's $1,000 face amount, we obtain the Dollar Price as a function of the yield-to-maturity. As Table 52 shows, this corresponds exactly to the presentation format of the standard Yield Book.

Understanding Yield-to-Maturity

This concept of the yield-to-maturity has many implications and interpretations, all closely related and, in fact, all mathematically equivalent.

First of all, we see that yield-to-maturity can be viewed as simply an alternative method for stating a bond's price. Given the market price, one can always determine the yield-to-maturity. Given the yield-to-maturity (to sufficient accuracy), one can always find the market price.

A second interpretation is that the yield-to-maturity corresponds to the interest rate on an "equivalent" savings account if the savings rate stays the same as the bond's yield-to-maturity. Consider a semiannually compounded savings account in which the investor made a deposit equal to the bond's current market value. As we have seen, if he proceeded to withdraw and to withhold funds in exact accordance with the bond's coupon schedule, then at maturity the account would contain a balance of precisely $1,000, the bond's redemption value. This interpretation is illustrated in Table 53.

This analogy to an equivalent savings account rate leads to the frequent use of the yield-to-maturity as a convenient basis for comparison between bonds with different coupons, maturities, and market prices. After all, if an investor had a choice between one savings account paying 6% and one paying 6½%, both insured and compounding semiannually, he would clearly put his money in the 6½% account.

For the insured savings account, the interest rate over a comparable compounding period essentially provides the absolute measure of investment merit if the rate is maintained. It is very tempting to put this analogy in reverse gear and say that this demonstrates that the yield-to-maturity is also the final and absolute measure of investment value in the bond market. However, as we pointed out in Chapter 1, this is not true. In the context of this analogy with a savings bank account, it must be recognized that there are three key points where the analogy breaks down. The first point is that the investor can usually schedule his withdrawals from a saving account as he chooses. This is not the case with a bond where the investor must purchase a very specific coupon flow and maturity point. Since the investor will generally have his own schedule for placing a time value on payments becoming available at different points in time, it may well be that two bonds having the identical yield-to-maturity but with different cash flows may have radically different investment values for a given investor. The analogy also fails with respect to the continuous availability of the savings account rate. The investor is usually free to compound his interest build-up in a savings account, even though he may not be sure of future rates. However, the coupon flow from a bond is forced and must be spent or reinvested in another instrument which need not, and in general will not, pay interest at the identical yield-to-maturity rate as the bond. Finally, the analogy also fails with respect to the availability of principal at a time prior to the maturity date. With the savings account, the amount of available principal is clearly specified at all times even though interest rates may rise or fall. On the other hand, as the bond investor knows only too well, the bond market provides both opportunity and risk with respect to capital values prior to maturity.

While these problems prevent the yield-to-maturity from being a final measure of investment value, it nonetheless serves the enormously important role of being a convenient, common yardstick for relating the cash flows of all bonds to their market prices.

A third interpretation of yield-to-maturity is that of a constant amortized-capital-plus-income percentage return over each semiannual period to maturity. Thus, in each semiannual period, the current yield is augmented (or reduced) by an amortized capital gain (or loss), so that a percentage return in book value equal to the yield-to-maturity is obtained every six months. This, of course, implies a hypothetical amortization schedule for the bond's price so as to achieve the needed capital gain in each six month period.

This view is closely related to the savings account analogy. In fact, Table 53 can also serve to illustrate this capital amortization schedule. If the bond's cost value were amortized in exact accordance with the balance in the savings account, then coupon income plus capital return would equal 3.25% in every six month period.

TABLE 53

How a 6 1/2% Savings Account With an Initial Deposit of $922.85 Supports the Same Cash Flow as a 4% Bond Maturing in 3 Years and 6 Months and Costing $922.85 for a Yield-to-Maturity of 6 1/2%

Semiannual Period Ending in	Bond	Savings Account: Starting Balance	x Interest Rate	= Interest Paid	Balance Before Cash Withdrawal	Cash Withdrawal
.5 Years	$20.00	$922.85	.0325	$29.99	$ 952.84	$20.00
1.0 "	20.00	932.84	.0325	30.32	963.16	20.00
1.5 "	20.00	943.16	.0325	30.65	973.81	20.00
2.0 "	20.00	953.81	.0325	31.00	984.81	20.00
2.5 "	20.00	964.81	.0325	31.36	996.17	20.00
3.0 "	20.00	976.17	.0325	31.73	1,007.90	20.00
3.5 "	1,020.00	987.90	.0325	32.10	1,020.00	1,020.00

This result is more clearly presented in Table 54. By consulting the Yield Book, it will be seen that this amortization schedule corresponds exactly to the 4% bond's Dollar Price at 3½ years, 3, 2½, 2, 1½, 1, and ½ years, all taken at the 6½% yield-to-maturity level. This is the idea behind the so-called "scientific amortization" of a bond's book value. By marking up the bond's price period-by-period to correspond with the original book yield-to-maturity level, the coupon plus amortized capital gain will always show a percentage return equal to this book yield-to-maturity. In this context of scientific amortization, it is interesting to observe that for bonds purchased at a discount the current yield component declines and

TABLE 54

Hypothetical Capital Gain Schedule Required to Insure a 3.25% Total Return Every Six Months (6.50% Annual Return) from a 4% Bond Maturing in 3 Years and 6 Months and Costing $922.85

Semiannual Period Ending in	Principal Value at Start of Each Period	Coupon Payment	Amortized Capital Gain $	Current Yield of Coupon Payment	Yield from Amortized Capital Gain	Total Return
Purchase	$922.85					
.5 Years	922.85	$20	$ 9.99	2.17%	1.08%	3.25%
1.0	932.84	20	10.32	2.14	1.11	3.25
1.5	943.16	20	10.65	2.12	1.13	3.25
2.0	953.81	20	11.00	2.10	1.15	3.25
2.5	964.81	20	11.36	2.07	1.18	3.25
3.0	976.17	20	11.73	2.05	1.20	3.25
3.5	987.90	20	12.10	2.02	1.23	3.25

the capital gain component grows with the passage of time. For bonds purchased at a premium and amortized downward on a scientific basis, the current yield component grows with time while the capital *loss* component also grows. Straight line amortization, which is popular, has the serious flaw of exaggerating the capital gain (or loss) in early years and understating it in later years. This is because it fails to take proper account of the effect of compounding.

Another interesting point with respect to scientific amortization is that the new book value in six months is readily computed from its book value today. Under scientific amortization, the total book return over the next six months must be

(Book Value Today) X (Semiannual Book Yield).

This return must consist of one coupon payment together with the amortized mark-up of book value, i.e.,

(1 Coupon) + (Gain in Book Value) =
(1 Coupon)
+ (Book Value in 6 Months)
– (Book Value Today)

Equating this expression with the previous one, we see that the total book return equals

(Book Value Today) × (Semiannual Book Yield)=
(1 Coupon)
+ (Book Value in 6 Months)
– (Book Value Today)

This equation is easily solved for the new book value under scientific amortization,

(Book Value in 6 Months) =
(Book Value Today) × (1+ Semiannual Book Yield)
– (1 Coupon)

This result can be illustrated with the bond in Table 54,

(Book Value in 6 Months) = \$922.85 × (1.0325) – \$20
= \$952.84 – \$20
= \$932.84

A fourth interpretation frequently associated with yield-to-maturity is in terms of the growth rate of the Future Value of a present investment. It is at this point where many errors are made. As we have seen in Chapter 1 and in Chapter 10, a key determinant of the Future Value is the interest rate at which coupon payments can be reinvested as they become available. Consequently, since yield-to-maturity fails to include any considered forecast of reinvestment rate, it cannot (except coincidentally) represent the real growth rate of fully compounded Future Value. In fact, it truly represents the growth rate of Future Value *only* when the reinvestment rate equals the yield-to-maturity itself.

In this chapter, we have focused on the concept of yield-to-maturity. To keep this focus clear, we have dealt only with special cases of bonds having a remaining life equal to a simple number of even semiannual periods, i.e., delivery falls on a coupon date. To develop a more thorough understanding of the Yield Book, we must treat the general case of any delivery date.

CHAPTER 13

Accrued Interest and Dollar Prices

In the preceding chapter, the yield-to-maturity concept was developed in the context of a bond having a remaining life corresponding to whole multiples of semiannual interest periods. In such cases, the bond's Present Value is well defined and consists solely of Principal Value free of any Accrued Interest. Such rounded calculations are adequate for all the theoretical problems discussed in this book, but it seems desirable here to go a step further.

In this chapter, therefore, we shall enlarge these concepts to cover a corporate bond having any given term to maturity. Our aim will be to illustrate the standard methods for computing the Dollar Price of any bond from its yield-to-maturity. Once we can perform this computation, the reverse process of finding the yield-to-maturity given the Dollar Price can be approached on a trial and error basis with a sequence of discount rates.

When a bond is purchased for delivery on a coupon date, the coupon payment will be paid in its entirety to the seller, while the buyer purchases the bond without any fraction of a coupon being due. However, as the delivery date extends beyond a coupon date, the seller is increasingly giving up an accrued fraction of the next coupon payment and becomes entitled to some form of compensation from the buyer. This compensation is referred to as the bond's

Accrued Interest. By convention, the Accrued Interest is computed as the coupon payment multiplied by a fraction of a semiannual period corresponding to the time held beyond the last coupon date.

Therefore the Accrued Interest can be calculated by a formula. Suppose the bond's remaining life consists of T full semiannual periods plus M months and D days. Then the next coupon payment would be due in M months and D days. If C is the coupon rate as a percentage of the $1000 face value, then the bond will pay $10 \times C$ coupon dollars per year, so that each semiannual coupon payment will be $5 \times C$ dollars. For example, for a 4% bond maturing in 3 years, 8 months, and 5 days, we would have $C = 4$, $5 \times C = \$20$, $T = 7$, $M = 2$, and $D = 5$, and the next coupon would be due in 2 months and 5 days. For corporate bonds, a 30 day month is always assumed by a marketplace convention.* Consequently, the total number of such days until the *next* coupon is

$$30\,M + D$$

By the same convention, there are 180 days in each coupon period, so that the number of (conventional) days *since* the last coupon payment is

$$180 - (30M + D) = 180 - (30 \times 2 + 5) = 180 - 65 = 115 \text{ days.}$$

Division of this sum by 180 will give us the fraction of a coupon due as Accrued Interest, i.e.,

$$\frac{180 - (30M + D)}{180} = \frac{115}{180} = .639$$

To obtain the Accrued Interest in dollars, AI, we must multiply this fraction by the coupon payment 5C,

$$AI = 5C\,\frac{(180 - 30M - D)}{180} = 20 \times .639 = \$12.78$$

Thus, for the above example of a 4% bond maturing in 3 years, 8 months, and 5 days, we would have an Accrued Interest of $12.78 per bond.

*Municipal bonds and most federal agency bonds are also calculated on the assumption of a 30 day month. Treasuries are calculated according to the exact number of days between coupons.

The Accrued Interest represents the growth in the interest component of a bond's value as the date of purchase approaches the next coupon payment date. This growth in value takes place independently of any changes in the underlying interest rate structure or in the value attached to comparable securities. In a sense, the addition of Accrued Interest prevents the bond's total realizable value from being an accurate measure of the bond's capital value.

In order to remove this distorting effect of the coupon payment cycle, market values are usually quoted in terms of Principal Value alone without Accrued Interest, where the Principal Value is simply defined to be the gross proceeds from sale less the Accrued Interest. The Principal Value provides a far better measure of the bond's capital value, both with respect to itself at earlier times and to other bonds. Since the Accrued Interest figure itself is a mechanical computation for a particular date of sale, the marketplace convention is to quote specific numbers only for the Principal Value, with the addition of Accrued Interest being implicitly understood. Only in the case of default or near default, or uncertainty of interest payments, are most U.S. bonds quoted "flat", i.e., with Accrued Interest as part of the price. Nevertheless, preferred stocks and many British bond issues are quoted flat. These go ex-dividend or ex-interest on the dates of record for payment.

Another convention in the bond market is to quote the Principal Value as a percentage of the bond's face value. This percentage quote is called the bond's "Dollar Price." In the usual case when the face value is $1,000 this has the effect of multiplying the Principal Value by the factor, $\frac{100\%}{1000} = .10$, i.e., the Dollar Price equals 1/10th of the Principal Value.

The Dollar Price together with its associated yield-to-maturity provide the foundation for all quotations used in buying and selling in the bond market.

In the preceding sections, we saw how a yield-to-maturity figure can be determined from a bond's market value and how, by its very definition, the market value can be reconstructed from the yield-to-maturity by using the latter as the discount rate in the Present Value formula. However, for simplicity's sake, these earlier calculations were done for the case of delivery falling on a coupon date, i.e., for a bond free of Accrued Interest. At this point, we shall proceed to generalize these results for a delivery date falling anywhere in the bond's coupon payment cycle.

First, consider a 4% bond with a 6.50% yield-to-maturity and a remaining life of 3 years and 8 months, i.e., exactly 2 months before the next coupon date. The Present Value at 6.50% of this bond's cash flow can be analyzed in three steps:

1) Take the Present Value of the principal at the *next* coupon date, $922.85 (by the same process as shown in Table 51).

2) Add the $20 coupon payment that will be received by the purchaser since he is buying the bond before the next coupon date. This gives us the sum of $942.85.

3) The above sum of $942.85 can be viewed as the bond's Present Value as of the next coupon date two months hence. In other words, today's buyer can view the bond's entire cash flow (when discounted at 6.50%) as being equivalent to a single lump sum of $942.85 paid at the end of two months. To discount this lump sum payment for the two month waiting period, one must multiply it by the Present Value of $1.00 due in two months discounted at 6.50% (i.e., due in one-third of a semiannual compounding period). This is just the cube root of the accrual factor for one period at 3¼% per period,

$$\frac{1}{(1.0325)^{1/3}} = \frac{1}{1.0107} = .9894$$

Performing this multiplication, we get the figure .9894 X $942.85 = $932.85 for today's Present Value of the bond's cash flow discounted at 6.50%. This is the so-called "exponential method" of interpolation between full compounding periods. It is generally considered to be the most theoretically correct method since compounding of the fractional-period accrual factors provides consistent results.

At a 6.50% yield-to-maturity, this 4% 3-year 8-month bond will have a market value (Principal Value plus Accrued Interest) equal to this Present Value of $932.85. However, this market value includes a certain amount of Accrued Interest for the 4-month period since the last coupon date. Using our formula for a C = 4% bond maturing in T = 7 semiannual periods, M = 2 months, and D = 0 days, we can compute this Accrued Interest,

$$AI = \frac{5C}{180} \quad (180 - 30M - D)$$

$$= \frac{5 \times 4}{180} \quad (180 - 30 \times 2 - 0)$$

$$= \frac{20}{180} \quad (120) = \$13.33$$

To determine today's Principal Value, we must subtract this $13.33 of Accrued Interest from the total market value of $932.85,

$$\$932.85 - \$13.33 = \$919.52$$

Expressing this Principal Value as a percentage of the bond's $1,000 face value, we obtain the Dollar Price of $91.95,

$$\frac{1}{10} \times 919.52 = 91.952$$

This Dollar Price corresponds to the figure quoted in the Yield Book for a 4% 3-year 8-month bond at a 6.50% yield-to-maturity.

The above computation is summarized in Table 55.

By carrying out the same steps for a C% bond with a Y% yield-to-maturity maturing in T semiannual periods and M months, we can develop the general formula for a bond's Dollar Price when Accrued Interest is due for an integral multiple of full months. This is given in the Appendix (#13).

With the aid of the method illustrated in Table 55 (and the formula provided in the Appendix), one can compute *all* the Dollar Prices in the Yield Book with the sole exception of those with maturities which are less than six months.

The method of Table 55 was developed on the assumption of a delivery date falling between coupon dates, i.e., when M is greater than zero but less than six. When the delivery does fall on a coupon

TABLE 55

Computation of the Dollar Price at a 6.50% Yield-to-Maturity of a 4% Bond Maturing in 3 Years and 8 Months

	Present Value @ 6.50% as of Next Coupon Date (Equals Present Value @ 6.50% of 4% Bond Maturing in 3 Years and 6 Months - See Table 51)	$ 922.85
+	Next Coupon Payable to Today's Buyer	20.00
=	Present Value @ 6.50% of Bond's Cash Flow as of Next Coupon Date 2 Months from Today	$ 942.85
x	Present Value @ 6.50% of $1.00 Paid in 2 Months (1/3rd Period at 3.25% Per Period)	.9894
=	Bond's Total Market Value (Principal Value Plus Accrued Interest) @ 6.50% Yield-to-Maturity (Present Value @ 6.50% of Bond's Cash Flow as of Today)	$ 932.85
-	Accrued Interest Attached to Bond (2/3rd of Coupon Period Accrued @ $20 Per Coupon Payment)	13.33
=	Bond's Principal Value	$ 919.52
x	To Express as % of $1,000 Face Value	x.10
=	Bond's Dollar Price	91.95

date (i.e., M = 0), then the coupon payment of 5C is foregone and cannot be *added* to the Present Value computation. At the same time, there is no Accrued Interest so that the formula amount,

$$\frac{5C}{180}\ (180 - 30M) = 5C$$

cannot be *deducted* from the market value. These two alterations cancel each other's effect. Consequently, this method can actually be used for any maturity (over six months) consisting of an integral multiple of full months.

When the bond's remaining life contains odd days, i.e., when its life must be expressed as T semiannual periods, M months, and D days, then the marketplace convention is to "linearly" interpolate between the Dollar Prices of bonds having maturities on the preceding and the following full month. For example, suppose one has a 4% bond maturing in 3 years, 7 months, and 5 days with a yield-to-maturity of 6.50%. The Dollar Price for the following month (T = 7, M = 2), i.e., for a bond maturing in T = 7 semiannual periods and M = 2 months, was already computed in Table 55 to be 91.95. For the preceding month, i.e., for a bond maturing in 3 years and 7 months (T = 7, M = 1), the yield formula provides us with a Dollar Price of 92.12. On the basis of the standard 30-day month, the delivery date falls (5/30)th of the way towards the following month, so that the interpolated Dollar Price becomes

$$92.12 + \left(\frac{5}{30}\right) \times (91.95 - 92.12) = 92.09$$

A formula for this method of "linear interpolation" is given in the Appendix (#14). With this interpolation formula and the "integral-month" Dollar Price formula one can determine the Dollar Price corresponding to a specified yield-to-maturity for any bond on *any* delivery date – except for those maturing in less than six months.

When the maturity is less than six months, then the marketplace convention is to treat the bond as a pure discount instrument and to develop the yield-to-maturity as a simple interest figure. For example, consider a 4% bond maturing in 2 months and having a 6.50% yield-to-maturity. The simple interest rate over the 2-month period to maturity is just

$$6\tfrac{1}{2}\% \times \frac{2}{12} = 1.083\%$$

Consequently, the bond's market value today will grow by a factor of

$$1.01083$$

over these 2 months. At maturity, we know that the bond will be worth its redemption value of $1000 plus the last $20 coupon payment. Consequently,

$$1.01083 \times (\text{Market Value Today}) = \$1{,}020$$

or

$$(\text{Market Value Today}) = \frac{\$1{,}020}{1.01083}$$

$$= \$1{,}009.07$$

The Accrued Interest for 4 months will be

$$\frac{4}{6} \times \$20 = \$13.33,$$

so that today's Principal Value must be

$$\$1{,}009.07 - \$13.33 = \$995.74$$

Expressing this Principal Value as a percentage of a $1000 face value, we obtain 99.57 which is the Yield Book result.

This example demonstrates the simple interest method used for bonds with maturities of less than six months. A general formula for this method is developed in the Appendix (#15).

When the bond matures in less than six months *and* has an odd number of days, i.e., when the life is not an integral multiple of months, then as before, one must linearly interpolate the Dollar Prices for the preceding and the following months.

With these techniques and the corresponding formulae (see the Appendix), one can reproduce any number in the Yield Book. One can also directly compute Dollar Prices and Accrued Interest figures for any remaining life (including odd days), any coupon rate (including non-multiples of 1/8%), and any yield-to-maturity (including non-multiples of 10 basis points).

This entire chapter has been oriented towards finding Dollar Prices from specified yield-to-maturity values. To proceed in the opposite direction, i.e., to compute yield-to-maturity values from specified Dollar Prices, the same techniques are used but one must solve for the yield-to-maturity through a trial and error search.

CHAPTER 14

The Yield to Call

Definition of the Yield-to-Call

When a bond is callable, i.e., redeemable prior to maturity at the issuer's option, the cash flow implicit in the yield-to-maturity figure is subject to possible early alteration. Most corporate bonds issued today are callable, but with a certain period of call protection before the call option can be exercised. At the expiration of this period the bond may be called at a specified call price which usually involves some premium over par. This call price may decline in steps towards par in accordance with a specified time schedule.

To provide some measure of the return in the event that the issuer were to exercise his call option at some future point, the yield-to-call is often computed and compared with the yield-to-maturity. This computation is based on the assumption that the bond's cash flow is terminated at the "first call date" with redemption of principal at the specified call price. For a given discount rate, the Present Value of this assumed "cash flow to call" can be determined in much the same fashion as in Chap. 11, *The Present Value of a Cash Flow*, and the yield-to-call is then defined as that discount rate which makes this Present Value figure equal to the bond's market value.

For example, suppose one has a 30-year 8¾% bond priced at 109¼ which is callable at 107 starting in 5 years. The cash flow *to maturity* consists of 60 semiannual coupon payments of $43.75 each followed by a redemption payment of $1,000. The yield-to-maturity turns out to be 7.94%. The cash flow *to an assumed call* in 5 years consists of 10 coupon payments followed by a redemption payment of $1,070. Using a 7% discount rate, the cash flow to call would lead to a Present Value of $1,112.39, computed as shown in Table 56. This figure exceeds the bond's $1,092.50 market value, so we would choose a higher rate, say 8%, for our next trial discount rate. At 8%, the Present Value of the cash flow to call is $1,077.70, i.e., less than the bond's market price. Searching with discount rates lying between 7% and 8% as shown in Table 57, one can pinpoint the yield-to-call as 7.663%.

In the Appendix (#16), we provide a formula relating the yield-to-call to the assumed call date and call price.

Methods for Computing the Yield-to-Call

Fortunately, there are specialized yield-to-call books which quickly provide the price or yield for a wide variety of coupons, yields, call prices and call dates. However, there are two methods which can be used for computing yield-to-call from the standard Yield Book.

The first method is based upon a scaling down of the cash flow so that the scaled-down redemption value is again $1,000. More precisely, one first obtains the scale-down factor by dividing the bond's $1,000 face value by the redemption value at call, 10 × CP, where CP is the call price:

$$\frac{1000}{10\,(\mathrm{CP})} = \frac{100}{\mathrm{CP}}$$

The coupon rate C is then multiplied by this scale factor to obtain the scaled-down coupon,

$$\left(\frac{100}{\mathrm{CP}}\right) \times \mathrm{C}$$

TABLE 56

Computation of the Present Value at a 7% Discount Rate of an 8 3/4% Bond Called in 5 Years at 107

	Redemption Payment	$1,070.00	
x	Present Value of $1.00 (Due at End of 10 Semiannual Periods @ 3.5% Discount Rate Per Period)	x .709*	
=	Present Value of Redemption Payment	$758.54	758.54
	Coupon Payment Semiannual	43.75	
x	Present Value of $1.00 Per Period (for 10 Periods @ 3.5% Discount Rate Per Period)	x 8.317*	
=	Present Value of Coupon Payments	$363.85	+ 363.85
	Total Present Value of Bond's Cash Flow @ 7% Discount Rate		$1,122.39
	Present Value as % of $1000 Face Value		112.24

*6 Digit Precision Used in Multiplication.

TABLE 57

Present Values of an 8 3/4% Bond Called in 5 Years at 107 and Having a Market Value of $1,092.50

Annual Discount Rate	Present Value of Cash Flow to Call
7.00%	$1,122.39
7.20	1,113.27
7.40	1,104.25
7.60	1,095.31
7.62	1,094.42
7.64	1,093.53
7.66	1,092.65
7.663 Yield-to-Call	1,092.50 Market Value
7.68	1,091.76
7.70	1,090.87
7.80	1,086.46
8.00	1,077.70

The same procedure is applied to the market value MV to obtain the scaled-down market value,

$$\left(\frac{100}{\text{CP}}\right) \times \text{MV}$$

A bond with this scaled-down coupon, maturing on the *call date* with a normal \$1,000 redemption value, and priced today at the scaled-down market value will then have the same cash flow *per invested dollar* as the original cash flow to call, i.e., the same coupon payment *per dollar invested today* and the same redemption payment *per dollar invested today*. Consequently, the yield-to-maturity (at the call date) of this scaled-down bond, as determined by the Yield Book, will be identical to the yield-to-call of the original bond.

As an example of this scale down method, the 8¾% bond callable at 107 in 5 years would lead to a scale factor of

$$\frac{100}{107} = .935$$

The corresponding scaled-down bond would then have a coupon rate of

$$.935 \times 8.75\% = 8.18\%$$

and a market value of

$$.935 \times \$1{,}092.50 = \$1{,}021.49$$

At a market value of \$1,021.49, *a 5-year* 8.18% coupon bond would have a yield-to-maturity of 7.66%, i.e., exactly the desired yield-to-call figure.

The second method for using the Yield Book to find yields-to-call involves segregating the cash flow to call into two components: 1) a coupon bond terminating at the call date, but with a \$1,000 redemption value, and 2) a lump sum payment on the call date of the call premium. The first component cash flow corresponds to a bond with the original coupon rate but maturing at the call date. Consequently, for a given discount rate, the Yield Book immediately provides the appropriate Present Value. The second component is just a future lump sum payment, whose Present Value can be quickly determined from the 0% coupon section of the Yield Book. Adding the Present Value figures for these two components, we obtain the Present Value of the overall cash flow to call at that discount rate. Continuing with the example used above, at a 7% discount rate, the Present Value of an 8¾% bond maturing in 5 years is computed as follows (see Table 56),

Present Value of $1,000 Redemption	$ 708.92
Present Value of Coupon Payments	363.85
Present Value of First Component Cash Flow	$1,072.77

The second component of cash flow, the call premium of $70 in 5 years, provides a Present Value of

$$.70892 \times \$70 = \$49.62$$

Adding these 2 figures together, we obtain a total Present Value of $1,122.39 for a 7% discount rate. This corresponds precisely with the results of the direct computation in Table 56. By trial and error search at various discount rates, one would eventually find that rate which gives two Present Value figures adding up to the bond's market value. This rate would then be the yield-to-call.

When the assumed call date does not fall on a coupon payment date, the simplest approach is to: 1) set the call date to the date of the last coupon payment prior to the call, and 2) then to adjust the call price, on a Present Value basis, to reflect the later actual payment of the redemption value plus the Accrued Interest due.

For delivery on a date other than a coupon payment date, the yield-to-call equation is adjusted in precisely the same fashion as the yield-to-maturity equation. These interpolation methods are described in detail in Chapter 13, *Accrued Interest and Dollar Prices.*

CHAPTER 15

Total Realized Compound Yield

Realized Compound Yield Over the Bond's Life

In Chapter I, we proposed the concept of total realized compound yield as an important value measure for investors seeking full compounding over the life of a long-term bond. It supplements yield-to-maturity in two ways: by including interest-on-interest for the full life of the investment at various assumed rates, and by including, where pertinent, interim price fluctuations. Thus, every bond offering can be related to four interest rates: 1) the coupon rate; 2) the yield-to-maturity (which can always be restated as the price); 3) the assumed reinvestment rate; and 4) the realized compound yield which is derived from the other three rates. The realized compound yield is a statement of the total cash flow derived from an investment, that is to say, the Future Value of the investment, expressed as an annualized interest rate. First, we will compute the Future Value in dollars of a bond investment, then the Future Value Per Dollar Invested and, finally, the interest rate required to produce just this Future Value. This is the realized compound yield.

The Future Value of an investment, as defined earlier, consists of the estimated total cash flow which the investment will generate as of some specified future point in time. The Future Value for a compounding investor includes *all* sources of return–principal, interest, and interest-on-interest. When the investment vehicle is a bond with a fixed schedule of coupon payments up to maturity, then the Future Value must include the time value ascribed to this coupon payment schedule. This time value factor is created by an explicit estimate of the interest rate(s) at which coupon payments can be reinvested–and compounded.

This estimate could theoretically consist of several reinvestment rates, each covering a specified future time period. However, in practice, one almost always works under the simplifying assumption of a single reinvestment rate. The following analysis will be carried out within the framework of this assumption of a single reinvestment rate.

We shall first consider the case when the point in time for assessing the Future Value corresponds with the bond's maturity. In this case, the bond's future capital value, if it remains in good standing, is completely predetermined and is usually equal to the $1,000 redemption value.

As an illustration, consider the example of a 30-year 4% bond priced at $671.82 where the yield-to-maturity (YTM) is 6.50%. To compute the Future Value at maturity, we must have an estimated reinvestment rate. In this example, we shall choose 6%. Table 58 presents a detailed schedule of how Future Value accumulates during the first and last few periods of the bond's life.

As we see from Table 58, the Future Value computation per se takes no account whatsoever of the bond's cost. A particular bond, at a specified reinvestment rate, provides the same Future Value at maturity regardless of its market cost today. Consequently, in order to become useful as a comparative investment measure, even for bonds having the same maturity, the Future Value figure must be divided by today's market cost to obtain a Future Value Per Dollar Invested Today. The Future Value computation can be carried out using either Compound Interest Tables or Tables 45 or 46. This method of computation is illustrated in Table 59. In the Appendix (#5), the general formula is derived for the Future Value Per Dollar at the bond's maturity.

TABLE 58

Schedule of the Future Value at Maturity of a
30-Year 4% Bond with a Market Cost of $671.82 (YTM = 6.50%)
at an Assumed 6% Reinvestment Rate

Perid Ending After	Funds Available for Reinvestment at Start of Period	Semiannual Reinvestment Rate		Interest-on-Interest	Coupon Payments	Principal Redemption	Addition to Funds Available for Reinvestment
.5 Years	$ 0	x .03	=	$ 0	$ 20	$ 0	$ 20.00
1.0	20.00	x .03	=	.60	20	0	20.60
1.5	40.60	x .03	=	1.22	20	0	21.22
2.0	61.82	x .03	=	1.85	20	0	21.85
2.5	83.67	x .03	=	2.51	20	0	22.51
3.0	106.18	x .03	=	3.19	20	0	23.19
28.5	2,823.08	x .03	=	84.69	20	0	104.69
29.0	2,927.77	x .03	=	87.83	20	0	107.83
29.5	3,035.60	x .03	=	91.07	20	0	111.07
30.0	3,146.67	x .03	=	94.40	20	1,000	1,114.40
Following Bond's Redemption =	$4,261.07						

Future Value = $4,261.07

Future Value Per Dollar Invested Today = $\frac{\text{Future Value}}{\text{Market Value}} = \frac{\$4{,}261.07}{671.82} = \$6.343$

The Future Value Per Dollar is tied to a precise maturity date in the future. This severely limits its usefulness as a comparative measure for competitive bond investments which do not have exactly the same maturity date. For this reason, and in order to approach the common standard of an annualized measure of investment return, it is very desirable to express the Future Value Per Dollar in terms of some average annual growth rate of Future Value, i.e., a rate of growth of wealth.

To define such a growth rate, we return to the analogy of an "equivalent" savings account. We can then define the fully realized compound yield to be that savings interest rate which, if fully compounded (semiannually) over the investment period, would compound a $1.00 initial deposit to a balance equal to the Future Value Per Dollar. In other words, the realized compound yield is that savings account rate which would provide the same Future Value as

TABLE 59

Use of Compound Interest Tables
to Compute the Future Value at Maturity Per Invested Dollar
for Same Example as in Table 58

	Coupon Payment	$ 20.00
x	Future Value of $1 Per Period for 60 Periods Compounded at 3% Rate Per Period	x 163.053
=	Future Value of Coupons and Interest-on-Interest*	3,261.07*
+	Future Value of $1,000 Redemption	+1,000.00
=	Total Future Value at Maturity	4,261.07
÷	Today's Market Cost	÷ 671.82
=	Future Value Per Dollar Invested	= 6.343

*This figure could also be obtained from Table 45A by multiplying the 30-year 6% factor of 815.267 by 4, the bond's coupon % rate.

TABLE 60

Finding the Realized Compound Yield for a
Future Value Per Dollar After 30-Years
(Same Example as in Table 58)

Annual Interest Rate		Future Value of $1.00 for 30 Years (60 Periods) at Indicated Interest Rate	
6.000%		$5.892	
6.250		6.336	
6.253		6.342	
6.254	Realized Compound Yield	6.343	Future Value Per Dollar
6.255		6.346	
6.260		6.355	
6.300		6.429	
6.400		6.619	
6.500		6.814	
7.000		7.878	

the bond itself over the same investment period. Since the Future Value figure includes the accrual from reinvestment of all available cash payments (or the potential accrual figure if these payments are withdrawn or spent), the "equivalent" savings account must also treat all interest payments as immediately reinvested. This is why the equivalent savings account must be fully compounded.

To actually determine the specific realized compound yield for a given bond, one must search the Compound Interest Tables for that interest rate giving a Future Value of $1 equal to a bond's Future Value Per Dollar Invested. For the example developed in Table 59, the Future Value Per Dollar was $6.343. From the Compound Interest Tables (see Tables 42A, B, C), for the 60 compounding periods corresponding to the bond's 30-year maturity, interest rates of 6%, 6½% and 7% give Future Values of $1 equal to 5.892, 6.814, and 7.878, respectively. From this, we would expect our realized compound yield figure for $6.343 to fall between 6% and 6½%. Table 60 shows the Future Value of $1 provided by rates in this interval, and we see that 6.254% is our figure for the realized compound yield of a Future Value of $6.343 Per Dollar invested.

The arrangement of the Compound Interest Tables can make this search a rather tedious process. Table 61 provides a more handy (although much abbreviated) format for finding the realized compound yield corresponding to a given amount of Future Value Per Dollar over a specified time period. Thus, for the above example, using Table 61, one would first proceed to the 30-year column, search down this column for the Future Value Per Dollar figure of 6.343, and then read off the resulting realized compound yield as lying between 6.20% and 6.40%. A standard interpolation would then provide a close approximation to the exact figure.

However, the realized compound yield (or effective yield, as it is sometimes called) can also be found from an *explicit* mathematical formula, which is provided in the Appendix (#17). With this formula, one can directly compute the realized compound yield from the Future Value Per Dollar without the necessity of going through a trial and error process. Finally, towards the end of this chapter we outline a short method to determine realized compound yield from the Yield Book itself.

TABLE 61

FUTURE VALUE OF $1 FOR SELECTED TIME PERIODS AND INTEREST RATES

Interest Rate	Number of Years of Semiannual Compounding											
	1/2	1	1 1/2	2	3	5	10	15	20	25	30	40
1.00%	1.005	1.010	1.015	1.020	1.030	1.051	1.105	1.161	1.221	1.283	1.349	1.490
2.00	1.010	1.020	1.030	1.041	1.062	1.105	1.220	1.348	1.489	1.645	1.817	2.217
3.00	1.015	1.030	1.046	1.061	1.093	1.161	1.347	1.563	1.814	2.105	2.443	3.291
4.00	1.020	1.040	1.061	1.082	1.126	1.219	1.486	1.811	2.208	2.692	3.281	4.875
5.00	1.025	1.051	1.077	1.104	1.160	1.280	1.639	2.098	2.685	3.437	4.400	7.210
5.20	1.026	1.053	1.080	1.108	1.166	1.293	1.671	2.160	2.792	3.609	4.665	7.795
5.40	1.027	1.055	1.083	1.112	1.173	1.305	1.704	2.224	2.903	3.789	4.946	8.426
5.60	1.028	1.057	1.086	1.117	1.180	1.318	1.737	2.290	3.018	3.978	5.243	9.109
5.80	1.029	1.059	1.090	1.121	1.187	1.331	1.771	2.358	3.138	4.176	5.558	9.845
6.00	1.030	1.061	1.093	1.126	1.194	1.344	1.806	2.427	3.262	4.384	5.892	10.641
6.20	1.031	1.063	1.096	1.130	1.201	1.357	1.842	2.499	3.391	4.602	6.245	11.500
6.40	1.032	1.065	1.099	1.134	1.208	1.370	1.878	2.573	3.525	4.830	6.619	12.427
6.60	1.033	1.067	1.102	1.139	1.215	1.384	1.914	2.649	3.664	5.070	7.015	13.428
6.80	1.034	1.069	1.106	1.143	1.222	1.397	1.952	2.727	3.809	5.321	7.434	14.509
7.00	1.035	1.071	1.109	1.148	1.229	1.411	1.990	2.807	3.959	5.585	7.878	15.676
7.20	1.036	1.073	1.112	1.152	1.236	1.424	2.029	2.889	4.115	5.861	8.348	16.935
7.40	1.037	1.075	1.115	1.156	1.244	1.438	2.068	2.974	4.277	6.151	8.846	18.294
7.60	1.038	1.077	1.118	1.161	1.251	1.452	2.108	3.061	4.445	6.455	9.372	19.760
7.80	1.039	1.080	1.122	1.165	1.258	1.466	2.149	3.151	4.620	6.773	9.930	21.342
8.00	1.040	1.082	1.125	1.170	1.265	1.480	2.191	3.243	4.801	7.107	10.520	23.050
8.20	1.041	1.084	1.128	1.174	1.273	1.495	2.234	3.338	4.989	7.457	11.144	24.892
8.40	1.042	1.086	1.131	1.179	1.280	1.509	2.277	3.436	5.185	7.823	11.805	26.879
8.60	1.043	1.088	1.135	1.183	1.287	1.524	2.321	3.536	5.387	8.208	12.504	29.023
8.80	1.044	1.090	1.138	1.188	1.295	1.538	2.366	3.639	5.598	8.610	13.244	31.336
9.00	1.045	1.092	1.141	1.193	1.302	1.553	2.412	3.745	5.816	9.033	14.027	33.830
9.20	1.046	1.094	1.144	1.197	1.310	1.568	2.458	3.854	6.043	9.475	14.856	36.520
9.40	1.047	1.096	1.148	1.202	1.317	1.583	2.506	3.966	6.279	9.939	15.733	39.422
9.60	1.048	1.098	1.151	1.206	1.325	1.598	2.554	4.082	6.523	10.425	16.660	42.550
9.80	1.049	1.100	1.154	1.211	1.332	1.613	2.603	4.200	6.777	10.934	17.641	45.924
10.00	1.050	1.102	1.158	1.216	1.340	1.629	2.653	4.322	7.040	11.467	18.679	49.561
11.00	1.055	1.113	1.174	1.239	1.379	1.708	2.918	4.984	8.513	14.542	24.840	72.476

The realized compound yield over a bond's life is thus seen as an explicit function of four independent variables: 1) the bond's life, 2) its coupon rate, 3) its market value, or *equivalently*, its current yield-to-maturity, and 4) the assumed reinvestment rate. Let us now explore the effect on the realized compound yield as these four independent variables take on various values.

First, let us fix the coupon rate at 4% and the maturity at 30 years, and explore the effect of varying yields-to-maturity (or market values) and reinvestment rates. The results are presented in Table 62.

We are immediately struck by the fact that when the reinvestment rate equals the yield-to-maturity rate, then and *only then* does the realized compound yield coincide with the yield-to-maturity. This is why the yield-to-maturity can be taken as a measure of the average growth rate of Future Value *only if* one is willing to assume reinvestment at this same rate.

Even if we were willing to make this assumption, we would still not have a consistent basis for comparing 2 bonds with different yields-to-maturity and hence different reinvestment assumptions.

Table 62 also shows, as we would of course expect, that the realized compound yield grows with increasing reinvestment rates. When the reinvestment rate is lower than the yield-to-maturity, then the realized compound yield will be pulled below the yield-to-maturity. On the other hand, when the reinvestment rate is greater than the yield-to-maturity, the realized compound yield will be raised above the yield-to-maturity. In fact, it turns out that the realized compound yield over a bond's *full life* always lies somewhere between the yield-to-maturity and the reinvestment rate.

Next, let us investigate the effect of time by fixing the coupon rate at 4% and the yield-to-maturity at 6.50%, and letting the maturity and reinvestment rate vary. This is done in Table 63.

The important lesson here is that while the realized compound yield coincides with the yield-to-maturity over the first half-year period, when there is of course no reinvestment at all, as the maturity period increases, the effect of the compounding grows increasingly stronger, and drives the realized compound yield away from the yield-to-maturity and towards the level of the reinvestment rate.

TABLE 62

Effect of Various Reinvestment Rates on the Realized Compound Yield for 30-Year 4% Bonds Priced at Various Yields-to-Maturity

Realized Compound Yields Over Bond's Life

	Reinvestment Rates							
Yield-to-Maturity	3%	4%	5%	6%	6 1/2%	7%	8%	9%
3%	3.00	3.39	3.82	4.28	4.52	4.78	5.31	5.87
4	3.61	4.00	4.43	4.89	5.14	5.39	5.92	6.49
5	4.18	4.57	5.00	5.47	5.71	5.97	6.50	7.07
6	4.71	5.11	5.53	6.00	6.25	6.50	7.04	7.61
6 1/2	4.96	5.36	5.79	6.25	6.50	6.76	7.30	7.86
7	5.21	5.60	6.03	6.50	6.74	7.00	7.54	8.11
8	5.66	6.06	6.49	6.96	7.21	7.46	8.00	8.57
9	6.09	6.48	6.91	7.38	7.63	7.89	8.42	9.00

TABLE 63

Effect of Various Reinvestment Rates
on
the Realized Compound Yield
for
4% Bonds Priced to Have a 6.50% Yield-to-Maturity

Realized Compound Yields Over Bond's Life

	Reinvestment Rate							
Maturity	3%	4%	5%	6%	6.5%	7%	8%	9%
0.50 Years	6.50	6.50	6.50	6.50	6.50	6.50	6.50	6.50
1.00	6.47	6.48	6.49	6.50	6.50	6.50	6.51	6.52
1.50	6.43	6.45	6.47	6.49	6.50	6.51	6.53	6.55
2.00	6.40	6.43	6.46	6.49	6.50	6.51	6.54	6.58
2.50	6.36	6.40	6.44	6.48	6.50	6.52	6.56	6.60
3.00	6.33	6.38	6.43	6.48	6.50	6.52	6.58	6.63
3.50	6.30	6.35	6.41	6.47	6.50	6.53	6.59	6.65
5.00	6.20	6.28	6.37	6.46	6.50	6.55	6.64	6.73
10.00	5.89	6.06	6.23	6.41	6.50	6.59	6.79	7.00
20.00	5.37	5.67	5.98	6.32	6.50	6.68	7.07	7.48
30.00	4.96	5.36	5.79	6.25	6.50	6.76	7.29	7.86
40.00	4.65	5.12	5.64	6.20	6.50	6.81	7.45	8.12
Perpetual	3.00	4.00	5.00	6.00	6.50	7.00	8.00	9.00

Finally, Table 64 shows the effect of various coupon rates, under a fixed maturity at 30 years and a yield-to-maturity of 6.50%. The results demonstrate that larger coupon rates increase the degree to which the realized compound yield diverges away from the yield-to-maturity and moves towards the reinvestment rate. At one extreme, the 0% coupon bond, there is no divergence whatsoever: the realized compound yield always equals the yield-to-maturity no matter what the reinvestment rate may be. This is, of course, due to the fact that such a 0% coupon bond has no schedule of coupon payments, and consequently there is no reinvestment problem at all. At the other extreme, the 9% premium bonds, one sees the greatest movement towards the reinvestment rate.

To summarize, we have seen that the realized compound yield calculated over a bond's life has several advantageous features compared with the conventional yield-to-maturity. These are:

(1) it properly allows for various possible future reinvestment rates and thus reflects the inherent uncertainties arising from different future rates;

(2) it provides a common yardstick for comparison of competitive bond investments at any assumed uniform reinvestment rate;

(3) it measures the growth rate of Future Value from all sources of return;

(4) it is commensurate with the yield-to-maturity under the assumption of reinvestment at the yield-to-maturity rate;

(5) it can be expressed in terms of an explicit mathematical formula which can be solved directly (i.e., without a trial and error search).

In addition, the concept of realized compound yield has a certain intrinsic flexibility. This flexibility reveals itself in the ease with which the concept can be extended to cover investment periods ending prior to or later than the bond's maturity.

TABLE 64

Effect of Various Reinvestment Rates and Coupon Rates
on
the Realized Compound Yield
for
30-Year Bonds
All Priced to have a 6.50% Yield-to-Maturity

Realized Compound Yield Over Bond's Life

	Reinvestment Rate							
Coupon Rate	3%	4%	5%	6%	6.5%	7%	8%	9%
0.00%	6.50	6.50	6.50	6.50	6.50	6.50	6.50	6.50
1.00	5.65	5.86	6.09	6.35	6.50	6.66	7.00	7.38
2.00	5.29	5.59	5.93	6.30	6.50	6.71	7.16	7.65
3.00	5.09	5.45	5.84	6.27	6.50	6.74	7.24	7.78
4.00	4.96	5.36	5.79	6.25	6.50	6.76	7.29	7.86
5.00	4.87	5.29	5.75	6.24	6.50	6.77	7.32	7.91
6.00	4.81	5.25	5.72	6.23	6.50	6.77	7.35	7.95
6.50	4.78	5.23	5.71	6.23	6.50	6.78	7.36	7.96
7.00	4.76	5.21	5.70	6.23	6.50	6.78	7.36	7.98
8.00	4.72	5.19	5.69	6.22	6.50	6.79	7.38	8.00
9.00	4.69	5.16	5.68	6.22	6.50	6.79	7.39	8.01

Realized Compound Yield Prior to Maturity

Suppose the investor purchased a 30-year 4% bond at $671.82 to yield 6.50%, but decided to sell this same bond 2 years later when it achieved a market value of $730.34. This market value at sale corresponds to a 6% yield-to-maturity. The consequent Future Value and the realized compound yield over this two year holding period are computed as shown in Table 65.

It should be noted that as long as the bond has the indicated market value at time of sale, the investor has achieved the resultant realized compound yield whether or not he actually sells the bond. The point is that this is the dollar sum which could be made available as of that point in time for a new investment decision, with continued holding of the same bond representing only one of the possible outcomes of that decision process. For this reason, in place of the term "holding period" we prefer to use the expressions "review period" or "workout period."

TABLE 65

Use of Compound Interest Tables to Compute the Future Value and Realized Compound Yield for a 30-Year 4% Bond Purchased at a Cost of $671.82 (YTM = 6.50%) with Reinvestment at an Assumed 6% Rate and Sold Two Years Later at a Market Value of $730.34 (YTM = 6.00%)

	Coupon Payment		$20
x	2-Year Future Value of $1 Per Period for 4 Periods (2 Years) at 3% Per Period		x 4.184
=	2-Year Future Value of Coupons and Interest-on-Interest*		83.68
+	2-Year Future Value of Principal (Market Value 2 Years Hence)		+730.34
=	2-Year Future Value		814.02
÷	Today's Market Cost	÷	671.82
=	2-Year Future Value Per Dollar	=	1.212
	Realized Compound Yield (Interest Rate Providing above Future Value Per Dollar in 2 Years)	=	9.833%

*This figure could also be obtained from Table 45A by multiplying the 2 year, 6% factor of 20.918 by 4, the bond's coupon % rate.

These calculations are strictly valid only in the context of a tax-free account. In taxable environments, various mathematical adjustments would naturally be required, but the basic principles underlying the development of the realized compound yield would still appear to be largely applicable.

In the Appendix (#6, #7, and #17), a general formula is provided for the Future Value Per Dollar and the realized compound yield over a workout period shorter than the bond's maturity.

Any capital gain (or loss) will naturally have a significant impact on the realized compound yield prior to maturity, especially over shorter review periods. To illustrate this effect, consider a 30-year 4% bond purchased at a yield-to-maturity of 6.50%, and then sold at various prices after various review periods. The resulting realized compound yields, under a fixed 6% reinvestment assumption, are shown in Table 66. The row of realized compound yields associated with a 6.50% yield-to-maturity at the end of each review period corresponds to the case of zero capital gain (or loss) beyond that due to amortization of the initial discount.

As the review period lengthens, the realized compound yield for a given change in yield-to-maturity grows closer and closer to the values in the "zero capital gain" row until all values coincide at the 30-year mark. This effect is the result of two factors at work. First, as the number of years to achieve it increases, a given capital gain (or loss) has a proportionately reduced impact on an annualized basis. Second, as the review period increases, the bond's remaining time to maturity grows correspondingly shorter, so that a given yield move gives rise to a decreasing move in capital value.

The above analysis reveals an important aspect of the realized compound yield. By explicitly incorporating estimates for the reinvestment rate and the end-of-review-period price, the realized compound yield relates a bond's return to the key elements of market risk and opportunity.

TABLE 66

Effect of Various Review Periods on the Realized Compound Yield of a 30-Year 4% Bond Purchased at $671.82 (YTM = 6.50%) With Reinvestment at 6% and Various End-of-Review-Period Market Values

Yield-to-Maturity at End of Review Period	Realized Compound Yield Over Review Period					
	Number of Years in Review Period					
	1 Year	2 Years	5 Years	10 Years	20 Years	30 Years
8.00%	-12.26	- 2.47	3.51	5.37	6.10	6.25
7.50	- 6.46	.34	4.44	5.69	6.17	6.25
7.00	- .23	3.32	5.41	6.03	6.24	6.25
6.80	2.40	4.56	5.82	6.17	6.27	6.25
6.60	5.11	5.83	6.23	6.31	6.29	6.25
6.50*	6.49*	6.48*	6.44*	6.39*	6.31*	6.25*
6.40	7.90	7.13	6.65	6.46	6.32	6.25
6.20	10.78	8.47	7.08	6.61	6.35	6.25
6.00	13.74	9.83	7.53	6.76	6.38	6.25
5.50	21.55	13.39	8.67	7.15	6.46	6.25
5.00	29.98	17.16	9.87	7.57	6.53	6.25

*Corresponds to scientific amortization.

Realized Compound Yield Beyond Maturity

We can also extend the realized compound yield concept to a future point beyond the bond's maturity.

The bond's maturity date is, in a sense, a rather artificial investment horizon. Presumably, an investor has planning periods which are convenient for his portfolio and his objectives. The evaluation of any particular investment instrument should be made within a time framework chosen by the investor, rather than pinned to an arbitrary characteristic like a bond's maturity date. By extending the realized compound yield concept to deal with *any* review period–whether shorter, equal, or longer than the bond's maturity–one has a theoretical tool for approaching this problem of fitting the evaluation of a given bond into the context of the investor's time plan.

To compute the realized compound yield over a period beyond the bond's maturity, one must first decide what assumptions to make regarding the reinvestment of 1) the Principal Value redeemed at maturity and 2) the Future Value arising from the compounding of coupon payments received up to maturity. There are many possible choices here, including differentiating the rate at which the principal amount is reinvested from the average rate used for the accumulated coupon dollars. However, for ease of illustration, we shall once again follow our earlier decision of selecting the simplest assumption: a single reinvestment rate for *all* cash payments throughout the review period. With this assumption, one can proceed to define first the Future Value to a point beyond maturity, and then the consequent realized compound yield.

To illustrate this case, let us return to our example of a 30-year 4% bond purchased at $671.82 to yield 6.50%. Suppose the investor wishes to evaluate this bond in the context of a 40-year planning period (perhaps in order to compare its return with that from a competitive bond investment with a 40-year maturity). Assuming a 6% reinvestment rate, we know from Table 58 that the 30-year Future Value of the bond will be $4,261.07 including accumulated coupons, interest-on-interest, and redeemed principal. For the 10 years remaining to the review point, we follow the

TABLE 67

Use of Compound Interest Tables to Compute
the Future Value and Realized Compound Yield Over a 40-Year Review Period
of a 30-Year 4% Bond Purchased at a Cost of $671.82 (YTM = 6.50%)
With All Reinvestment at an Assumed 6% Rate

	Future Value of Bond (Principal and Interest) at 30-Year Maturity		$4,261.07
x	10-Year Future Value of $1 at 6%	x	1.806
=	4C Year Future Value		$7,695.49
+	Today's Market Cost	+	671.82
=	Future Value Per Invested Dollar	=	11.455
	Realized Compound Yield to Achieve This Future Value Per Dollar over 40-Years	=	6.19%

procedure decided upon earlier and reinvest this entire sum at the same reinvestment rate as before maturity, namely, 6%. From Table 42C, we see that for each $1 invested at 6% compounded semi-annually, we will accumulate over a 10-year period an amount equal to the 10-year Future Value of $1, or $1.806. Multiplying this growth factor by the $4,261.07 invested, we find that the investment would generate an estimated 40-year Future Value of $7,695.49. Dividing this figure by the market cost, we determine the Future Value Per Dollar and then the realized compound yield. The steps in this computation are summarized in Table 67.

In the time between the redemption date and the end of the review period, all funds are being compounded at the reinvestment rate. Consequently, as the length of this time interval beyond maturity grows, the reinvestment rate assumes increasing importance and the realized compound yield converges towards the reinvestment rate. This is illustrated in Table 68.

This "beyond redemption" evaluation also proves useful in analyzing a callable bond to a review point beyond its assumed call date. For example, suppose we wished to evaluate over an eight-year period an 8¾% bond purchased at $1,092.50 (YTM = 7.94%, YTC = 7.663%) and assumed to be called 5 years later at 107 (see

TABLE 68

Effect of Various Reinvestment Rates on the Realized Compound Yield for a 30-Year 4% Bond Purchased at $671.82 (YTM = 6.50%) Over Various Review Periods Beyond the 30-Year Maturity

Time Review Period Extends Beyond 30-Year Maturity	Review Period	Realized Compound Yield							
		Reinvestment Rate							
		3%	4%	5%	6%	6.5%	7%	8%	9%
0 Years	30 Yrs.	4.96	5.36	5.79	6.25	6.50	6.76	7.30	7.86
1 "	31 "	4.90	5.31	5.76	6.25	6.50	6.76	7.31	7.90
2 "	32 "	4.84	5.27	5.74	6.24	6.50	6.77	7.34	7.93
3	33 "	4.78	5.23	5.72	6.23	6.50	6.78	7.36	7.96
4 "	34 "	4.73	5.20	5.69	6.22	6.50	6.78	7.38	7.99
5 "	35 "	4.68	5.16	5.67	6.22	6.50	6.79	7.39	8.02
10 "	40 "	4.47	5.02	5.59	6.19	6.50	6.82	7.47	8.15
20 "	50 "	4.18	4.81	5.47	6.15	6.50	6.85	7.57	8.32
30 "	60 "	3.98	4.68	5.39	6.13	6.50	6.88	7.65	8.43

TABLE 69

Use of Compound Interest Tables to Compute the Future Value and Realized Compound Yield Over an 8-Year Period of a 30-Year 8 3/4% Bond Purchased at a Cost of $1,092.50 (YTM = 7.94%) but Called 5 Years Later at 107 with all Reinvestment at an Assumed 6% Rate

	Coupon Payment	$43.75
x	5-Year Future Value of $1 Per Period for 10 Periods at 3% Per Period (Table 42C)	x11.464
=	5-Year Future Value of Coupons and Interest-on-Interest	501.55
+	5-Year Future Value of Called Principal	+1,070.00
=	5-Year Future Value of Called Bond	1,571.55
x	3-Year Future Value of $1 (6 Periods at 3% Per Period - Table 42C)	x1.194
=	8-Year Future Value	1,876.43
÷	Today's Market Cost	÷ 1,092.50
=	Future Value Per Invested Dollar	1.718
	Realized Compound Yield	6.877%

Table 57). We will assume a 6% reinvestment rate throughout the 8 year period. The computation would then proceed as indicated in Table 69.

In all of the preceding discussion of Future Values and realized compound yields, we have chosen review periods consisting of an integral number of semiannual periods. To extend this result to review periods having an odd number of months and/or days, the interpolation techniques described in Chapter 13 should be used in order to obtain results consistent with the standard yield-to-maturity computation.

Realized Compound Yield and the Recovery of Book Loss

The Future Value and realized compound yield can also be useful in contexts where a book loss must be recovered in order to justify a Pure Yield Pickup Swap. This general problem of correctly computing recovery times for such proposed swaps is described in some detail in Chapter 7. The investor wants to determine the time required for the improvement in his "book cash flow" from the swap to accumulate to the point of equaling an initial book loss.

This accumulation of "book cash flow" consists of 1) coupon payments, 2) interest-on-interest (which will show up in the income account, at least indirectly, no matter what the accounting treatment may be), and 3) gain or loss in book capital value in accordance with whatever amortization procedure is being used. However, if we define the capital gain (or loss) over a specified time to correspond with the book gain (or loss) determined by the amortization scheme, then the above definition of "accumulation of book cash flow" just becomes the gain in Future Value. For a given time period, by subtracting the gain from just holding the H-bond from the gain achieved from the number of P-bonds that would be obtained through executing the swap, we can determine the accumulated book improvement to that future time. Moreover, when this improvement just equals the initial book loss. then the elapsed time corresponds to the required recovery time.

This method can be generalized so that the mathematics and tables of Future Value can be directly applied to computing accumulated gains from swaps in a given book value environment. The mathematical details are given in the Appendix (#19).

The realized compound yield computation can also prove useful in connection with book loss problems. In fact, the realized compound yield can provide a quick indication of whether or not a swap will recover the book loss. If a P-bond has a realized compound yield equal to or greater than that of the H-bond as of the H-bond's maturity, then the swap will recover the book loss by the maturity of the H-bond. This result holds for any book value amortization method as long as the P-bond's book value at the H-bond's maturity is used in computing the P-bond's Future Value Per Dollar and realized compound yield.

As indicated in Chapter 7, it is the authors' feeling that the framework of book value places artificial and irrelevant constraints on the investment decision-making process. It tends to freeze portfolios and hold down the rate of return. Nevertheless, there are many portfolio managers who simply have no choice: they are required to justify any swap as an improvement within their bookkeeping framework.

Using the Yield Book to Find Realized Compound Yields

Throughout this book we have emphasized the concept of realized compound yield as a comprehensive guide to bond values. It reveals the fully compounded growth rate of any investment under varying reinvestment rates and thus permits consistent comparisons between alternate investments. We have demonstrated how realized compound yields can be calculated by the use of Compound Interest Tables.

However, for those who find it more convenient to use only the Yield Book, there is a straightforward method of deriving realized compound yields from any standard Yield Book which includes

"0%" coupon tables, which most do. This is demonstrated in Table 70. The only independent data required are the terms and price of the bond and assumptions on the future reinvestment rate or rates.

TABLE 70

Method for Finding Realized Compound Yield Over the Life of a Bond Using Only the Yield Book

A 30-Year 4% Bond Purchased to Yield 6.50% with a Reinvestment Rate Assumption of 6%

1. Value of bond at today's market to yield 6.50% — $671.82
2. Hypothetical Value of bond today at YTM of 6% (Reinvestment Rate) — $723.20
3. Divide (1) above by (2) above $\frac{671.82}{723.20} = .9289$
4. Find price of "0%" coupon 30-year bond at YTM = 6% (Reinvestment Rate) $16.97
5. Multiply (3) above by (4) above .9289 x 16.97 = $15.76
6. Find YTM of 30-Year "0%" coupon bond with Dollar Price of (5) above. This is the realized compound yield. — 6.26%

(Add Accrued Interest, if any, to Principal Value in steps 1 and 2.)

In this case the realized compound yield lies about halfway between the yield-to-maturity and the reinvestment rate. We have seen that it always is somewhere between these two rates if the bond is held to maturity.

The example used in Table 70 is the same one used in Tables 59 and 60 to illustrate the procedure based on the Compound Interest Tables. The reasons why the Yield Book can be used as in Table 70 to calculate realized compound yield are complex (see Appendix—#20).

The method outlined in Table 70 applies only where the desired time period coincides with the life of a bond. If it is desired for reasons discussed above to measure realized compound yields for periods *beyond* the life of a bond, the same method can be used with a slight adjustment in step 4 and 6 to account for the longer review period as follows:

Step 4 (Table 70). Find dollar price for "0%" coupon bond with a longer maturity coinciding with the longer review period.

Step 6 (Table 70). Find YTM for "0%" coupon bond with the same longer maturity coinciding with the review period.

Finally if it is desired to measure realized compound yields for a period *shorter* than the life of a bond, the same method may be used but a preliminary calculation must be made. This is the "scale-down" technique discussed in Chapter 14. However, this entails a much more complicated calculation and the use of the Compound Interest Tables seems preferable in these cases.

Appendix

(See Glossary of Symbols at the End)

With the aid of the following general formulae, most significant bond yield calculations can be quickly performed by standard computers.

1. *The Future Value of $1 (CH 8)*

   The T half-year Future Value of \$1 @ R = $(1 + R)^T$
   " " " " " " " \$P @ R = $P(1 + R)^T$

2. *The Present Value of $1 (CH 9)*

   The Present Value of \$1 to be Received in T Half Years @ R = $\dfrac{1}{(1 + R)^T}$

   The Present Value of \$P to be Received in T Half Years @ R = $\dfrac{P}{(1 + R)^T}$

3. *The Future Value of $1 Per Period (CH 10)*

   The T Half Years Future Value of \$1 Per Period @ R =

$$\frac{(1 + R)^T - 1}{R}$$

   For the Future Value of any amount (A) per period, multiply the above by A.

For the Future Value of a coupon flow, multiply the above by the amount of the semiannual coupon (5C).

(Note that in all these formulae R, the interest rate, is assumed to be greater than zero.)

4. *Interest-on-Interest*

From the total Future Value of the compounded coupon flow (#3 above), subtract the total of coupon payments, i.e., the amount T X 5C.

5. *Future Value of a Bond at Maturity*

$$\$1{,}000 + 5C\left(\frac{(1+R)^T - 1}{R}\right)$$

if maturity is exactly T semiannual periods from today, redemption value is $1,000 and each coupon received is reinvested at R.

6. *Future Value of a Bond Prior to Maturity*

In #5 above, substitute assumed future Principal Value at end of review period for $1,000, and the number of semiannual periods to review (W) for T.

7. *Future Value Per Dollar Invested Today*

Divide #5 or #6 above by today's market value.

8. *Present Value of $1 Per Period (CH 11)*

Present Value of $1 per period for T periods @ R

$$= \frac{1}{R} - \frac{1}{R\,(1+R)^T}$$

This is the sum of the Present Values of each payment.

For the Present Value of any amount of level payments, such as a coupon flow, multiply the above by the amount of each payment.

9. *Present Value of A Bond*

This is the sum of the Present Value of the redemption payment and the Present Value of the coupon flow. It is

$$= \frac{5C}{R} + \frac{1}{(1+R)^T}\left(1{,}000 - \frac{5C}{R}\right)$$

This is also the Present Value of a lump sum payment equal to a bond's Future Value at maturity at the same interest rate R.

10. *Market Value of a Bond and its Yield-to-Maturity (CH 12)*

Since yield-to-maturity (Y) is defined as that discount rate (R) which provides a Present Value of a bond equal to its Market Value (MV),

$$MV = \frac{5C}{Y} + \frac{1}{(1+Y)^T}\left(1000 - \frac{5C}{Y}\right)$$

11. *Accrued Interest (CH 13)*

$$AI = 5C\left(\frac{180 - 30\,M - D}{180}\right)$$

This assumes the conventional 30-day months.

12. *The Principal Value (PR)*

The Principal Value is defined as Market Value (MV) less Accrued Interest. The Dollar Price of a bond (DP) is defined as its Principal Value expressed as a percentage of its redemption value.

13. *Dollar Price of a Bond Derived From Yield-to-Maturity*

For bonds maturing in an integral number of semiannual periods, the Dollar Price (DP) equals $\frac{MV}{10}$, so that using #10 above,

$$DP = \frac{C}{2Y} + \frac{1}{(1+Y)^T}\left(100 - \frac{C}{2Y}\right)$$

or if maturity is in integral months but not an integral number of semiannual periods,

$$DP = \frac{1}{(1+Y)^{M/6}}\left[\frac{C}{2} + \frac{C}{2Y} + \frac{1}{(1+Y)^T}\left(100 - \frac{C}{2Y}\right)\right] - \frac{C\,(180 - 30M)}{360}$$

The above formulae are for bonds having a maturity of 6 months or longer.

14. *Interpolation for Dollar Price of a Bond with Odd Days*

Where DP (T,M,D) is the Dollar Price of a bond with a maturity of T = full semiannual time periods to maturity, plus M = additional months, plus D = additional days,

$$DP\,(T,M,D) = DP\,(T,M,0) + \frac{D}{30} \times \left[DP\,(T,M+1,0) - DP\,(T,M,0)\right]$$

15. *Dollar Price of a Bond With Maturity Under Six Months*

$$DP = \frac{100 + C/2}{1 + \frac{MY}{6}} - \frac{C}{2}\left(\frac{180 - 30M}{180}\right)$$

16. *Yield-To-Call (CH 14)*

That discount rate which makes the Present Value of the bond's cash flow to call equal to its market value,

$$MV = \frac{5C}{YTC} + \frac{1}{(1+YTC)^{CT}}\left[10\,(CP) - \frac{5C}{YTC}\right]$$

17. *Realized Compound Yield (E) (CH 15)*

That interest rate at which the semiannually compounded

Future Value of \$1 will equal the "Future Value Per Dollar Invested Today" of the investment. Thus,

$$E = (FVPD)^{1/W} - 1$$

18. *Future Value of a Bond Over Review Period Beyond Maturity*

Future Value Per Dollar Invested Today =

$$\frac{(1 + R)^{W - T}}{MV} \times \left[1{,}000 + 5C \left(\frac{(1 + R)^{T} - 1}{R}\right)\right]$$

19. *Time to Recover a Book Loss*

This is an artificial concept because there is an *immediate* benefit to the portfolio's cash flow whenever a P-bond promises a larger realized compound yield than the H-bond over the H-bond's life. Nevertheless, the calculation of "time to recover" is popular. For this calculation to be performed correctly, it is *essential* to compare the book loss with the difference in Future Values (P-bond less the H-bond) including amortized principal, coupons and interest-on-interest under identical reinvestment rate assumptions. This last step is often omitted, leading to grossly misleading results.

To obtain a formula, suppose the net proceeds HMV from the sale of an H-bond with amortized book value HBV are invested on a swap in P-bonds, each costing PMV. For any given review date, let HFV and PFV denote the Future Values of the H-bond and P-bond, respectively, on a book cost basis. Then the net book benefit NB from the swap will be

$$NB = \left[\left(\frac{HMV}{PMV}\right) PFV\right] - HFV$$

as of this review date. Immediately following the swap, this net gain will be negative, just equalling the book loss BL, i.e.,

$$\begin{aligned} NB &= \left[\left(\frac{HMV}{PMV}\right) PMV\right] - HBV \\ &= -(HBV - HMV) \\ &= -BL \end{aligned}$$

For a productive Pure Yield Pickup Swap, this net loss will decline until it reaches and then passes the zero mark. At this point when the net just equals zero, the book loss is recovered.

We can express the net gain formula in terms of Future (book) Values Per (market) Dollar,

$$NB = HMV \left[\left(\frac{PFV}{PMV}\right) - \left(\frac{HFV}{HMV}\right)\right]$$

At recovery, NB = 0, and we see that

$$\frac{PFV}{PMV} = \frac{HFV}{HMV}$$

so that the realized compound yields must also be equal at this point.

20. *Rationale Underlying Yield Book Method for Finding Realized Compound Yield*

The procedure leads to finding a solution E for the equation,

$$\frac{100}{(1+E)^W} = \left[\frac{MV}{\begin{pmatrix}\text{Present Value of Bond's} \\ \text{Cash Flow at Discount} \\ \text{Rate R}\end{pmatrix}}\right] \frac{100}{(1+R)^W}$$

$$= \frac{100\ MV}{\begin{pmatrix}\text{Future Value at Review} \\ \text{of Bond's Cash Flow with} \\ \text{Reinvestment at R}\end{pmatrix}}$$

$$= \frac{100}{FVPD}$$

or

$$(1 + E)^{W} = FVPD$$

Glossary of Symbols

A	Amount of a future payment.
AI	Accrued interest.
BL	Book loss.
C	Coupon rate expressed as a percentage per annum.
CP	Call price.
CT	Number of semiannual periods from today to call date.
D	Number of days that the bond's remaining life exceeds an integral number of months.
DP	Dollar Price of a bond.
E	Realized compound yield, expressed as a decimal rate per semiannual period.
FVPD	Future Value Per Dollar invested today.
H-bond	In a swap, the bond now *h*eld and to be sold.
HBV	The H-bond's current amortized book capital value.
HFV	The H-bond's Future Value on a book basis, i.e., the accumulated book dollars from coupons, interest-on-interest, and amortized capital value provided by the H-bond as of some future review point.
HMV	The H-bond's current net sale value.
M	Number of integral months that the bond's maturity exceeds an integral number of semiannual periods.
MV	Market value of a bond.
NB	Net book benefit from swap up to some future review point.
P	Principal amount.
P-bond	The bond *p*roposed for *p*urchase in a swap.
PFV	The P-bond's Future Value on a book basis as of some review point (see HFV).
PMV	The P-bond's current net cost.
PR	Principal Value.
R	Reinvestment rate (or discount rate) expressed as a decimal rate per semiannual period.

T	Number of semiannual periods to maturity.
W	Number of semiannual periods until the end of the review period.
Y	Yield-to-maturity expressed as a decimal rate per semiannual period.
YTM	Yield-to-maturity.
YTC	Yield-to-call expressed as a decimal rate per semiannual period.

Index

ABOUT BLOOMBERG

Bloomberg L.P., founded in 1981, is a global information services, news, and media company. Headquartered in New York, the company has nine sales offices, two data centers, and 94 news bureaus worldwide.

Bloomberg, serving customers in 126 countries around the world, holds a unique position within the financial services industry by providing an unparalleled range of features in a single package known as the BLOOMBERG PROFESSIONAL® service. By addressing the demand for investment performance and efficiency through an exceptional combination of information, analytic, electronic trading, and Straight Through Processing tools, Bloomberg has built a worldwide customer base of corporations, issuers, financial intermediaries, and institutional investors.

BLOOMBERG NEWS®, founded in 1990, provides stories and columns on business, general news, politics, and sports to leading newspapers and magazines throughout the world. BLOOMBERG TELEVISION®, a 24-hour business and financial news network, is produced and distributed globally in seven different languages. BLOOMBERG RADIO℠ is an international radio network anchored by flagship station BLOOMBERG® 1130 (WBBR-AM) in New York.

In addition to the BLOOMBERG PRESS® line of books, Bloomberg publishes *BLOOMBERG MARKETS*® and *BLOOMBERG WEALTH MANAGER*®. To learn more about Bloomberg, call a sales representative at:

Frankfurt:	49-69-92041-0	São Paulo:	55-11-3048-4500
Hong Kong:	852-2977-6000	Singapore:	65-6212-1000
London:	44-20-7330-7500	Sydney:	61-2-9777-8600
New York:	1-212-318-2000	Tokyo:	81-3-3201-8900
San Francisco:	1-415-912-2960		

FOR IN-DEPTH MARKET INFORMATION and news, visit the Bloomberg website at www.bloomberg.com, which draws from the news and power of the BLOOMBERG PROFESSIONAL® service and Bloomberg's host of media products to provide high-quality news and information in multiple languages on stocks, bonds, currencies, and commodities.

ABOUT THE AUTHORS

Martin L. Leibowitz joined Morgan Stanley in April 2004 as a managing director in the research department. For the prior nine years he was vice chairman and chief investment officer of TIAA-CREF, the world's largest pension fund, with more than $300 billion in assets. For the preceding twenty-six years, he was with the investment banking firm of Salomon Brothers where he became the director of global research and member of the executive committee.

Dr. Leibowitz is the author of five books and more than one hundred forty articles. Ten of his articles have received the *Financial Analysts Journal* Graham and Dodd Award for excellence in financial writing. The Association for Investment Management Research (AIMR) singled him out to receive two of its highest and most select awards: the Nicholas Molodovsky Award in 1995 and the James R. Vertin Award in 1998. In 1995, he received the Distinguished Public Service Award from the Public Securities Association and became the first inductee into the Fixed Income Analysts Society's Hall of Fame. In 2003, he was elected a fellow of the American Academy of Arts & Sciences, and named a distinguished fellow of the Institute for Quantitative Research and Finance. *Pensions & Investments* magazine included Dr. Leibowitz in its list of thirty individuals who, through their ideas and research over the years, have "made the most dramatic difference in the management of pension funds and other institutional assets."

Dr. Leibowitz is vice chairman of the board of trustees for both the Carnegie Corp. and the Institute for Advanced Study at Princeton. He earned a bachelor's and a master's degree in physics from the University of Chicago and a Ph.D. in mathematics from New York University.

Sidney Homer, who died in 1983, was the founder and general partner in charge of Salomon Brothers' bond market research department. He was at various times in his fifty-year career a bond salesman, bond trader, stock and bond analyst, and institutional bond buyer. Best known for his pioneering and analytical studies of bond market history and relative values and the economic forces which create bond market trends, he is the author of several books including *A History of Interest Rates, The Bond Buyer's Primer,* and *The Price of Money.* He was inducted posthumously into the Fixed Income Analysts Society's Hall of Fame in 1997.

Mr. Homer graduated magna cum laude from Harvard College with a concentration in philosophy.